RAILROAD BANKRUPTCIES AND MERGERS FROM CHICAGO WEST 1975–2001:
FINANCIAL ANALYSIS AND REGULATORY CRITIQUE

RESEARCH IN TRANSPORTATION ECONOMICS

Series Editor: Martin Dresner

Volumes 1–6: Research in Transportation Economics – Edited by B. Starr McMullen

RESEARCH IN TRANSPORTATION ECONOMICS   VOLUME 7

RAILROAD BANKRUPTCIES AND MERGERS FROM CHICAGO WEST 1975–2001:

FINANCIAL ANALYSIS AND REGULATORY CRITIQUE

BY

MICHAEL CONANT

Walter A. Haas School of Business, University of California, Berkeley, USA

2004

ELSEVIER
JAI

Amsterdam – Boston – Heidelberg – London – New York – Oxford – Paris
San Diego – San Francisco – Singapore – Sydney – Tokyo

ELSEVIER B.V.	ELSEVIER Inc.	**ELSEVIER Ltd**	ELSEVIER Ltd
Sara Burgerhartstraat 25	525 B Street, Suite 1900	**The Boulevard, Langford Lane**	84 Theobalds Road
P.O. Box 211, 1000 AE	San Diego, CA 92101-4495	**Kidlington, Oxford OX5 1GB**	London WC1X 8RR
Amsterdam, The Netherlands	USA	**UK**	UK

© 2004 Elsevier Ltd. All rights reserved.

This work is protected under copyright by Elsevier Ltd, and the following terms and conditions apply to its use:

Photocopying
Single photocopies of single chapters may be made for personal use as allowed by national copyright laws. Permission of the Publisher and payment of a fee is required for all other photocopying, including multiple or systematic copying, copying for advertising or promotional purposes, resale, and all forms of document delivery. Special rates are available for educational institutions that wish to make photocopies for non-profit educational classroom use.

Permissions may be sought directly from Elsevier's Rights Department in Oxford, UK: phone (+44) 1865 843830, fax (+44) 1865 853333, e-mail: permissions@elsevier.com. Requests may also be completed on-line via the Elsevier homepage (http://www.elsevier.com/locate/permissions).

In the USA, users may clear permissions and make payments through the Copyright Clearance Center, Inc., 222 Rosewood Drive, Danvers, MA 01923, USA; phone: (+1) (978) 7508400, fax: (+1) (978) 7504744, and in the UK through the Copyright Licensing Agency Rapid Clearance Service (CLARCS), 90 Tottenham Court Road, London W1P 0LP, UK; phone: (+44) 20 7631 5555; fax: (+44) 20 7631 5500. Other countries may have a local reprographic rights agency for payments.

Derivative Works
Tables of contents may be reproduced for internal circulation, but permission of the Publisher is required for external resale or distribution of such material. Permission of the Publisher is required for all other derivative works, including compilations and translations.

Electronic Storage or Usage
Permission of the Publisher is required to store or use electronically any material contained in this work, including any chapter or part of a chapter.

Except as outlined above, no part of this work may be reproduced, stored in a retrieval system or transmitted in any form or by any means, electronic, mechanical, photocopying, recording or otherwise, without prior written permission of the Publisher.
Address permissions requests to: Elsevier's Rights Department, at the fax and e-mail addresses noted above.

Notice
No responsibility is assumed by the Publisher for any injury and/or damage to persons or property as a matter of products liability, negligence or otherwise, or from any use or operation of any methods, products, instructions or ideas contained in the material herein. Because of rapid advances in the medical sciences, in particular, independent verification of diagnoses and drug dosages should be made.

First edition 2004

Library of Congress Cataloging in Publication Data
A catalog record is available from the Library of Congress.

British Library Cataloguing in Publication Data
A catalogue record is available from the British Library.

ISBN: 0-7623-1079-0
ISSN: 0739-8859 (Series)

∞ The paper used in this publication meets the requirements of ANSI/NISO Z39.48-1992 (Permanence of Paper).
Printed in The Netherlands.

CONTENTS

LIST OF TABLES	*vii*
INTRODUCTION	*ix*
1. RAILROAD REGULATION AND MISALLOCATION OF RESOURCES	*1*
2. ROCK ISLAND BANKRUPTCY	*27*
3. MILWAUKEE ROAD BANKRUPTCY	*47*
4. ILLINOIS CENTRAL MERGER AND SALES OF LINES	*71*
5. UNION PACIFIC MERGERS: 1982 AND 1988	*89*
6. BURLINGTON NORTHERN – SANTE FE MERGER	*103*
7. UNION PACIFIC MERGER OF SOUTHERN PACIFIC	*117*
APPENDIX: MAPS	*135*
INDEX	*151*

LIST OF TABLES

Number	Title	Page
1.1	Route Milage By Density Categories, 1975	4
1.2	Route Miles and Density Categories of Selected Class 1 Railroads, 1975	6
1.3	Main Line Corridors of Consolidation Potential, 1975	8
1.4	Road and Operating Statistics of Class I Railroads	17
1.5	Employment By Railroads	19
2.1	Economic Performance of the Rock Island and The Union Pacific Railroads For 1974	29
2.2	Analysis of Six Railroad Lines Between Chicago and Omaha, 1975	31
2.3	Chicago, Rock Island & Pacific Railroad Comparative Profit and Loss Data	34
3.1	Milwaukee Road Line Densities, 1976	49
3.2	Chicago, Milwaukee, St. Paul & Pacific Railroad Comparative Profit and Loss Data	54
3.3	Financial Results and Predictions for Combined Soo/Milwaukee	64
4.1	Financial Results of the I.C. and G.M.&O., 1971 and I.C.G., 1973	73
4.2	Illinois Central Gulf Railroad Route Miles and Financial Results	76
4.3	Illinois Central Gulf Milage Operated By States in 1973 and 1996	81
5.1	Financial Results of Applicant Railroads, 1981	90
5.2	Western Pacific Railroad Before Merger Financial Results and Estimated Losses if Maintenance of Way and Structures Had Been at High Standard	93

5.3	Western Pacific Railroad Financial Results	94
5.4	Union Pacific Railroad and Missouri Pacific Railroad Financial Results After Merger	95
5.5	Missouri-Kansas-Texas Railroad Before Merger Financial Results and Estimated Losses if Maintenance of Way and Structures Had Been at Missouri Pacific Standard	98
6.1	Financial Results of Burlington Northern and Santa Fe, 1994	106
6.2	Burlington Northern-Santa Fe Projected Annual Cost Savings	110
6.3	Burlington Northern-Santa Fe Railway Co. Financial Results	111
7.1	Financial Results of Union Pacific and Southern Pacific, 1995	119
7.2	Southern Pacific Transportation Co. and Subsidiaries Financial Results	120
7.3	Union Pacific-Southern Pacific Merger Surface Transportation Board's Restatement of Cost Savings	123
7.4	Union Pacific Railroad Company Income Statement	128

INTRODUCTION

This study of the law and economics of railroad bankruptcies and mergers was designed to review critically the negative effects of the regulatory system and the delays of the bankruptcy courts in dealing with excess capacity in lines and yards of carriers. A significant part of the study is the application of the economics of cross-subsidization. Limited users of net-loss branch lines, such as farmers, elevator operators and some local merchants, exerted political pressure to block abandonments of lines under the vague public interest standard of the Interstate Commerce Act. They expected major shippers on main lines to pay high enough freight rates to subsidize them. The political power of agricultural interests in the United States Senate has gained their voters many subsidies, such as price supports for farm products, empty superhighways in areas of low population, ethanol subsidies and significant barriers to rail line abandonments. Before the major postwar bankruptcies that began with Penn-Central in 1970, the Interstate Commerce Commission was noted for a costly administrative procedure and a hopeless policy of trying to save weak railroads. The retention of excess capacity meant the rejection of efficiency criteria and imposed costs on the entire railroad industry.

This study is in many aspects a sequel to my 1964 volume, *Railroad Mergers and Abandonments* (Berkeley: University of California Press, 1964). That volume began with a chapter entitled "Route Capacity, Excess Capacity and Overinvestment". The current volume centers on the Staggers Act of 1980 and the final moves to solve the problem of excess capacity. While the Penn Central bankruptcy of 1970 was the subject of many studies, the two midwest bankruptcies treated here in Chapters 2 and 3 have not received great comment. The objective here is to make an economic and legal analysis of the origins and inevitability of these bankruptcies with emphasis on the regulatory system that had hindered reduction of excess capacity. The later chapters demonstrate in detail the effectiveness of the Staggers Act and a new regime at the ICC under the chairman, economist Darius Gaskins and his successors. Using efficiency criteria, the new ICC members approved mergers and abandonments and the sale of net-loss lines to new short-line and regional railroads. These new smaller carriers were not bound by the union contracts whose work rules imposed great costs on the Class I carriers.

The action of Congress to terminate the ICC at the end of 1995 was the final acknowledgement that a so-called independent regulatory commission had not been insulated from congressional and other political forces. The ICC had not been a public agency serving the interests of Americans as consumers. To the contrary, it condoned monopoly in collective rate-making by railroad traffic bureaus and largely impeded railroads in reduction of excess capacity. The functions of the ICC concerning mergers were transferred to the executive branch, the Department of Transportation's new Surface Transportation Board (STB).But this was near the end of the great railroad merger movement. The only western merger left to be approved by STB in 1996 was of the Union Pacific and the Southern Pacific.

This study does not treat the special statutes and ICC rulings designed to protect and to sustain the income of railroad workers who lost jobs because of railroad mergers. The extensive literature on this topic is reviewed in the excellent study of Professor Herbert R. Northrup, *Railroad Labor Protective Programs in Mergers: Generous Public Policy for a Favored Few*, 23 Transportation Law Journal 176 (1995).While the costs to the carriers of labor income protective programs for displaced workers were significant, they were not large enough to affect the decisions to merge. To the extent that these costs affected the income of the carriers treated in this study, it is recorded in the financial data herein.

The author is indebted for critical comments on the manuscript for this book to Professor Theodore Keeler and Professor Frederick Morrissey, a former member of the California Public Utilities Commission.Professor Robert E. Gallamore made helpful suggestions for expanded explanations in some of the chapters. These submissions have been incorporated in the revised manuscript with special thanks from the author. Karl Nygren, a leading attorney in railroad mergers, gave valuable assistance. A great debt is owed to my computer assistant, Cynthia Lee, who worked long hours to complete the manuscript.

1. RAILROAD REGULATION AND MISALLOCATION OF RESOURCES

There is a very large literature on the misallocation of resources resulting from regulation of railroads. American railroads were built before the coming of hard roads. Investment by rival carriers in multiple parallel lines between major cities and in thousands of miles of branch lines did not anticipate the coming of paved highways and the great rivalry of motor carriers.[1] Investment in passenger trains and thousands of small-town stations did not anticipate the overwhelming development of the private automobile for shorter trips and air carriers for longer trips.[2]

In a free market, resources are reallocated over time in order to adjust to technological change. But in the regulated railroad industry, the ability of firms to exit net-loss functions was greatly impeded by the political system. Parallel railroads, paying high real estate taxes for rail routes and union wages to maintain roadbeds and rails were not allowed to abandon one line and contract for trackage rights over the neighboring line.[3] Likewise, state public utility commissions would not permit discontinuance of most net-loss passenger service, or were slow to do so.

The forced continuance of net-loss passenger service was a prime example of government-mandated cross-subsidization.[4] Railroads, facing intense competition from motor carriers for many classes of freight, were expected to subsidize net-loss passenger service by charging higher freight rates. This forced cross-subsidization, in reality an imposed public service function, was one key factor leading to railroad bankruptcies. The reason a long-run net-loss economic activity is labeled a public service function is that no private enterprise could survive financially with such a burden. It is elementary economics that when the average cost function of a service is at all points above the demand function, such activity in a private enterprise must be discontinued.

The Class 1 railroads reported aggregate losses from passenger and allied services of over $420 million in 1965 and over $476 million in 1970.[5] While these figures of fully allocated costs overstate the possible avoidable losses from discontinuance of passenger service because they include some joint passenger-freight expenses, they do indicate that the burden of passenger losses was great. The New York, New Haven & Hartford Railroad, with large passenger losses on lines into New York, filed for bankruptcy on July 4, 1961.[6] The Penn Central, which had passenger service losses of $100 million in 1968, filed for bankruptcy on June 21, 1970.[7] In October, the national government rescued the railroads and took over passenger service with passage of the National Rail Passenger Service Act of 1970.[8] Thus, the burden of net losses of rail passenger service was shifted to the taxpayers of the nation, the overwhelming majority of whom would not find rail passenger service useful. The one main line with sufficient traffic density so that its revenues cover its costs except for interest on capital is the one from Boston to New York and Washington D.C. This rail line, purchased from Conrail and a short line in Michigan are the only lines owned by Amtrak. The profound social issue is whether, except for a few short routes between large cities, all the rest of Amtrak should be subsidized by government when public ground transport is available from private enterprise bus companies.[9] The task is one of ranking national government spending priorities.

The decision of the Congress to create the National Railroad Passenger Corp. (Amtrak) after the bankruptcies of the major northeast railroads was prompted by the possibility that all passenger service in the area would be discontinued. The legal background to this crisis was the just compensation rights in the eminent domain clause of the Fifth Amendment to the Constitution. Statutory compulsion of bankrupt railroads to continue net-loss services such as transporting passengers when it was clear that this service would never become profitable would have to be financed from the railroads' invested capital. This cannibalizing of railroad corporate capital to the detriment of creditors in order to retain passenger service would be governmental confiscation. In *Brooks-Scanlon v. Railroad Commission*, Justice Oliver Wendell Holmes stated that "A carrier cannot be compelled to carry on even a branch at a loss, much less the whole business of carriage."[10] This dictum on the constitutional right to abandon particular net-loss branches of an overall net-loss railroad was supported by later decisions.[11] The constitutional right to discontinue net-loss services on a net-loss railroad is an application of the same logic as that for branch lines. The leading case on the right to discontinue net-loss passenger services on a net loss railroad was *Mississippi R. R. Comm'n v. Mobile & O.R.R.*[12] While operating at a deficit and without obtaining permission from the state railroad commission, the railroad discontinued operation of six passenger trains. The district court enjoined enforcement of the commissions order to restore service and the U.S. Supreme Court affirmed. When it came to the New Haven Railroad, the Supreme Court permitted delays that seemed contrary to the earlier decision.[13]

EXCESS CAPACITY

Excess capacity is the definition for investment in physical plant that is underutilized and consequently does not earn a market rate of return. In the railroad industry, excess capacity is primarily found in route miles of line with low density of traffic. Before the liberalizations of the 1976 and 1980 statutes, the key barrier to the exit of capital from low density lines was the regulation of abandonments by the Interstate Commerce Commission.[14] While the great proportion of small line abandonments were granted, the long administrative proceedings and their cost were a substantial deterrent to filing such petitions by railroad. In some instances, it may have been less costly just to stop maintenance of way and hope that shippers would find alternative transport for their commodities. This would be primarily a shift to motor carriers.

Even with very low maintenance expenditure on low-density lines for freight trains with maximum speed limited to 10 miles per hour, the transportation cost of trains with few cars and numerous stops for switching one or two cars at a time is very high. Consequently, the cost of moving a ton of freight one mile on a branch line is likely to be significantly higher than moving each ton at high speed on long trains on high-density main lines. The economic result is another aspect of cross-subsidization of low-density traffic by high-density traffic. The rate regulation prior to 1980 would not allow higher rates per mile on branch lines than main lines in order to compensate for the higher costs. In many cases, of course, higher rail rates would cause shippers to switch to motor carriers, thus relieving the railroad of the duty to maintain its line.

Econometric studies of traffic density point out that miles of road or miles of track must be held constant in order to distinguish changes in density from changes in the scale of the firms. Studies by Harris[15] and Keeler[16] centered on the relation of unit rail costs and traffic density. In spite of different specifications of the cost function, their results were very similar. Costs per unit were shown to decline sharply with increasing density but they became constant once density reached about 35 to 40 million gross ton-miles per mile of road per year. This minimum efficient density could be achieved on a single track line with a high level of maintenance of way and centralized traffic control. Both the Harris and Keeler studies of the mid-1970s estimated the break-even level of traffic density at about 8 million gross ton-miles per mile of road per year.

Table 1.1. Route Milage By Density Categories, 1975.

Density Categories (Millions of gross ton-miles per mile per year)	Route Milage (thousands)	Percent of Total Route Milage[a]
A-Mainlines (20 million or more)	50.1	26.3
B-Mainlines (5 million to 20 million)	48.3	26.5
A-Branchlines (1 million to 5 million)	40.4	21.2
B-Branchlines (less than 1 million)	51.6	27.1
Total Milage Measured	190.4	

Source: U.S. Department of Transportation, *Final Standards, Classification, and Designation of Lines of Class 1 Railroads in the United States*, Vol. 2, 137 (1977).
Note: [a] percentages total 100.1 due to rounding.

The most detailed information on freight line densities in the United States became available from the Department of Transportation which carried out a study required by the Railroad Revitalization and Regulatory Reform Act of 1976.[17] The data for 1975 reported by Class 1 railroads show that they operated 207,097 miles of road including trackage rights over other railroads.[18] They owned 172,428 miles of road. As shown in Table 1.1, the density study assembled data on 190,400 miles of road. The A-Mainlines of 20 million or more gross ton-miles per mile of road per year totaled 50,100 miles of road. This 26.3% of national route milage carried two-thirds of all traffic.[19] The B-Mainlines of 5 million to 20 million gross ton-miles per mile of road per year totaled 48,300 miles of road. Together, these two mainline categories constituted 52.8% of the total route milage. The two categories labeled Branchlines totaled 92,000 miles of road or 48.3% of the total. If one combines the weakest 10,000 route miles of A-Branchline with the 51,600 miles of B-Branchline, the statistics show that almost one third of the rail milage of the nation carried a total of only 1% of the gross ton-miles per mile.[20]

Another classification of the Department of Transportation placed each line segment within one of six density categories by gross ton-miles per mile of road (GTM).

They were as follows:[21]

Density Class	GTM
1	0–1
2	1–5
3	5–10
4	10–20
5	20–30
6	over 30

Levin combined this data with the Federal Railroad Administration's network model so that the data permitted a tabulation of the distribution of each railroad's route milage by density class.[22] For his analysis, Levin combined density classes 1 through 3 (0 to 10 GTM) into one group labeled Low Density Lines (LDLs). For the 60 railroads that were tabulated, he notes that LDLs accounted for 63.2% of total route miles but carried only 18% of the GTM. The average GTM per mile of road was three million.

Another comparison of Levin's LDL (0 to 10 GTM) group with the A and B-Branchlines in Table 1.1 shows that only density classes 1 plus 2 (0 to 5 GTM) are labeled branchlines. Density class 3 (5 to 10 GTM) is the bottom part of B-Mainlines in Table 1.1. For example, almost all of the Chicago and North Western main line from Minneapolis to Council Bluffs, Iowa, was in density class 3. It was labeled as A-Mainline, apparently because the last 27 miles were over the main line from Chicago to Council Bluffs and in Class 5. Similarly, the 545-mile Rock Island line from Topeka, Kansas to Tucumcari, New Mexico was labeled A-Mainline though only the first 81 miles to a Missouri Pacific connection were in Class 5, and 259 miles of the line were Class 3.

Levin then centered his analysis on density Class 6, which he labeled highest density lines (HDL). He calculated that these lines operated at approximately minimum efficient density as estimated by prior econometric studies. The HDL represented only 10.9% of Class 1 railroad milage but they carried 33.8% of national GTM, averaging 33.3 million GTM per mile. In between LDL and HDL are density classes 4 and 5 with 10 to 30 GTM, constituting 25.9% of national railroad milage and 48.2% of GTM.

Data derived from the Levin study are presented in Table 1.2 in order to demonstrate for 1975 the key traffic density characteristics of leading Class 1 railroads that are treated in detail in later chapters. For each carrier, the table indicates which percentage of its route miles and which percentage of its gross ton-miles are in each of the three density categories. The strongest railroads financially in 1975 were those with the largest HDL percentages of route miles and gross ton-miles. These were the Santa Fe, the Southern Pacific and its subsidiary, St. Louis-Southwestern, and the Union Pacific. The Burlington Northern was also financially strong with 83.8% of its gross ton-miles in the high plus medium categories.

The weakest railroads financially were those with the largest percentage of LDL route miles and gross ton-miles. The Chicago & North Western, the Milwaukee Road and the Rock Island, all operating numerous net-loss branchlines in the upper Midwest, had more than 70% of route miles in LDLs. Both Milwaukee Road and the Rock Island, with minimal high density lines, were about to move into bankruptcy reorganization. The North Western was weak

Table 1.2. Route Miles and Density Categories of Selected Class 1 Railroads, 1975.

CARRIER	Route Miles Classified	Gross Ton-Miles (Millions)	Low Density Lines		Medium Density Lines		High Density Lines	
			Percent of Route Miles	Percent of GTM	Percent of Route Miles	Percent of GTM	Percent of Route Miles	Percent of GTM
Sante Fe	12,209.1	156,948.3	57.6	11.9	22.1	32.8	20.3	55.3
Burlington Northern	20,859.1	204,218.8	65.1	16.2	26.8	54.9	8.1	28.9
Milwaukee Road	8,889.5	52,894.0	77.2	37.2	22.6	61.5	0.2	1.4
Chicago North Western	9,567.4	64,979.2	79.1	28.1	15.4	43.7	5.5	28.2
Rock Island	6,220.6	46,218.3	71.9	36.9	28.0	63.6	0.1	0.5
Illinois Central	8,919.1	77,861.4	73.6	34.9	22.4	48.9	4.0	16.2
M-K-T	1,797.7	16,402.0	58.7	23.7	40.0	71.4	1.3	4.9
Missouri Pacific	7,536.8	78,752.0	61.1	19.3	31.8	57.0	7.1	23.7
St. Louis-San Francisco	4,480.5	40,518.8	63.0	19.4	37.0	80.6	0	
St. Louis-Southwestern	1,198.6	22,934.0	38.8	5.5	25.3	28.9	35.9	65.6
Soo Line	4,158.3	27,148.9	75.9	32.3	24.1	67.7	0	
Southern Pacific	10,551.4	169,603.1	48.6	8.4	21.4	26.3	30.0	65.3
Union Pacific	8,356.5	114,870.4	58.7	11.6	16.3	24.8	25.0	63.6
Western Pacific	1,046.1	18,669.5	21.5	5.7	60.6	59.2	17.9	35.1

Source: Richard C. Levin, *Regulation, Barriers to Exit and the Investment Behavior of Railroads*. In Gary Fromm, (Ed.), *Studies in Regulation* (Cambridge; MIT Press, 1981) as derived from data from the U.S. Department of Transportation.

financially but was saved from bankruptcy by its key exchange of trains with the strong Union Pacific near Omaha. Thus, 28.2% of North Western gross ton-miles were in high-density. The Soo Line was another carrier with 75.9% of its route miles in low-density and none in high-density, but Soo Line was a subsidiary of Canadian Pacific which could subsidize its losses. The Illinois Central had 73.6% of its route miles in low-density branches, but it operated the prime high-density line from Chicago to New Orleans.

The St. Louis-San Francisco had 80.6% of its gross ton-miles in medium density lines in the South and was destined to be acquired by the Burlington Northern. The Missouri Pacific and Western Pacific, with significant high density lines, were acquired by Union Pacific in 1980. The much weaker MKT was acquired by Union Pacific in 1988.

Another aspect of main line excess capacity studied by the U.S. Department of Transportation was entitled Corridors of Consolidation Potential. Recognizing that some of these corridors overlap, the total milage of the main line corridors listed in Table 1.3 was 18,900 miles.[23] This study was the first governmental recognition that for railroads, with high fixed costs, having more firms in the market did not result in effective competition. Rather, it the result was many low-density main lines, an inefficient level of operations. The expansion of highways after World War I and the development of larger motor trucks brought the great rivalry to railroads of motor carriers. The building of the four-lane interstate highways after World War II increased this rivalry and accentuated the problem of excess capacity of railroad main lines. Most railroads could not earn a market rate of return on investment.

The remedy of consolidating main lines was a total rejection by the Department of Transportation of the earlier ICC policy that mergers of parallel lines or similar trackage rights should be denied in order to protect rival weak railroads. The fundamental fact that increased traffic density was the key to increased railroad efficiency had been ignored.

But the financial crises of major railroads presented the truth that the only long-run remedy was structural realignment and the abandonment of some main lines.

The density and capacity data in Table 1.3 demonstrated the need for the remedy of consolidation of main lines, but it is accepted that the capacity figures are rough estimates. In example 1, Chicago to Pittsburgh, the two Conrail lines, formerly New York Central and Pennsylvania Railroad, had a total capacity of 258 million gross ton-miles while the total density of all four roads was only 163 million gross ton-miles. Similar situations were calculated in all ten examples. In example 4, Chicago to Kansas City, the Burlington Northern and the Santa Fe had a combined line capacity of 221 million gross ton-miles while all

Table 1.3. Main Line Corridors of Consolidation Potential, 1975.

Corridor	Number of Railroads	Total Miles of Line (all railroads)	Shortest Route (miles)	Total Line Densities (MGT)	Total Line Capacities (MGT)
1 Chicago to Pittsburgh	4	1,802	438	163	384
2 Chicago to Buffalo	4	2,145	506	129	264
3 Chicago to Southern Gateways	7	2,167	284	102	194
4 Chicago to Kansas City	8	3,933	448	175	383
5 Dallas-FortWorth to Houston	5	1,494	266	81	151
6 Chicago to Omaha	5	2,370	448	123	233
7 Kansas City/Omaha to Colorado	6	3,631	544	127	247
8 Chicago to Minneapolis	5	2,179	404	111	306
9 Chicago to St. Louis	5	1,389	257	95	205
10 Chicago to Detroit	4	1,158	264	85	195

Source: U.S. Department of Transportation, *Final Standards, Classification, and Designation of Lines of Class 1 Railroads in the United States*, Vol. 1, pp. 47–48 (1977).
Note: MGT = Millions of Gross Ton-Miles per Mile of Road.

eight carriers had a total density of only 175 million gross ton-miles. Another major inefficiency in this corridor was the Chicago & North Western which directly served a large number of industries in the Chicago area. The North Western line to Kansas City branched from its line across Iowa and was 544 route miles, compared with the short route of the Santa Fe which was only 448 miles. Furthermore, the average line density of the North Western was reported in the consolidation study as 33 million gross ton-miles, but this applied only to the A-Mainline across Iowa. The B-Mainline south to Kansas City had density of less than 20 million gross ton-miles.

In example 6, from Chicago to Omaha, the Burlington Northern and the Chicago & North Western had a combined line capacity of 156 million gross ton-miles while all five carriers had a total density of 123 million gross ton-miles. As detailed in Chapters 2 and 3, the Rock Island and Milwaukee Road both later filed bankruptcy. The Rock Island line from Illinois to Omaha was sold to a regional railroad, and the Milwaukee Road main line across Iowa was abandoned and most of the tracks removed.

In example 8, from Chicago to Minneapolis, the Milwaukee Road alone had a line capacity of 135 million gross ton-miles while the combined line density of all five carriers was only 111 million gross ton-miles. If one combines the Milwaukee Road with the Burlington Northern, the capacity was 205 million gross ton-miles or nearly twice the average density of five carriers. While the Milwaukee Road and the parallel Chicago and North Western were unable to agree on merger terms, it is surprising that no agreements could be reached for trackage rights for through trains. This would have enabled the North Western to reduce some main line to branch lines and abandon others.

REMEDIAL LEGISLATION

The Railroad Revitalization and Regulatory Reform Act of 1976[24] (4R Act) brought radical change to railroad regulation. Under sections 202 and 205, rate regulation was relaxed enough to end cross-subsidization of rates on some classes of goods by higher minimum rates set on others. A rate which equaled or exceeded variable cost of providing a service was presumed to contribute to the going concern value of the carrier unless intervenors could rebut the presumption by clear and convincing evidence.[25] No maximum rate was to be found unreasonable unless the ICC should find that the proponent carrier had market dominance for such service, i.e. absence of effective competition from other carriers or modes of transportation.[26] This section was destined to promote contests before the ICC over whether a railroad was dominant in the area of a given rail line. In effect, the ICC definition of dominance applied to such a large percentage of railroad rates that it largely prevented carrier freedom in ratemaking.[27]

The 4-R Act amended the Department of Transportation Act to enable the Secretary of Transportation to develop and make available recommendations for mergers, consolidations and other unifications or coordination projects for rail services, including joint use of tracks or other facilities.[28] This was a radical new policy of Congress to favor efforts to achieve a more efficient, economical and viable rail system in the private sector. It was a clear rejection of the former ICC policy of trying to maintain numerous parallel rail lines and sacrifice efficiency. The Secretary was enabled to conduct studies to determine potential cost savings and improvements in the quality of rail services expected to result from the unification or coordination of two or more railroads. The data in Tables 1.2 and 1.3 are derived from these studies. The aim was the elimination of duplicative and overlapping operations, the utilization of the shortest and most efficient routes, the exchange of trackage rights, and the combination of facilities.

When requested by one or more railroads, the Secretary was authorized to hold conferences with respect to proposed railroad unifications or coordinations to which the ICC, local governments and all interested parties would be invited. Whenever such merger or coordination proposed was submitted to the ICC for action, the Secretary was authorized to appear before the ICC in the proceeding.

Merger procedures were revised in order to reduce greatly the allowable time for hearings and decision by the ICC.[29] Once all parties had received notice of a proposed merger and filed comments or inconsistent applications, the ICC was required to conclude evidentiary proceedings within 240 days and render a final decision within 180 days thereafter. In Chapter 2, there is a summary of the 11 year contest before the ICC between the Chicago & North Western and the Union Pacific over which carrier should be permitted to acquire the Rock Island Railroad.

The 4-R Act also provided for financial assistance for railroad rehabilitation.[30] The Secretary of Transportation was authorized to issue guarantees for obligations of railroads to acquire new equipment or rebuild them and for work on track, roadbed, structures, communications and terminals. A rail fund was established in the treasury to finance these improvements. Rail funds were to be supplied to railroads demonstrating need for assistance for rehabilitation of facilities in exchange for redeemable preference shares issued by the carriers. As to railroads in bankruptcy, the Secretary was authorized to purchase trustee certificates from the carriers.

As to abandonments, in 1972 the ICC had adopted a rule shifting the burden of proof for abandoning light density lines. The new rule established a rebuttable presumption that abandonment should be permitted for any railroad showing fewer than 34 carloads per mile per year over the lines under petition.[31] If there was no public objection, the abandonment was immediately granted. If shippers filed protests, upon hearing they had to carry the burden of showing that public convenience and necessity required continued service. The 34-car-rule was upheld by the courts as within the statutory authority of the ICC to make rules and regulations.[32] The 4-R Act also set time limits for the ICC to render decisions in abandonment cases.[33]

The Staggers Rail Act of 1980[34] was enacted with the strong backing of Conrail and the U.S. Federal Railroad Administration in an effort to supplement the 4-R Act of 1976 in relieving the financial crises of the railroads. The consensus of the industry was that further deregulation followed by economic change induced by market forces was necessary for survival.[35] The goals of the Staggers were stated as follows:[36]

(1) to assist the railroads of the Nation in rehabilitating the rail system in order to meet the demands of interstate commerce and the national defense;
(2) to reform Federal regulatory policy so as to preserve a safe, adequate, economical, efficient, and financially stable rail system;
(3) to assist the rail system to remain viable in the private sector of economy;
(4) to provide a regulatory process that balances the needs of carriers, shippers, and the public; and
(5) to assist in the rehabilitation and financing of the rail system.

The first function of the Staggers Act was to deregulate most ratemaking. The enacted policy was "to allow, to the maximum extent possible, competition and the demand for services to establish reasonable rates for transportation by rail."[37] In order to effect this, the added policy was "to require rail carriers, to the maximum extent practicable to rely on individual rate increases, and to limit the use of increases of general applicability."[38] Absent market dominance by the railroad, a rate that contributed to the going concern value of a carrier was conclusively presumed not to be below a reasonable minimum. The statutory test was "A rate for transportation by rail that equals or exceeds the variable cost of providing the transportation is conclusively presumed to contribute to the going concern value of such rail carrier."[39]

The Staggers Act redefined market dominance so that it became of minor significance to ratemaking. The regulation of maximum rates applied only when rates exceeded a statutory ratio of rates to variable costs.[40] The original limitation rate 160%. After 1984, the ICC was empowered to set the percentage rates indicating dominance between 170% and 180% of variable cost.[41] From data submitted by the railroads, the ICC would determine the railroad cost adjustment factor. This percentage of change would be published by the ICC quarterly, thus enabling the carriers to raise rates as costs rose and still not be accused of market dominance.

Upon challenge by a shipper, the first burden on the railroad was that it had presented valid cost evidence that the rate did not exceed the percentage limit above variable cost set by the ICC. Even if the railroad failed in this burden of proof, market dominance was not presumed. The shipper had the burden of evidence that it did not face a transport market with enough alternatives equal to effective competition. The four types of competition considered by the ICC were interrailroad, intermodal such as motor carriers, geographic competition and product competition.[42]

The Staggers Act contained a section authorizing freedom of contract between railroads and shippers.[43] Railroads could offer lower rates for multi-car shipments or for a whole service of shipments over a stated period of time. For each contract, nonconfidential information contained therein had to be filed with the ICC for approval. The ICC was ordered to publish special tariff rules for such contracts in order to assure that the essential terms of the contract were available to the public in tariff format. Other provisions allowed shipper complaints of harm from the effects of contract tariffs. More than 79,000 contract rates had been filed by the end of 1988, an estimated 60% of all Class 1 freight traffic.[44]

The increased rate flexibility under the Staggers Rail Act enabled railroads to retain and regain boxcar service. In 1983, the ICC exempted railroad boxcar service from regulation, ending rate regulation based on contents.[45] In 1988, the ICC Office of Transportation Analysis concluded that aggressive pricing enabled railroads to retain boxcar traffic they otherwise would have lost to motor carriers.[46]

The Staggers Act also had a special set of provisions concerning the cancellation of joint rates and imposition by railroads of joint-rate surcharges.[47] Where a railroad participating in a joint rate could demonstrate that its revenues were less than 110% of its variable costs of rendering its part of the haul, that railroad could impose a surcharge on the joint rate. Such surcharge could be applied without the concurrence of any other rail carrier. A rail carrier could cancel the application of a joint rate to a through route in which it participated, without the concurrence of any other rail carrier.[48] In 1984, the ICC modified the regulations to provide that reasonably expected costs might be assigned to single-line traffic as well as joint line traffic originating or terminating on the surcharged line.[49]

The Staggers Act greatly limited the antitrust exemption for railroad rate bureaus.[50] Rail carriers were not to discuss or enter agreements on single line rate except for purposes of general rate increases. Carriers were barred from discussing or agreeing on rates related to a particular interline movement unless that carrier practicably participated in that movement. Thus a railroad had to be a direct connector to a joint-line movement of trains in order to be free to discuss joint rates with the other connecting railroad. Consequently, the ICC issued a decision barring agreements between the four major geographical rate bureaus because they severely lessened competition.[51] Thereafter, the number of joint rate proposals submitted to the rate bureaus dropped dramatically.[52]

As to railroad mergers, the Staggers Act adopted a distinction between mergers that involved two Class 1 railroads and those that did not. For mergers of two Class 1 railroads, the Act added a fifth criterion for approval to the four criteria adopted in the Transportation Act of 1940. The five criteria were as follows:[53]

(1) the effect of the proposed transaction on the adequacy of transportation to the public;
(2) the effect on the public interest of including, or failing to include, other rail carriers in the area involved in the proposed transaction;
(3) the total fixed charges that result from the proposed transaction;
(4) the interest of rail carrier employees affected by the proposed transaction; and
(5) whether the proposed transaction would have an adverse effect on competition among rail carriers in the affected region or in the national rail system.

Where the merger did not involve two Class 1 railroads, the approval criteria were only two:[54]

(1) as a result of the transaction, there is likely to be substantial lessening of competition, creation of a monopoly, or restraint of trade in freight surface transportation in any region of the United States; and
(2) the anticompetitive effects of the transaction outweigh the public interest in meeting significant transportation needs.

The addition of the fifth criterion when the proposal concerned two Class 1 railroads was not innovative since the effect on alleged competition had long been an aspect of the public interest standard. While the Transportation Act of 1920[55] relieved the railroads from the operation of the antitrust laws when a unification was approved by the ICC, the requirement for the commission to draw a comprehensive plan for consolidation of railroads had as one criterion the preservation of competition.[56] In fact, the comprehensive consolidation plan failed primarily because it was designed to save weak railroads by causing strong railroads to absorb them.[57]

As to mergers that did not involve two Class 1 railroads, the public interest standard no longer applied. The specified standards of lessening of competition, creation of monopoly, or restraint of trade were highly unlikely to apply to Class II railroads, whether short line or regional. Even acquisitions of a Class II railroad by a Class I railroad would be unlikely to have anticompetitive effects.

The Staggers Act gave the ICC power to exempt from the regulatory hearing process any transaction that was not necessary to carry out the transportation policy enunciated in the code.[58] This was especially applicable to new short-line carriers when they bought branch lines from Class 1 railroads and to existing short-line carriers when they bought lines abandoned by nearby Class 1 railroads. Most requests for authority to acquire rail lines after 1980 were for exemptions by Class II railroads. The ICC concluded that a case-by-case handling of these exemptions involved a burdensome and unnecessary expenditure of resources both by the petitioners and the commission. Since most requests to create or acquire an additional line by a Class II or Class III railroad were unopposed, the ICC in 1985 amended its acquisition regulations.[59] The carrier was merely required to file a notice of exemption that would be effective seven days after it was filed. The effective date was revised in 1988 to 21 days after filing. The ICC would publish a notice of the filing in the Federal Register within 30 days of the filing.

The ICC also issued an exemption for all railroad trackage agreements except those sought in response to a rail consolidation proceeding.[60] The finding was that trackage rights provided carriers with alternative, shorter, and faster routes that enhanced a carrier's competitive position. Most trackage rights promoted efficiency for the operator and still maintained the quality of service for shippers. Increasing traffic density on the most efficient rail line between two points with two carriers sharing the costs would not only lower average total costs of operation. The tenant carrier could reduce its former main line to branch line status with less maintenance or even sell that section to a short-line railroad. The only real issue between the trackage owner and the tenant railroad was the amount of compensation for trackage rights.[61]

As to abandonments of rail lines, the Staggers Act reduced the time allowed for proceedings.[62] Unprotested applications could result in abandonment in 75 days. In protested cases, investigation was to be completed in 135 days as compared with 24 months allowed under the 4-R Act of 1976, and a final decision had to be rendered within 255 days from the date of application.

The Act directed that when the ICC found that a line could be abandoned, the finding had to be published in the Federal Register. With 10 days, any person or firm could offer the carrier a subsidy or offer to purchase the line. If an offer to purchase did not lead to an agreement with the carrier, either party could request the ICC to set the compensation. The statutory standard was fair market value.[63] In its first decision to set compensation on sale of a net-loss branch line, the price was set at nonrail liquidation value.[64] In 1987 the ICC adopted rules for continuing rail service by requiring a carrier to accept a subsidy, or to sell or lease a line to a financially responsible person before approval of an exempt abandonment.[65]

Starting in 1983, the ICC issued rules exempting rail line abandonments when the line had been out of service for two years. This exemption was later expanded to include discontinuance of trackage rights.[66] The appeals courts held these rules necessary to effectuate relevant goals of the national transportation policy adopted in the Staggers Act.[67]

Just before enactment of the Staggers Act, the ICC issued rules to allow evidence of opportunity costs in abandonment proceedings.[68] If a railroad was denied abandonment of a net-loss rail line, the funds that could be recovered from abandonment would not be available to reinvest in profitable lines of the carrier. This was the opportunity cost that had not previously been recognized in abandonment cases. This new policy was upheld on appeal after passage of the Staggers Act.[69] An adequate rate of return was to be computed each year by using the findings of the Commission's annual revenue adequacy proceedings adjusted for taxes and inflation. For 1983, the ICC found the appropriate rate of return to be used in calculating a railroad's opportunity cost to be 22.3%.[70]

Another significant regulatory change by the ICC was termination of the DT&I Conditions to merger approvals. These general conditions had been imposed in 1950 and did not identify specific carriers or individual gateways.[71] Condition 1 required a consolidated carrier to "maintain and keep open all routes and channels of trade via existing junctions and gateways" unless otherwise authorized by the ICC. Another condition required a consolidated carrier to continue "present traffic and operating relationships." The conditions were highly anticompetitive. A consolidated carrier was generally barred from lowering rates on its new single-line route below the rates on any competing joint-line routes in which it had participated. If connecting carriers did not agree to lower corresponding joint rates, some routes or gateways would in effect be closed. The ICC policy was to keep all carriers in the market no matter how inefficient. The consolidated carrier could not alone cut rates in order to increase its line density and pass savings on to shippers.

In 1979 the ICC adopted a limiting policy and found the DT&I conditions unnecessary in a case.[72] It held that it would impose the conditions only if the consolidation would result in (1) impairment of a protesting carrier's ability to provide essential services, or (2) the loss of adequate transportation service to shippers. In 1982, the ICC finally made an official finding that the DT&I traffic protection conditions were anticompetitive and contrary to the public interest.[73] All DT&I conditions that had been imposed in past rail merger cases were revoked unless parties that were involved could demonstrate a public interest in continuing them. Notice was given that DT&I conditions would not be imposed in future merger cases.

EFFECTS OF DEREGULATION

In the twenty years since passage of the Staggers Act, the economic structure of the railroad industry and the interfirm rivalry of the carriers has changed radically.[74] The number of Class I railroads has dropped from 106 in 1960 to 74 in 1975, 39 in 1980, 14 in 1990, and eight in 2000.[75] Some western carriers, such as the Rock Island Railroad and the Milwaukee Road were bankrupt and dismembered. Many more ceased separate existence through mergers and are the subjects of Chapters 4 through 7 herein.

The great changes in the Class I railroads in the last half-century are presented in Table 1.4. As reported to the ICC, the miles of road operated by U.S. railroads, including leased lines and trackage rights over other carriers, decreased from 226,101 miles in 1950 to 120,022 miles in 2000, drop of 47%. From the passage of the Staggers Act in 1980, the miles operated decreased by over 56,000. The small decrease from 1995 to 2000 results from the large grants in trackage rights to rivals in order to secure ICC approval of mergers. The Burlington Northern-Santa Fe merger and the Union Pacific-Southern Pacific merger are prime examples, as explained in Chapters 6 and 7.

The miles of road owned by Class I railroads also decreased by over 50% in the last half century to a total of 100,839 in 2000. This includes, 1,589 miles owned by Canadian railroads. The decrease since passage of the Staggers Act in 1980 is from 152,229 miles to 100,839 miles in 2000, or 33.7%. The abandonments of railway line approved by the ICC from 1980 to 1995, when the ICC was terminated, totaled 30,180 miles.[76] A large majority of these lines were not removed but were sold to short-line or regional carriers for continued operation. These acquisitions by new small carriers who were noncarriers before the purchase were facilitated by fact that these sales were not railroad consolidations. In this class of cases, the ICC had discretion not to order income protection for workers of the selling Class I railroad who lost jobs.[77] As Judge Richard A. Posner stated in upholding the ICC decision not to impose income

Table 1.4. Road and Operating Statistics of Class I Railroads.

Year	Miles of Road Operated	Miles of Road Owned	Revenue Ton-Miles (Millions)	Revenue Per Ton-Mile (Cents)[a]	Intermodal Traffic (Trailers and Containers)
1950	226,101	208,756	588,578	n.a.	
1955	224,475	190,843	623,615	1.370	
1960	220,228	188,097	572,309	1.403	
1965	213,167	180,113	697,878	1.266	1,664,929
1970	209,836	176,745	764,809	1.428	2,363,200
1975	207,097	172,428	754,252	2.041	2,238,117
1980	176,457	152,229	918,958	2.867	3,059,402
1985	161,037	140,921	876,984	3.043	4,590,952
1990	133,189	114,930	1,033,969	2.657	6,206,782
1995	124,871	105,434	1,305,688	2.401	7,936,172
2000	120,022	99,250	1,465,960	2.257	9,176,890

Sources: U.S., I.C.C., *Transport Statistics in the United States* (1950–1995); Surface Transportation Board, *Statistics of Class I Freight Railroads in the United States* (1995–1999); Association of American Railroads, *Railroad Facts* 26, 27, 30, 44 (2001).
Note: n.a. = not available.
[a] The freight revenue per ton-mile indexed in constant 1990 dollars would show 1990 at 2.657, 1995 at 2.118, and 2000 at 1.890. *Railroad Facts* 31 (2001).

protection in the sale by Chicago & North Western of a 208-mile line to Fox River Valley Railroad:

> The decision to sell a line is not a decision about the utilization of labor or about wages, work rules, working conditions, job rights, etc. It is a decision to reduce the extent of the railroad's business, akin to a manufacturer's decision to curtail its output or to retire unneeded capacity without replacing it. It is not a decision about labor inputs.[78]

The total route lines of non-Class I railroads in the United States in 1999 was over 49,000 miles.[79] From 1980 to 1992, 285 short line and regional railroads were created with 27,688 miles of line.[80] John Riley of the Federal Railroad Administration explained why net-loss lines of Class I railroads could have lower costs when acquired by new, smaller lines:

> The smaller railroad has lower overhead. It can maintain a less costly equipment inventory. It will normally maintain its tracks to different standards. And, most important, the small railroad, whether it is union or non-union, is not likely to be encumbered by the strict craft lines and work rules that tend to typify major carrier agreements. So what that means is that the short line carrier can use the talents of a single employee on multiple tasks rather

than employing several individuals on a full-time basis when their services are needed only a portion of the time.[81]

An example was the Chicago and North Western line from Winona, Minnesota west across both Minnesota and South Dakota to Rapid City. This 637-mile line was reported in 1975 to have less than five million gross ton-miles of traffic per mile of road.[82] The line was sold to the new Dakota Minnesota & Eastern in 1986 and was operating successfully in 1996.[83]

The revenue ton-miles measure the quantity of goods carried by railroad for shippers, as distinguished from all the fuel and other products carried for rail operations. As noted in Table 1.4, the revenue ton-miles went from 918,958 million in 1980 to 1,465,960 million in 2000, a 59.5% increase. While part of this gain was due to growth in national output of goods, a significant part was diversion of traffic from motor carriers as rail rates decreased. Part of this was the great growth in intermodal traffic, trailers and containers on flat cars (TOFC/COFC). As noted in Table 4, this traffic tripled from three million in 1980 to nine million in 1999. A report to Congress noted this impact:

> Goods not carried in TOFC/COFC service would likely be carried by trucks. Spurred in part by greater rate-making flexibility and ICC's exemption of this traffic from regulation under the Staggers Rail Act, railroads were able to design price packages that make this business attractive to shippers and others.[84]

Revenue per ton-mile, as one measure of income, is recorded in Table 1.4. The actual dollar figures show a decrease from 2.867 cents in 1980 to 2.257 cents in 2000. But in real terms, rate rivalry caused a greater drop. In 1990 constant dollars, the decrease was from 2.657 cents in 1990 to 1.890 cents in 2000. Gallamore calculated the great increase in factor productivity. Ton-miles per constant dollar of operating expense increased almost 2.5 times between 1980 and 1995.[85] Most other indicators of railroad economic performance also improved. This resulted from a combination of two economic forces, deregulation and innovation that reinforced each other. Railroad industry structure with net-loss investment in excess capacity of low-density lines impaired investment in new expensive technology. With the dramatic reduction in Class I line milage, investment could be concentrated on high-density main lines. New high-productivity, multi-function machines for maintenance of way are a prime example of substituting capital for labor in the production process.[86]

Lower freight rates resulting from the competitive effect of deregulation increased the pressure on carriers to reduce their workforce in order to lower operating costs. The history of employment reduction is noted in Table 1.5. As to the period after the adoption of the Staggers Act, employment by Class I railroads decreased from 458,000 in 1980 to 168,000 in 2000, a decrease of

Table 1.5. Employment By Railroads (Thousands of Persons).

	All Railroads	Class I Railroads
1955	1,239	1,058
1960	909	780
1965	753	640
1970	640	566
1975	548	488
1980	532	458
1985	372	302
1990	296	216
1995	265	188
2000	246	168

Source: Association of American Railroads, *Railroad Facts* 56 (2001).

63%. With the backing of the federal railway labor laws, the powerful railway labor unions had long ago bargained the Class I carriers into full crew agreements for trainmen. This meant four or five workers on each freight train.[87] In the 1990s, the Class I railroads finally bargained the unions into reducing crew size on through freight trains to two, with three crew men on trains where more switching was required.[88]

CONCLUSION

The Surface Transportation Board has published two detailed bulletins on the decline in railroad rates since passage of the Staggers Act.[89] While nominal published rates have dropped about 20% between 1980 and 2000, an index of inflation-adjusted rates shows a drop of about 50%. The indexes drop for 1999 alone was 2.7%.[90] While this is overwhelming evidence of interrailroad competition and intermodal competition, it occurred while the number of railroads in every district declined radically through mergers. The economists of the Department of Justice who contended that fewer railroads would result in less railroad competition and higher rates have been totally disproved. The key is the great productivity gains by the railroads since 1980. Losses from excess capacity disappeared as miles of road owned by Class I carriers dropped 33.7%.[91] Revenue ton-miles increased 56% with a 52% decrease in employees, 28% fewer locomotives and 23% fewer freight cars in service.

The issue arises concerning which parties benefited by reduced rates. A weak hypothesis is that if nominal rates had not been reduced 20% since 1980, the freight revenues of Class I railroads in 1999 of $32,680 million would be only

80% of the total. If one ignores the fact that 20% higher rates would have caused a significant drop in demand as some shippers switched to motor carriers, the savings were $8,170 million. Certain shippers point out that none of this reduced cost of doing business showed up in their net profits. The STB bulletin contained the answer:

> The fact that neither railroads nor shippers have captured the majority of these savings suggests that rail customers – because they tend to operate in highly competitive markets for widely available commodities such as coal, grain, or chemicals – have been forced to pass along the bulk of these savings to their own customers. Thus the ultimate beneficiaries of increases in railroad productivity appear to have been consumers.[92]

STB points out that because the prices of many commodities shipped by rail have fallen even more than their respective freight rates, for many shippers transport costs are a larger fraction of the delivered price today than in the past. Corn, wheat, and coal at mines in the Powder River Basin are noted examples.[93]

The final conclusion is that the Class I railroads have significantly benefited by their reduced miles of road and growth in productivity. In 1980, when the bankruptcies of the Rock Island and of the Milwaukee Road were being heard in court, the net revenue from railway operations of all Class I carriers was $1,280 millions with an operating ratio of 95.35%.[94] By 1990, the aggregate net revenue from railway operations was $3,674 million and the operating ratio was 87.03. In 1999, the aggregate net revenue from railway operations was $5,476 million and the operating ratio was 83.67.

NOTES

1. See Albro Martin, *Enterprise Denied: Origins of the Decline of American Railroads, 1897-1917* (New York: Columbia University Press, 1971); Alfred D. Chandler, *The Railroads: the Nation's First Big Business* (New York: Harcourt, Brace & World, 1965).

2. See Theodore E. Keeler, *The Economics of Passenger Trains*, 44 J. Business 148–174 (1971).

3. See Michael Conant, *Railroad Mergers and Abandonments* 113–131 (Berkeley: University of California Press, 1964); Richard C. Levin, *Regulation, Barriers to Exit, and the Investment Behavior of Railroads* in *Studies in Public Regulation*, Gary Fromm, ed. (Cambridge: MIT Press, 1981) (Cited hereinafter as Levin, *Regulation*).

4. As to cross-subsidization of different classes of shippers that was effected by the regulated rate system, see Theodore E. Keeler, *Railroad, Freight and Public Policy* 25–26 (Washington D.C., Brookings Institution, 1983); Ann F. Friedlaender and Richard H. Spady, *Freight Transport Regulation* 106–108 (Cambridge: MIT Press, 1981); George W. Hilton, *The Basic Behavior of Regulatory Commissions*, 62 Amer. Econ. Rev. 47–54 (May 1972). For a renowned judge's critique of minimum rate regulation, see Henry J. Friendly, *The Federal Administrative Agencies: The Need for Better Definition of Standards* 106–140 (Cambridge: Harvard University Press, 1962).

5. U.S., I.C.C., *Transport Statistics in the United States* 30 (1960); *Id.* 60 (1965). As to the history of the railroad passenger deficit, see Conant, *Railroad Mergers and Abandonments, supra* note 3, at 132–165; U.S., I.C.C., *Investigation of Costs of Intercity Rail Passenger Service* (1969).

6. In re New York, N.H.&H. R.R., 289 F. Supp. 451, 456 (D. Conn. 1968). See note *New Haven Railroad Reorganization Proceedings, or the Little Railroad that Couldn't*, 78 Harv. L. Rev. 861 (1965); Michael Conant, *Merger Valuation of Net Loss Railroads*, 42 ICC Practitioners J. 281–287 (1975).

7. In re Penn Central Transportation Co., 384 F. Supp. 895, 902 (Special Ct., Reg. Rail Reorg. Act, 1974). See U.S. Cong., House, Committee on Interstate and Foreign Commerce, *Inadequacies of Protections for Investors in Penn Central and other Railroads*, 92d Cong., 1st Sess. (1971); U.S. Cong., House, Committee on Banking, *The Penn Central Failure and the Role of Financial Institutions*, 92d Cong., 1st Sess. (1972).

8. Rail Passenger Service Act of 1970, 84 Stat. 1327 (1970), 49 U.S.C.A. 24301 (1997).

9. See Steven A. Morrison, *The Value of Amtrak*, 33 J. Law and Econ. 361 (1990). In 1999, Amtrak operated passenger service on 22,741 miles of road and carried 21.5 million passengers. Its 1999 operating revenues were $1,864.6 million and its operating expenses were $2,786.4 million, resulting in a net operating loss of $921.8 million. Association of American Railroads, *Railroad Facts* 77 (2000).

10. Brook-Scanlon Co. v Railroad Comm'n, 251 U.S. 396, 399 (1920). See Railroad Comm'n v. Eastern Texas R. R., 264 U.S. 79 (1924); Bullock v. Railroad Comm'n, 254 U.S. 513 (1921).

11. See Annotation, 10 A.L.R. 2d 1121, 1130–1134 (1950); Note: *Takings and the Public Interest in Railroad Reorganization*, 82 Yale L. J. 1004 (1975).

12. 244 U.S. 388 (1917).

13. Between its 1961 bankruptcy and its 1969 inclusion in Penn-Central, the operating losses of the New Haven eroded the debtors estate (bondholders' interests) in excess of $60 million. New Haven Inclusion Cases, 399 U.S. 392, 490 (1970). The Court concluded, "But in the circumstances presented by this litigation we see no constitutional bar to that result." *Id.*, at 491. See NYNH&H R.R. Co., Trustees Discontinuance of All Interstate Passenger Trains, 327 I.C.C. 151 (1966) (some discontinuances granted and others denied).

14. U.S. Department of Transportation, *Railroad Abandonments and Alternatives: A Report on Effects Outside the Northeastern Region* 9–34 (1976). See Donald W. Larson and Robert C. Vogel, *Railroad Abandonment: Optimal Solutions and Policy Outcomes*, in Kenneth D. Boyer and William G. Shepherd, eds. *Essays in Honor of James R. Nelson* 65–82 (E. Lansing: Michigan State University Press, 1981).

15. Robert G. Harris, *Economics of Traffic Density in the Rail Freight Industry*, 8 Bell J. Econ. 556 (1977); Robert G. Harris, *Economic Analysis of Light Density Rail Lines*, 16 Logistics and Trans. Rev. 3 (1980). For an earlier study of the conomics of density and railroad linkages in the West, see U.S. Department of Transportation, *Western Railroad Mergers* 19 (1969).

16. Theodore E. Keeler, *Railroad Costs, Returns to Scale, and Excess Capacity*, 56 Rev. of Econ. and Stat. 201 (1974).

17. 90 Stat. 33 (1976); U.S. Department of Transportation, *Final Standards, Classification, and Designation of Lines of Class 1 Railroads in the United States* (1977) (cited hereinafter as *Final Standards*).

18. U.S., I.C.C., *Transport Statistics in the United States* 6 (1975).
19. U.S. Dep't. of Trans., 1 *Final Standards, supra* note 17, at Al.
20. *Id.*
21. *Id.*, Vol. 2 at 138.
22. Levin, *Regulation, supra* note 3, at 186–189.
23. U.S. Dep't. of Trans., 2 *Final Standards, supra* note 17, at 47–48.
24. Public Law 94-210 (Feb. 5, 1976), 90 Stat. 31. See Paul W. MacAvoy and John W. Snow, eds. *Railroad Revitalization and Regulatory Reform* (Washington D.C.: American Enterprise Institute, 1977).
25. RRRR Act, Section 202, 90 Stat. 34.
26. 49 U.S.C. §10705 (1976). *See* 1 Special Procedures for Making Findings of Market Dominance, Final Report, 355 I.C.C. 12 (1977); S. Rep. No. 499, 94th Cong., 2d Sess. 46, *reprinted in* 1976 U.S. Code Cong. & Ad. News 14, 60.
27. Upon challenge by the railroads, this approach was upheld. *See* Atchison, T.&S. F. Ry. v. ICC, 580 F.2d 623 (D.C. Cir. 1978).
28. RRRR Act, Section 401, 90 Stat. 61, 49 U.S.C. 1654. See Richard C. Levin and Daniel H. Weinberg, *Alternatives for Restructuring the Railroads: End to End or Parallel Mergers?*, 17 Economic Inquiry 371 (1979).
29. RRRR Act, Section 402, 90 Stat. 62.
30. *Id.*, Section 4501, 90 Stat. 65–67.
31. 49 C.F.R. §§ 1121.20-1121.24 (1972).
32. Commonwealth of Pennsylvania v. United States, 301 F. Supp. 208 (M.D.Pa., 1973), *affirmed*, 414 U.S. 1017 (1973).
33. RRRR Act, Section 802, 90 Stat. 127-130, 49 U.S.C. 1a.
34. Public Law 96-448 (Oct. 14, 1980), 94 Stat. 1895. For background to the statute, *see* H.R. Rep. No. 1035, 96th Cong., 2d Sess. 38, *reprinted in* 1980 U.S. Code Cong. & Ad. News 3978–3983.
35. See Richard D. Stone, *The Interstate Commerce Commission and the Railroad Industry* 113–151 (Westport, CT: Praeger, 1991).
36. 94 Stat. 1879, 49 U.S.C. 10101a (1980).
37. *Id.*
38. *Id.*
39. *Id.*
40. Section 202, 94 Stat. 1900, 49 U.S.C. 10709 (1980).
41. Section 203, 94 Stat. 1901, 49 U.S.C. 10707a (1980).
42. *Market Dominance Determinations and Considerations of Product Competition*, 365 I.C.C. 118 (1981), *affirmed sub nom.* Western Coal Traffic League v. I.C.C., 719 F. 2d 772 (5th Cir. 1983), *cert. denied*, 104 S. Ct 2160 (1984). See Product and Geographic Competition, 2 I.C.C. 2d 1 (1985).
43. Section 208, 94 Stat. 1908, 49 U.S.C. 10713 (1980). See Railroad Transportation Contracts, 367 I. C. C. 9 (1982); U.S., I.C.C., *Report on Railroad Contract Rates Authorized by Selection 208 of the Staggers Rail Act of 1980* (1984).
44. Stone, *The Interstate Commerce Commission, supra* note 35, at 161.
45. Exemption From Regulation-Boxcar Traffic, 367 I.C.C. 425, 446 (1983), *affirmed in part, vacated in part, and remanded to ICC*, Brae Corp. v. United Staes, 740 F. 2d 1023, 1070 (D.C. Cir. 1984), *cert. denied*, 471 U.S. 1069 (1985). The general exemption of boxcar rates was upheld. Only the exemption of joint rates was remanded for further review. See Railroad Exemption – Export Coal/Boxcars, 1 I.C.C. 2d 287, 289

(1985); Boxcar Hire and Car Service, 3 I.C.C. 2d 1 (1986); Exemption from Regulation-Boxcar Traffic, 3 I.C.C. 2d 23 (1986).
46. U.S., I.C.C., *Effects of the Boxcar Exemption* (1988).
47. Section 217, 94 Stat. 1916, 49 U.S.C. 10705a (1980); Light Density Line Surcharge, 367 I.C.C. 99 (1981), *aff'd sub nom.*, Alldrege Grain and Storage Co. v. I.C.C., 720 F.2d 481 (8th Cir. 1983).
48. See Intramodal Rail Competition, 1 I.C.C. 2d 822 (1985).
49. Reasonably Expected Costs, 365 I.C.C. 819 (1982); 1 I.C.C. 2d 252 (1984).
50. Section 219, 94 Stat. 1926, 49 U.S.C. 10706(a). Congress created the antitrust exemption for rate bureaus in 1948. 62 Stat. 472 (1948). In spite of antitrust prosecution, control of rail rates by rate bureaus had been continuous since about 1900. See Conant, *Railroad Mergers and Abandonments, supra* note 3, at 31.
51. Western Railroads-Agreement, 364 I.C.C. 635 (1981), 365 I.C.C. 918 (1982).
52. See Railway Age 12 (Sept. 13, 1982).
53. Section 228, 94 Stat. 1931, 49 U.S.C. 11344(b).
54. *Id.*
55. 41 Stat. 456 (1920).
56. 41 Stat. 482.
57. James M. Herring, *The Problem of Weak Railroads* 99–124 (Philadelphia: University of Pennsylvania Press, 1929).
58. Section 213, 94 Stat. 1913, 49 U.S.C. §10505 (1980).
59. Class Exemption-Acq. & Oper. Of R. Lines under 49 U.S.C. 10901, 1 I.C.C 2d 810 (1985), *affirmed*, Illinois Commerce Commission v. I.C.C., 817 F. 2d 145 (D.C. Cir., 1987), revised at 4 I. C.C. 2d 408, 822. Under the ICC Termination Act of 1995, 109 Stat. 803, Class II rail carriers were required to provide adversely affected railroad employees a maximum of 1 year of severance pay. Class Exem. For Acq. Or Oper. Under 49 U.S.C. 10902, 1 S.T.B. 95 (1996).
60. Railroad Consolidation Procedures-Trackage Rights Exemption, 1 I.C.C 2d 270 (1985). See Conant, *Railroad Mergers and Abandonments, supra* note 3, at 100–109.
61. See William B. Tye, *Pricing Trackage Rights to Preserve Post-Merger Rail Competition on Equal Terms*, 24 Logistics and Transportation Review 317 (1988).
62. Section 402, 94 Stat. 1941, 49 U.S.C. 10903 (1980).
63. 94 Stat. 1944. The ICC concluded that fair market value was to be defined as the greater of net liquidation value or going concern value. Abandonment of R.R. Lines & Discontinuance of Serv., 365 I.C.C 249 (1981).
64. Chicago and North Western Transp. Co.-Abandonment, 363 I.C.C 956 (1981), *affirmed*, Chicago and North Western Transp. Co. v. United States, 678 F.2d 665, 668 (7th Cir. 1982). See Conant *Merger Valuation of Net Loss Railroads, supra*, note 6.
65. Exempt. Of Rail Abandonment-Offers of Finan. Assist., 4 I.C.C 2d 164 (1987).
66. Exemption of Out of Service Rail Lines, 366 I. C.C. 885 (1983); 1 I.C.C. 2d 55 (1984), 2 I.C.C 2d 146 (1986).
67. Illinois Commerce Com'n v. I.C.C, 848 F.2d 1246 (D.C. Cir. 1988). The ICC did not have to conduct an evidentiary hearing before it could exempt a carrier's application for abandonment. State of W. Va. Ex Rel. Manchin v. I.C.C, 841 F.2d 1162 (D.C.Cir. 1988).
68. Abandonment of R. Lines-Use of Opportunity Costs, 360 I.C.C 571 (1979).
69. Farmland Industries, Inc. v. United States, 642 F.2d 208 (7th Cir. 1981).
70. Abandonment of R. Lines-Use of Opportunity Cost, 367 I.C.C 734 (1983).

71. Detroit T. & I.R.Co. Control, 275 I.C.C. 455, 492 (1950).
72. Norfolk & W.Ry.Co.-Control-Detroit T. & I.R.Co., 360 I.C.C. 498 (1979).
73. Traffic Protective Conditions, 366 I.C.C. 112 (1982), *reversed and remanded*, Detroit, Toledo & Ironton R.Co. v. U.S., 725 F. 2d 47 (6th Cir. 1984). While termination of all future imposition of the DT&I condition was upheld, retrospective termination was limited. The Court held "that the Commission must conduct individual hearings on each previously approved merger before it can find that revocation of DT&I conditions imposed on that merger is appropriate." *Id.* at 51.
74. See Curtis M. Grimm and Robert Windle, *The Rationale for Deregulation*, in James Peoples, ed., *Regulatory Reform and Labor Markets* (Boston: Kluwer Academic Publishers, 1998); Clifford Winston, Thomas M. Corsi, Curtis M. Grimm, and Carol A. Evans, *The Economic Effects of Surface Freight Deregulation* (Washington, D.C.: Brookings Institution, 1990); Christoph A. Vellturo, Ernst R. Berndt, Ann F. Friedlaender, Judy Shaw-Er Wang Chiang, and Mark H. Showalter, *Deregulation, Mergers, and Cost Savings in Class I U.S. Railroads, 1974–1986*, 1 J. Econ. & Manag. Strategy 339 (1992).
75. U.S., I.C.C., *Transport Statistics in the United States* (1960–1990); U.S., Surface Transportation Board, *Statistics of Class I Freight Railroads in the United States* (2000).
76. U.S., I.C.C., *Annual Reports* (1980-1995). See U.S., General Accounting Office, *Railroad Abandonmnets: Abandonment Activity and Shipper Views on Rail Service Loss* 21–28, 52 (1987).
77. Simmons v. I.C.C., 760 F. 2d 126 (7th Cir. 1985); Black v. I.C.C., 762 F. 2d 106 (D.C. Cir. 1985).
78. Chicago & North Western v. Railway Labor Exec., 908 F. 2d 144, 152 (7th Cir. 1990).
79. Association of American Railroads, *Railroad Facts* 45 (2000).
80. Michael W. Babcock, Marvin Prater, and John Morrill, *A Profile of Short Line Railroad Success*, 34 Transport. J. 21, 23 (1994). See John F. Due, *New Railroad Companies Formed to Take Over Abandoned or Spun-Off Lines*, 24 Transportation J. 30 (1984); John F. Due and Suzanne D. Leever, *The Post-1984 Experience with New Small and Regional Railroads*, 33 Transportation J. 40, 42 (1993); Curtis M. Grimm and Harry J. Sapienza, *Determinants of Shortline Railroad Performance*, 32 Transportation J. 5 (1993).
81. U.S. Cong., Senate, Committee on Commerce, Science, and Transportation, *Short Line and Regional Railroads*, Hearing, 99th Cong., 2d Sess., 2-3 (1988). See U.S. Department of Transportation, *Deferred Maintenance and Delayed Capital Improvements on Class II and Class III Railroads, A Report to Congress* (1989).
82. 2 *Final Standards*, *supra* note 17, at 113, 149.
83. F. D. 30889, Dakota Minnesota & Eastern-Class Exemption (Aug. 18, 1985); Traffic World 42 (Jan. 29, 1996).
84. U.S., General Accounting Office, *Railroad Regulation: Economic and Financial Impacts of the Staggers Rail Act of 1980*, 23 (1990). See Improvements of TOFC/COFC Regulations, 3 I.C.C. 2d 869 (1987); Robert E. Gallamore, *State of the Art of Intermodal Freight Transport in the United States,* in Intermodal Freight Transport in Europe and the United States 17 (Lansdowne, VA: Eno Transportation Foundation, 1998).
85. Robert E. Gallamore, *Regulation and Innovation: Lessons from the American Railroad Industry*, in J. A. Gómez-Ibáñez, W. B. Tye and C. Winston, eds., *Essays in Transportation Economics and Policy* 495 (Washington D.C.: Brookings Institution

Press, 1999); Wesley W. Wilson, *Cost Savings and Productivity in the Railroad Industry*, 11 J. Regulatory Econ. 21 (1997).

86. See Gus Welty, *For Railroads, a M/W Wish List*, Railway Age 61 (Aug. 1997).

87. See, e.g. U.S. Cong. Senate, Committee on Commerce, *Penn-Central and Other Railroads*, 92d Cong., 2d Sess., 159 (1972); Joseph R. Daughen and Peter Binzen, *The Wreck of the Penn Central* 219 (Boston: Little Brown, 1971).

88. See Gallamore, *Regulation and Innovation, supra* note 85, at 502; David E. Davis and Wesley W. Wilson, *Deregulation, Mergers, and Employment in the Railroad Industry*, 15 J. Regulatory Econ. 5 (1999).

89. U.S. Surface Transportation Board, *Rail Rates Continue Multi-Year Decline* (1998); *Id.* (2000).

90. *Id.* at 1.

91. See Table 1.4, *supra*.

92. U.S., S.T.B., *Rail Rates Continue Multi-year Decline* 3 (2000). See Steven A. Morrison and Clifford Winston, *Regulatory Reform of U.S. Intercity Transportation*, in J. S. Gomez-Ibáñez, W. B. Tye and Clifford Winston, *Essays in Transportation Economics and Policy, supra* note 85, at 469, 488-489.

93. U.S., S.T.B., *Rail Rates Continue Multi-year Decline* 3 (2000).

94. Association of American Railroads, *Railroad Facts* 12, 14 (2000).

2. ROCK ISLAND BANKRUPTCY

The Chicago, Rock Island & Pacific Railroad Company filed bankruptcy on March 17, 1975. Following a strike of union workers in August 1979, the Railroad was declared cashless on September 26, 1979 and the ICC ordered another carrier to provide temporary service on Rock Island lines.[1] Under operation by the bankruptcy trustee from 1975 to 1980, the Rock Island suffered net losses totaling $210,627,230 and increased its debt by at least $200,000,000.[2] On January 25, 1980, Judge Frank J. McGarr of the Reorganization Court found the Rock Island not capable of being reorganized as a going concern and ordered bankruptcy trustee William M. Gibbons to commence liquidation of the assets. Following recommendation of the ICC, on June 2, 1980, Judge McGarr confirmed total abandonment of all Rock Island rail lines subject to the sale or lease of such lines as other carriers wished to bargain to acquire.[3]

The issue of whether some part of the Rock Island lines could be reorganized under the bankruptcy laws and emerge with a reasonable probability of operating at a net profit was a subject of intense debate. From the beginning of the bankruptcy, the outspoken major bondholders argued that it could not.[4] They proposed immediate dismemberment of the carrier and sale of its viable lines to other carriers followed by abandonment of the remainder. Trustee Gibbons, from the bias of his position as head of the railroad, disagreed and convinced Judge McGarr to let him try for reorganization for almost five years. A key factor supporting Gibbons's viewpoint was the low long-term debt of the Rock Island. The Rock Island had been in bankruptcy from 1933 to the end of 1947 and had been relieved of much of its debt.[5] Its long-term bonds on December 31, 1974 were $97,875,000 as compared to assets listed on a cost basis of $423.8 million, the ratio of bonds to asserted assets being 23%.[6] But the company had net losses every year since 1965. Consequently, the bondholders argued correctly in 1975 that even if the Rock Island were relieved by the reorganization court of having to pay $4 million per year in interest on long-term debt, it was still not potentially viable.

When the Union Pacific proposal to merge the Rock Island was before the Interstate Commerce Commission, Jervis Langdon, then Rock Island president, testified that he felt that the Rock Island could not survive as an independent entity.[7] He pointed to its inherently weak position as a rival for traffic in its own territory because of (a) the absence of important local traffic at Rock Island stations, and (b) the vulnerability of Rock Island's interline business.[8] Langdon noted that at that time, 76.4% of Rock Island's freight revenues originated or terminated at 55 major stations, and that at these stations Rock Island shared traffic with an average of 4.2 other railroads. Not only had rail rivalry left the Rock Island with a small slice of the total volume of traffic, but the growing market share of motor carriers had a severe impact. Langdon further noted that on important interline business, the Rock Island was disfavored. It had no financial ties to any of the western carriers, but it did offer one of the shortest routes to major west coast cities in combination with Southern Pacific.

Bankruptcy trustee Gibbons had to be aware of all these facts. This view is supported by Gibbons' search for a financially strong merger partner in his 1976 petition to intervene in the Missouri Pacific's merger of its two subsidiaries, Texas & Pacific and Chicago & Eastern Illinois.[9] Since these three carriers were already a coordinated system, no diversion of traffic would result, so that ICC denial of the petition for inclusion of the Rock Island in the Missouri Pacific was affirmed.[10]

ECONOMIC PERFORMANCE

The economic performance of railroads can be measured in many ways, but they are meaningful only on a comparative basis.[11] Table 2.1 presents a number of these measures for the bankrupt Rock Island and for the profitable Union Pacific. The Rock Island can be viewed as exemplary of the weak midwest roads, operating primarily in the area of great excess capacity east of the Missouri River. The Chicago, Milwaukee, St. Paul & Pacific and the Chicago & North Western were also examples. The 1974 estimated rates of return on net railroad assets for the three carriers were: Rock Island–0; Milwaukee Road–0; North Western–2.03%. In contrast, the Union Pacific was the financially strongest example of large-scale western railroads, operating mainly in areas of few parallel lines. The Santa Fe, the Southern Pacific, and the Burlington Northern were also examples. The 1974 estimated rates of return on net railroad assets of these carriers were: Union Pacific–6.11%; Santa Fe–3.46%; Southern Pacific–2.81%; Burlington Northern–2.90%. The fact that in 1974 none of these carriers had a rate of return equal to the riskless 8% long-term U.S. government bonds was indicative of the need for structural reorganization of the entire United States rail system.

One common measure of economic performance of railroads is the density of traffic, namely, the net ton-miles of revenue freight per mile of road per

Table 2.1. Economic Performance of the Rock Island and The Union Pacific Railroads for 1974.

	Rock Island	Union Pacific	Ratio of Rock Island to Union Pacific (percent)
Miles of road	7,361	9,464	77.8
Ton-miles of traffic[1] (millions)	19,738.8	55,625.5	35.5
net ton-miles per mile of road	2,683,728	5,877,593	45.7
net ton-miles per freight car day	1,691	2,617	64.6
Freight revenues per mile of road	$46,943	$101,281	46.3
Net railway operating income per mile of road	–$3,013	$13,070	
Maintenance of way expense per mile of road	$6,210	$13,806	45
Maintenance of way expense per equated track mile	$5,511	$10,872	50.7
Transportation expenses per 1,000 equated ton miles	$8.64	$6.11	141.4

Sources: Annual Report to the Interstate Commerce Commission as compiled in Moody's Transportation Manual (1975).
[1] Net tons of goods carried multiplied by the distance carried.

year. This is affected by the aggregate demand for traffic in the operating area, the number of rival railroads, the number and size of major shippers located on each individual railroad, and the proportion of road that is main lines as opposed to branch lines. As noted in Table 2.1, the 1974 net ton-miles per mile of road for the Rock Island were 2,683,728, while for the Union Pacific figure was 5,877,593. Thus, the density of traffic on the Rock Island was only 45.7% of the Union Pacific. A second economic performance is net ton-miles per freight car day, but this may differ for carriers hauling farm products as compared with those hauling steel, coal and autos. This measure of the efficiency in the use of cars in 1974 was 1,691 for the Rock Island and 2,617 for the Union Pacific. The Rock Island was 64.6% of the Union pacific. The result of the much lower traffic density on the Rock Island was that freight revenues on the Rock Island, per mile of road, were only 46.3% of those on the Union Pacific. The Union Pacific earned $13,070 per mile of road in 1974 before fixed charges, while the Rock Island lost $3,013 per mile of road.

The Union Pacific's dense traffic on most main lines could not be carried without first-class maintenance of way. The Union Pacific spent $13,806 per mile of road or $10,872 per mile of track for maintenance in 1974. This was twice the expenditure of the Rock Island. As a result, the Union Pacific could run longer and faster trains than less-maintained roads. This is reflected in transportation expense per ton mile. As noted in Table 2.1, it is $6.11 for the Union Pacific and $8.64 for the Rock Island. The latter was 141% of the former.

EXCESS CAPACITY

The Rock Island, like most carriers east of the Missouri River, had low or negative rates of return on investment on most lines because of low densities of traffic. The exceptions were a few high-density main lines. The low densities on a majority of lines can be traced to the excess capacity created in the industry before the advent of motor carriers by the building of numerous parallel routes between most large cities.[12]

At the end of 1974, the Rock Island reported that it had 4,659 miles of main line, 1,713 miles of branch lines, 46 miles of leased line and trackage rights over 943 miles of road of other carriers.[13] But some main lines had little traffic. As noted in Chapter 1, Table 1.2, 71.9% of the line owned by the Rock Island in 1975 had density of less than 10 million gross ton-miles, averaging 3.8 million gross ton-miles per mile of road. Of the 7,361 miles of road, only two main routes could be estimated still to be profitable in 1975, but deferred maintenance of road caused slow orders so that shippers sought other carriers. The two routes of densest traffic were the 494-mile route from Chicago to Omaha and the 1,414-mile route from Minneapolis to Houston and Galveston.[14] On the Chicago-Omaha route, the section east of Davenport had a 1975 density of 27 million gross ton-miles per year, but west of Davenport, the average density was only 11.5 million gross ton-miles.[15] On the Minneapolis-Houston route, the 1975 density ranged from seven million gross ton-miles from Minneapolis to Allerton, Iowa, to 23 million gross ton-miles from Kansas City to Dallas.[16] The segment from Dallas to Houston was operated jointly by Rock Island and Burlington Northern and still reported only seven million gross ton-miles per year.

The excess capacity problem applied even to the Rock Island's main line from Chicago to Omaha. As shown in Table 2.2, the six lines between Chicago and Omaha included four short routes whose distances ranged from 484 miles to 494 miles. The Chicago & North Western and the Burlington Northern each had over 80% of its routes double tracked. The Milwaukee Road and the Burlington Northern each had over 60% of its routes equipped with centralized traffic control. Since the estimated optimum capacity of a double-track line with automatic block signals is 186 million gross tons per route mile per year, it

Table 2.2. Analysis of Six Railroad Lines Between Chicago and Omaha, 1975.

Railroad	Length of the line (miles)[a]	Percent Double-Tracked	Average Density[b]	Line Capacity	Fastest Transit Time (hours)
Milwaukee Road	488.0	40	12	29	16
Chicago & North Western	484.4	89	45	75	12
Burlington Northern	494.0	91	35	81	12.75
Rock Island Lines	493.0	48	19	30	14
Illinois Central Gulf	515.0	6	12	18	20
Norfolk and Western	645.6	7	N.A.	N.A.	24

Source: U.S. Cong., House, Committee on Interstate and Foreign Commerce, *Railroad Revitalization*, Hearing on H. R. 6351, 94th Cong., 1st Sess., 1975, p. 179; U.S. Dept. of Transportation, *Final Standards, Classification and Designation of Lines of Class 1 Railroads in the United States*, Vol. 1, 1977, pp. 47–48.
[a] All mileages were computed form the *Rand McNally Handy Railroad Atlas of the United States*, 1973.
[b] Millions of gross ton-miles per mile of road.

was clear that the aggregate of 70 million gross tons of these six carriers could be hauled easily on one of them.[17] Secretary William Coleman of the United States Department of Transportation in his testimony to Congress, used this corridor to illustrate the excess capacity problem of American railroads.[18]

In the Chicago-Omaha corridor, the two railroads with the densest traffic were the Chicago & North Western and the Burlington Northern with an average of over 35 million gross ton-miles per mile of line. Both of these lines had sufficient traffic to run through trains in the corridor. As noted in Table 2.2, they had the fastest running time of 12 hours and $12\frac{3}{4}$ hours, respectively. The relatively low density of the Rock Island main line across Iowa existed despite the fact that it was the only railroad directly connecting the large cities of Davenport and Des Moines with each other and with Chicago and Omaha. The Chicago & North Western controlled a bypass of Omaha to a direct connection with the Union Pacific at Fremont, Nebraska. This not only shortened the time for shipments from the west coast to Chicago but also enabled the transfer of full trainloads between carriers without meeting major terminal congestion at Omaha. The Burlington Northern had the advantage of controlling major traffic on its lines in and near Chicago and of having the shortest direct route from Chicago to Denver.

It is thus apparent that the borderline profitability of most of the Rock Island main lines was, first, related to the oversupply and the consequent excess capacity of railroad facilities in its territory. From Davenport to Kansas City the Rock Island and the Milwaukee Road had parallel lines about ten miles apart and both had light traffic and were poorly maintained.[19] Even the Minneapolis-Houston route, one with some of the carrier's densest traffic, paralleled other routes. From Minneapolis to Kansas City, the North Western was a nearby under-utilized rival.[20] From Wichita to Fort Worth, the Santa Fe was parallel and about twenty-five miles away. From Dallas to Houston, there were five parallel lines. A similar multiplicity of routes existed between Kansas City and St. Louis. Even when rival routes were some distance away, they might represent substantial excess capacity in the industry. The Rock Island line from Tucumcari, New Mexico, to Kansas City was the main connection for the Southern Pacific to Kansas City. Even so, the 1973 density on the southern half of this route, which represented the traffic to and from the Southern Pacific, was only 5.8 million net ton-miles per mile road per year, or 12.4 million gross ton-miles.[21] The Southern Pacific was negotiating in early 1976 to buy this line, since the bankrupt Rock Island could not maintain it properly, and the Southern Pacific proposed to spend $100 million to rehabilitate it.[22] The objective was to secure a route to St. Louis that was 400 miles shorter than its existing route.

The second major reason the Rock Island was so much weaker than most parallel lines is that many of its lines were not the most efficient in terms of distance, curvature, and grades. The line from St. Louis to Kansas City, for example, had a 1973 density of 1.5 million net ton-miles per mile of road or 3.1 million gross ton-miles per mile of road.[23] It was 298 miles long compared to 279 on the Missouri Pacific. The other aspects of these rival routes were also superior. This Rock Island line should have been a prime candidate for abandonment rather than rehabilitation. A similar argument could possibly be made for other Rock Island main lines. The lines west of Omaha and those between Amarillo and Memphis might or might not have been candidates for immediate abandonment, but their low densities indicate that investment should not have been made to bring them up to first-class standard for fast-freight.

FINANCIAL ANALYSIS

The key accounting figures for predicting the future of a railroad are those for net railway operating income. This is the figure in carrier annual reports that separates results from railroad operations from secondary activities such as managing land or timber businesses. Profits from sideline businesses cannot offset railroad losses in most instances for more than a short time. The idea that non-regulated business should cross-subsidize the key regulated rail operations just postpones recognition of the regulatory policies causing losses. The

ICC policies limiting line abandonments and the large costs of administrative hearings in abandonment cases were prime examples.

The annual profit and loss data reported in Table 2.3 indicate the extreme financial weakness of the Rock Island as early as 1965, ten years before the carrier filed bankruptcy. The string of net losses began in 1965. While the Rock Island had a very small net railway operating income in 1965 and 1966, that key measure of railroad success or failure jumped to a $14 million loss in 1967 and remained negative thereafter. The continuing net railway operating losses convinced the Rock Island executives that that the railroad was heading toward bankruptcy and they spent much time in the 1960s negotiating for a merger with another railroad that could keep Rock Island lines solvent. But that failed, and by early 1975, before the bankruptcy, the oil companies had put the Rock Island on a prepay basis to sell it fuel. Rock Island President, John W. Ingram, said at a Senate hearing when the United States Railway Association imposed a long delay before denying the Rock Island a $100 million loan for rehabilitation, "I think the Rock Island crisis is perhaps the most mishandled problem I have ever seen, and I consider the Government's approach to the situation to be a travesty of nonfeasance and bureaucratic apathy."[24] The Federal Railroad Administration held an opposing view. They knew that failure of the Rock Island was imminent. They viewed a governmental bail-out of Rock Island as a waste of rail subsidy funds.

The net railway operating losses of the Rock Island before bankruptcy, 1967 through 1974, aggregated $92,988,000. Before 1971, an undetermined amount of this loss must be allocated to the sum of both interstate and commuter passenger service. Passenger revenues dropped from $8.5 million in 1967 to $4.8 million in 1970. After 1970, passenger revenues averaged $5 million per year, most of it from Chicago commuter service with a net loss about $2 million per year.[25] The Chicago Regional Transportation Authority was created in 1974 and in 1976 the R.T.A. granted the Rock Island $1.8 million to offset part of the carrier's loss from commuter operations.[26] Starting in 1977, the R.T.A. acquired 80 new Budd bilevel passenger cars, most of which were allocated to the Rock Island commuter lines.[27] Thereafter, R.T.A. purchased 50 new locomotives most of which were allocated to the Rock Island commuter lines.[28]

The years of deferred maintenance[29] of line before the 1975 bankruptcy meant many Rock Island trains had to operate under slow orders and the carrier had significantly increased numbers of accidents.[30] This meant poor service to shippers, who consequently would make every possible effort to drop Rock Island service and switch to another rail carrier. As noted in Table 2.3, this in turn led to the large net railway losses from 1975 to September, 1979, when the Rock Island became cashless. The total net railway operating losses from 1975

Table 2.3. Chicago, Rock Island & Pacific Railroad Comparative Profit and Loss Data (Thousands of Dollars).

Year	Operating Revenue	Net Railway Operating Income	Net Income	Working Capital
1965	210,790	2,479	−1,451	203
1966	230,366	1,228	−3,639	−3,074
1967	221,885	−14,049	−16,677	−10,879
1968	239,346	-6,518	−4,805	−349
1969	259,584	−7,877	−9,831	−2,013
1970	273,465	−14,359	−16,640	−10,835
1971	291,808	−4,315	−6,415	−10,659
1972	305,290	-5,503	−5,855	−14,062
1973	329,002	−18,185	−14,980	−22,924
1974	367,615	−22,182	−23,097	−24,542
1975	321,571	−32,051	−31,166	17,670
1976	341,320	−25,115	−25,047	9,362
1977	362,921	−38,483	−34,834	−8,085
1978	365,749	−18,736	−21,162	−27,231
1979	263,442	−79,291	−93,860	−40,138

Source: U.S. Interstate Commerce Commission, *Transport Statistics in the United States* (1965–1978); Chicago, Rock Island & Pacific Railroad Co., *Annual Report* to the Securities and Exchange Commission (1979).

through 1979 were $193,676,000. Essentially all the 1979 operating revenues were in the first nine months before the ICC had to direct other carriers to operate temporarily over the Rock Island routes, but the net operating railway loss in the final quarter of 1979 was $10,465,000.

CANCELLED UNION PACIFIC PROPOSAL

The proposed merger of the Rock Island into the Union Pacific was cancelled by the Union Pacific because the conditions to merger set by the ICC made it unprofitable. The merger plan was incorporated in an agreement of the carriers in May, 1963. It was in the administrative process for more than eleven years. The ICC finally rendered a divided decision in the case in October, 1974.[31] The Union Pacific was permitted to merge the northern half of the Rock Island, except the line from Denver to Omaha, which was to go to the Denver and Rio Grande Western Railroad. The Southern Pacific was permitted to purchase the southern half of the Rock Island except the line from Amarillo to Memphis, which was conditionally allocated to the Santa Fe. The Santa Fe was allowed to purchase this segment on condition that it also merge the financially weak Missouri-Kansas-Texas.

The ICC clearly favored the merger of the Rock Island into the financially strong Union Pacific because the Rock Island was a chronically weak carrier in jeopardy of bankruptcy.[32] Union Pacific resources would be used to rehabilitate under-maintained key lines of the Rock Island. But the commission feared that the traffic diversion from the North Western and the Milwaukee Road to the acquired Rock Island lines could bankrupt those two carriers.[33] One can understand the magnitude of the potential traffic diversion after the merger only if one knows the prior traffic flows and interchanges of the Union Pacific. The Union Pacific conducted through-train interchanges with the North Western at Fremont, Nebraska, and with the Burlington at Grand Island Nebraska.[34] The 1964 data showed that of the 425,999 total carloads interchanged by the Union Pacific at Omaha, Fremont or Grand Island, 36.8% were with the North Western, 24.6% with the Burlington, and 17.9% with the Milwaukee.[35] Only 5.5% had been interchanged with the Rock Island.

Having no workable solution to the very large potential diversion of traffic from the usual interchange carriers of the Union Pacific to its acquired Rock Island lines, the ICC attempted to postpone the issue by imposing conditions on the merger that prevented realization of the expected economies from merged operations.[36] For five years after merger, the Union Pacific would be required to deliver to the North Western and to the Milwaukee Road at the Omaha gateway 100% of the average number of loaded cars delivered to those carriers in the five years before the merger year. A similar traffic maintenance condition would be imposed on both the Union Pacific and Santa Fe toward the St. Louis-San Francisco Railway and the Kansas City Southern Railway at their junction points. Similar conditions would be imposed on the Union Pacific and Southern Pacific toward the Missouri-Kansas-Texas. In all these conditions, the acquiring carriers would be required to indemnify the protected carriers for any decrease in the normal amount of traffic delivered to them. A further condition would bring the holding companies of the acquiring carriers under ICC jurisdiction.

The ICC opinion summarized the basic problem in reaching its decision:

> The Commission is, thus, faced with a dilemma. On the one hand, there is a clear public need to preserve the services of the Rock Island, which a UP-RI merger would accomplish; but, on the other hand, the transaction could jeopardize the existence of other carriers or weaken them to the extent they will not be able to provide essential and necessary services. On balance, all of the advantages likely to result from the proposed mergers, if achieved

at the cost of the bankruptcy or the serious weakening of several other carriers, would result in a net impairment of the national transportation system. We conclude, then, that merger of the Union Pacific and Rock Island, primarily because it would preserve the Rock Island, would be consistent with the public interest; but, only subject to the conditions set forth hereinafter, for the protection of other carriers.[37]

The Union Pacific also had an incentive to withdraw from its 1964 exchange-of-stock offer to Rock Island shareholders because the Rock Island's financial condition had worsened greatly by 1974. Union Pacific had offered one share of Union Pacific $1.80 convertible preferred stock for each share of Rock Island common. Each share of the Union Pacific preferred was convertible into 0.85 share of Union Pacific common. The offer also guaranteed Rock Island shareholders a dividend of $0.45 quarterly from July 1, 1964 to June 30, 1967. At the time the proposal was submitted to Union Pacific's shareholders in early 1965, data in the Notice of Meeting showed both carriers were profitable in the years 1960 to 1964.[38] But if the Rock Island had expended funds for first-rate maintenance of its main lines, it would have been a net loss railroad from 1960 to 1964.[39] The managerial issue was whether the Rock Island Board of Directors should not have chosen to declare dividends and instead should have expended those funds on maintenance of way. However, the total dividends of the Rock Island in the five years were $6.50 or 70% of the Union Pacific's $8.30. As a result, the market price of Rock Island common stock in 1964 averaged about 68% of the price of Union Pacific common. On this basis, the exchange ratio of 0.85 share of Union Pacific for a Rock Island share was not just very generous, it lacked foundation. On May 11, 1965, however, the exchange was approved by 82.7% of the Union Pacific common votes and 79.3% of the Union Pacific preferred.

The merger valuation of the Rock Island assets at the time of shareholder approval in 1965 can be derived from the value attached to the securities in the exchange. The Union Pacific $1.80 convertible preferred was valued at $40 per share and the Union Pacific common at $47.[40] Since the Rock Island common shares were to be traded one-for-one with Union Pacific convertible preferred, the Rock Island common can also be valued at $40 per share. The 2,916,911 Rock Island shares at the end of 1964 thus had an assumed value of $116,676,400. In this case, the shareholders' equity on the books of the Rock Island of $301,646,931 was overvalued by almost $185 million or 150%. The $155.8 million equity surplus was an accounting fiction and there had not been a true basis for dividends from 1960 to 1964. Furthermore, if the $184,970,491 overvaluation of the equity is subtracted from the asserted total assets of $497,220,028 at the end of 1964, the corrected and true asset valuation was $312,249,537.

The report of the administrative law judge showed the division of the Rock Island assets between the Union Pacific and the Southern Pacific on a pro forma basis on the expected date of execution, December 31, 1967.[41] On that date the Rock Island had 2,921,161 shares outstanding and a corrected asset valuation of $310,317,108. If the overvaluation of Rock Island assets is attributed to road and structures, the net depreciated value of these is reduced to $191 million. All transportation property had a corrected net depreciated valuation of $241 million. The Southern pacific agreed to purchase 38.8% of the assets (cost minus depreciation) for $120 million. Of this, $107.7 million was attributed to transportation property, $6.5 million investment in affiliated companies, and $5.8 million to materials and supplies.[42] Southern Pacific agreed to pay 45% of the $241 million corrected value of transportation property for 38.8% of transportation assets because this portion had over 65% of the earning power of the whole railroad.

In the eight years, 1965 through 1973, the relative financial strength of the two carriers, the value of their assets based on their earning power, changed radically. Union Pacific's earning per common share continued to increase, and this figure was after Federal and state income taxes. The Rock Island had continuous deficits after 1965 and no income taxes. The difference in earnings per common share exceeded $6 in every year since 1966. The stated book value of the shareholders' equity in the Rock Island decreased by $75.3 million between 1964 and 1973. Some of these startling changes were in the record before the ICC administrative law judge when he signed his final report on February 9, 1973. Since no party objected to the 1964 exchange ratio of shares, however, he approved it as a matter of course. The ICC also approved the exchange ratio but noted that the parties might want to renegotiate it.

In light of all these facts, the 1964 valuation of the Rock Island, based on historical accounting income data, had to be discarded. The reasonable prediction in 1974 was that, over the economic horizon, the Rock Island could not earn a positive income. Consequently, the only rational valuation of the entire line was liquidation value.

ROCK ISLAND DISMEMBERMENT

The Interstate Commerce Commission made a finding on September 26, 1979 that the Rock Island was cashless and unable to operate. The issue of whether the ICC should direct other railroads to operate on all Rock Island lines was highly contested. The Chicago & North Western President asserted that about 80% of Rock Island freight traffic could be served directly by rival railroads.[43] The Federal Railroad Administration opposed directed service on all Rock Island lines as a waste. Only railway labor would gain from continued multiple service to major cities. Nonetheless, the ICC directed service by other railroads on all Rock Island lines.

The ICC ordered the Kansas City Terminal Railway Company to provide directed service, at government expense, over the Rock Island routes.[44] This order was renewed twice for a total of 171 days.[45] These operations continued through March 23, 1980, when lack of funds prevented further continuance under federal subsidy.[46] On March 28, 1980, the ICC issued unsubsidized directed service orders to some 15 railroads to operate on various routes of the Rock Island for 240 days from the first directed service on October 5, 1979.[47] The Commission emphasized the permissive nature of these orders, so that each carrier could weigh the costs and benefits before accepting or rejecting the order. The orders of the ICC setting the compensation for permissive use of the Rock Island lines were upheld on appeal.[48]

A specific directed service order had been issued to the St. Louis Southwestern Railway, a subsidiary of the Southern Pacific for temporary authority to operate the Rock Island line between Santa Rosa, New Mexico and Kansas City and on to St. Louis, a distance of 965.2 miles.[49] The Southern Pacific and the trustee of the Rock Island had much earlier entered an agreement on June 21, 1978 for the sale and purchase of these lines for $57 million.[50] On June 6, 1980, the ICC finally approved the transaction, one week after the president signed the Rock Island Railroad Transition and Employee Assistance Act.[51] The Southern Pacific also secured the Rock Island's 65-mile trackage rights over the Union Pacific from Topeka to Kansas City. The 604-mile line from Santa Rosa to Topeka, the only segment to become an SP main line, was operative but undermaintained. The rehabilitation cost of this segment was estimated by consulting engineers to be $169.6 million and reduced by SP to $117.9 million.[52]

The Rock Island 298-mile route from Kansas City to St. Louis had not been maintained and service on the line had been embargoed since summer, 1979.[53] There was no evidence that local shippers required service on the line.[54] Independent consulting engineers estimated the rehabilitation cost for the line with the addition of centralized traffic control that would facilitate fast freight trains to be $81 million.[55] It is likely that Southern Pacific bargained for this segment only to counter the bid of Missouri Pacific, which already had a more direct and efficient line between Kansas City and St. Louis. In fact, Southern Pacific had been trying unsuccessfully to negotiate trackage rights over either the Missouri Pacific or the Norfolk & Western on that route. The Southern Pacific was able to save the $81 million rehabilitation cost by securing trackage rights in 1982 over the Missouri Pacific line from Kansas City to St. Louis.

Southern Pacific intervened in the merger case of Union Pacific to acquire the Missouri Pacific and was granted those trackage rights by the ICC as a condition of merger approval.[56]

On May 23, 1980, the ICC recommended abandonment of the entire Rock Island system and on June 2, 1980, the reorganization court ordered the abandonment.[57] Three days earlier, the Rock Island Railroad Transition and Employee Assistance Act became law.[58] This enabled extension of directed service orders to various carriers that were operating parts of the Rock Island routes while the trustee negotiated sales or leases of those lines to the carriers.[59] By September 1982, about half of the 7500 route miles had been sold or leased to other carriers. The longest route that was leased went to the Chicago & North Western which was paying $425,909 per month for 746 miles in Minnesota and Iowa.[60] This included 430 miles of the key north-south 480-mile "spine line" between the Twin Cities and Kansas City and branch lines serving major grain producers. It was only after three years of leasing that the Chicago & North Western received ICC approval to purchase 720 miles of the lines for $93 million or $129,167 per mile.[61] The Rock Island route was superior to the parallel North Western route in distance, grades, weight of rail, signaling system, curvature and passing sidings.[62] The Rock Island had not maintained the spine line, and during the three leasing years the North Western had spent about $20 million on maintenance of way to keep them operable.[63]

The main line of the Rock Island from Chicago to Omaha of 493 miles was divided between three carriers. On March 20, 1980, the ICC issued a directive service order to the Chicago Regional Transportation Authority to operate the 40.6-mile Chicago to Joliet commuter service.[64] The line was conveyed to the R.T.A in 1983. The Baltimore & Ohio Railroad (later part of the Chessie system) contracted a long-term lease on the 74 miles between Joliet and Bureau, Illinois plus 25 miles of trackage rights to move freight over the commuter lines north of Joliet.[65] In 1984, the trustee sold the 379 miles of line from Bureau to Omaha to Heartland Rail Corp. for $31 million.[66] Heartland was financed in part by a $15 million loan from the Iowa Rail Finance Authority. Heartland leased the line to the Iowa Interstate Railroad which also secured trackage rights over the Baltimore and Ohio segment to Joliet and over the R.T.A. commuter lines into Chicago yards. The 1991 data on line densities in Illinois indicate that the Iowa Interstate Railroad had mostly local traffic and very little from Class 1 carriers. The Iowa Interstate had less than five million gross tons of freight traffic per mile annually.[67] The Union Pacific, which by 1991 had acquired trackage rights over the Chicago & North Western, and the Burlington Northern both had lines from Omaha to Chicago with over 25 million gross tons of freight traffic per mile annually.[68]

The Rock Island line from Davenport, Iowa to Kansas City paralleled the line of the Milwaukee Road. The carriers had long had agreements for the Milwaukee Road to operate over the Rock Island lines for about 42 miles between Polo, MO and Kansas City and for about 26 miles between Davenport and Muscatine, Iowa. Rock Island's line capacity was estimated to be about $2\frac{1}{2}$ times that of the Milwaukee Road. Both lines had significant deferred maintenance. As early as 1977, with support from the Federal Railroad Administration, the carriers entered an agreement for the Milwaukee to use Rock Island tracks for through trains.[69] Milwaukee Road would avoid spending $5.7 million on maintenance of way and still be able to offer local service on its own line at reduced speeds. By the time that the Rock Island became cashless in 1979, the deferred maintenance on its line had become much worse and service on that line was embargoed in 1980. In 1982, the northern 64 miles of the line from Davenport to Washington, Iowa was offered for sale by the Rock Island trustee, and the bankrupt Milwaukee Road won the line with a bid of $17 million.[70] The other 101 miles of the Rock Island tracks, south to Allerton junction with the main Minneapolis-Kansas City line, were sold to a dealer in used track who removed them.

The Rock Island line from Topeka, Kansas to Limon, Colorado paralleled other lines and none of the Class 1 carriers in the region indicated an intent to acquire it. The Denver & Rio Grande Western, which desired trackage from Colorado to Kansas City did not bid for the Rock Island line with its deferred maintenance. Rather, the D. & R.G. intervened in the proceeding before the ICC of the Union Pacific to control the Missouri Pacific and was granted 619 miles of trackage rights over the Missouri Pacific from Pueblo, Colorado to Kansas City.[71] In order to maintain service on part of the Rock Island lines, two short-line railroads received temporary authority from the ICC, which set lease payments. The Mid States Port Authority, a governmental agency formed by 14 Kansas counties, bid for 450 miles of the line, mostly in Kansas, but extending to Limon, Colorado.[72] These lines were operated by the Kyle Railroad.[73]

The 630-mile Rock Island line from Salina, Kansas to Dallas was bought in parts by the Oklahoma-Kansas-Texas Rail Users Association and the State of Oklahoma.[74] The state purchased the 351 miles of the abandoned line in Oklahoma for $15 million and other lines both East and West of El Reno. The Users Association was financed by a $40 million loan from the Federal Railroad Administration.[75] The operator was the Oklahoma, Kansas and Texas Railroad, a subsidiary of the Missouri-Kansas-Texas Railroad.[76]

Because of the many sales of lines to Class 1 carriers and to new regional and short-line carriers, most of the Rock Island lines were not actually abandoned and removed. Of the 4773 miles of main line and the 1721 miles of branch lines at the end of 1975, only 1400 miles were designated for removal in September, 1982.[77] This included 1049 miles of line over which no trains were operating and no other carrier had shown an interest to buy or lease. Numerous factors contributed to the ability of other railroads to make segments of the Rock Island profitable when integrated into their systems. The lines from Santa Rosa, NM, to Topeka bought by the Southern Pacific and the line from the Twin Cities to Kansas City bought by the North Western are prime examples. In other cases, state government helped finance some of the short-line railroads to purchase branch lines.

CONCLUSION

The Rock Island Railroad had been one of the financially weakest railroads since the coming of motor carrier competition after World War I. It had been in bankruptcy for 15 years during the depression of the 1930s and during World War II. On its key routes, rival railroads had strategic advantages over the Rock Island. On the Chicago-Omaha Route, for example, the Chicago & North Western had superior connection with the Union Pacific that bypassed the Omaha rail yards. The rival Burlington, with lines from Chicago to Colorado, also offered faster service to the West. From Chicago to southern California, the through route of the Santa Fe offered superior service than the Rock Island which had to transfer trains to Southern Pacific at Santa Rosa, New Mexico. Furthermore, the Rock Island had failed to maintain its main line from Topeka to Santa Rosa. As a consequence, the Southern Pacific switched freight cars destined for St. Louis to its subsidiary, the St. Louis Southwestern, even though this added 400 miles to the total trip.

The problem of low-density branch lines was especially severe on the Rock Island because it lacked high-density main lines whose earnings could cross-subsidize the net loss branches. As noted in Chapter 1, Table 1.2, in 1975, the Rock Island route miles with low density were 71.9% of Rock Island's total milage. The barriers to rail line abandonments imposed by the Interstate Commerce Commission and the legal expense to carriers for proceedings with uncertain outcomes greatly limited the success in reducing investment in net loss lines.

The alternate possible solution for a net loss railroad was to seek merger with a connecting carrier. The primary objective was to create new single-line service that would divert traffic from rival carriers. In the 1930s, when both the Rock Island and the St. Louis-San Francisco were in bankruptcy reorganization, the Rock Island sought merger with the SL-SF. This attempt was unsuccessful.

The program of the Union Pacific to acquire the Rock Island resulted in agreement in 1963. Union Pacific, expecting to retain just the northern half of the Rock Island, planned to shift its main trainload traffic away from the Chicago & North Western near Omaha. But this would sacrifice the exchange at Fremont, Nebraska with the North Western that efficiently bypassed the possible congestion of moving whole trains through Omaha railroad yards. It now seems clear that the Union Pacific was better off that the ICC added so many financial condition to approval of the merger that it caused the Union Pacific to cancel it. Later, the Union Pacific acquired the North Western.

The key financial lesson that was learned from the failed Union Pacific attempt to acquire the Rock Island was that this agreed price for a net-loss carrier was too high. The price was based mainly on the ratio of the dividends paid by the two carriers. But the Rock Island was failing to maintain its main rail lines in order to pay dividends. This policy in effect deliberately hid the fact that the Rock Island was deferring recognition of its losses in the years before the acquisition agreement. The lesson to be learned from this failure is that accounting systems should be revised to force railroads with long-term net-loss divisions to write down those assets on the balance sheets to salvage value.

NOTES

1. Statement of bankruptcy trustee William M. Gibbons in U.S. Cong., Senate, Committee on Commerce, Science, and Transportation, *Milwaukee Railroad and Rock Island Railroad Amendments Act*, Hearing, 97th Cong., 1st Sess., 1981, at 64.

2. Statement of Terry F. Moritz on behalf of the Rock Island creditors in *Id.*, at 75.

3. Chicago, R.I. & P.R. Co. Abandonment, 363 ICC 150 (1980).

4. A Rock Island creditors group sued unsuccessfully to overturn approval by the bankruptcy court of the trustee's issuance of $22 million of trustee's certificates for maintenance of the railroad and to enter a 15-year lease for 56 new locomotives. Matter of Chicago, R.I. & P.R. Co., 545 F. 2d 1087 (7th Cir. 1976). See *Wall Street Journal*, July 23, 1975, 6; *Id.*, Feb. 27, 1976, 3.

5. Chicago, R.I. & P.Ry. Co. Reorganization, 257 I.C.C. 265, 307 (1944); In re Chicago, R.I. & P.Ry. Co., 160 F. 2d 942 (7th Cir. 1947), cert. denied 332 U.S. 793 (1947).

6. *Moody's Transportation Manual* 175 (1975).

7. Union Pacific proposal, F. D. 23286 was reported with Chicago & N. W. Ry. Co.-control-Chicago, R.I. & P.R. Co. 347 I.C.C. 556 (1974). See record testimony of Jervis Langdon, Jr., 16.

8. *Id.* at 8 to 14.

9. Missouri Pacific R. Co.-Merger-Texas and P.R. Co. and Chicago & E.I.R. Co., 348 I.C.C. 414 (1976).

10. Gibbons v. United States, 559 F. 2d 408 (5th Cir. 1977), cert. denied 435 U.S. 950 (1978).

11. For rates of return on Class 1 railroads, see U.S., I.C.C, *Transport Economics,* new series, Vol. II, No. 4, 1975, pp. 12–13.

12. A list of the rival railroads paralleling the Rock Island was included in the testimony of Commissioner Stafford in U.S. Cong., Senate, Committee on Commerce, *Financial Condition of the Rock Island Railroad*, Hearings on S. 917, 94th Cong., 1st. Sess., 1975, 70. See U.S. Department of Transportation, *Western Railroad Mergers* 19–32 (1969).

13. Chicago, Rock Island & Pacific RR Co., Annual Report to the Interstate Commerce Commission, Dec. 31, 1974, 99.

14. Derived from rail line segment study in U.S. Department of Transportation, *Final Standards Classification, and Designation of Lines of Class 1Railroads in the United States*, Vol. 2, 178–180 (1977).

15. *Id.*

16. *Id.*

17. U.S. Dept. of Transportation, *Rail Service in the Midwest and Northeast Region*, Vol. 1, p. 5 (1974).

18. U.S. Cong., House, Committee on Interstate and Foreign Commerce, *Railroad Revitalization*, Hearings on H. R. 6351, 94th Cong., 1st Sess., 1975, 174–180. See earlier analysis in Michael Conant, *Railroad Mergers and Abandonments* 17–18 (Berkeley: University of California Press, 1964).

19. *Financial Condition of the Rock Island Railroad, supra* note 12, at 91.

20. From 1970 to 1975, the North Western spent $20 million upgrading its line between Des Moines and Kansas City. There were no reports of attempts by North Western to negotiate coordinated service with the Rock Island, followed by abandonment of the less efficient line. *Id.*, at 131.

21. *Id.*, at 77.

22. *Moody's Transportation Service*, May 2, 1975, 1184.

23. *Financial Condition of the Rock Island Railroad, supra* note 12, at 77.

24. *Id.*, at 80.

25. *Id.*, at 93.

26. *Moody's Transportation Manual* 900 (1982).

27. Railway Age, Feb. 11, 1980, at 46.

28. *Id.*

29. Statement of John Ingram in *Financial Condition of the Rock Island Railroad, supra*, note 12, at 104, listing the rail lines needing rehabilitation because of deferred maintenance at estimated cost of $50 million.

30. *Id.*, at 89, noting the cost of accidents on the Rock Island in 1974 was $14 million.

31. Chicago & N.W. Ry. Co.-Control-Chicago, R.I. & P.R. Co., 347 I.C.C. 556 (1974). See Richard Saunders, *Merging Lines: American Railroads 1900–1970*, 347–353 (Dekalb: Northern Illinois University Press, 2001).

32. On the financial weakness of the Rock Island, resulting in great deferred maintenance, see 347 I.C.C., at 691.

33. *Id.*, at 598.

34. On the efficiencies of avoiding congested railroad yards by interchanging entire trains outside yards, see *Railway Age,* Sept. 24, 1979, at 22–24.

35. 347 I.C.C. at 702.

36. 347 I.C.C. at 616.

37. 347 I.C.C. at 600.

38. Union Pacific Corp., Notice of Meeting, March 22, 1965, p. 14.

39. For the five years, 1960 to 1964, the Rock Island expenditures for maintenance of way and structures per equated track mile averaged $2,642, the total equaling 11.7%

of operating revenues. The Union Pacific comparative figure of $4,082 per equated track mile can be used as a standard for high maintenance. For Rock Island to have had the same high level of maintenance as Union Pacific, Rock Island would have had to spend an estimated additional $13 million per year on maintenance. The result would have been maintenance of way expenditures in the years 1960 to 1964 equaling 18.3% of operating revenues. The consequences would have been large operating losses for the carrier. See *Moody's Transportation Manual* 385 and 825 (1970).

40. Chicago & North Western RR.-Control-Chicago, Rock Island & Pacific RR., F. D.-22688, et. al., *Report and Order Recommended by Administrative Law Judge*, p. 630.

41. *Id.*, at 637.

42. *Id.*, at 669.

43. See *Financial Condition of the Rock Island Railroad, supra* note 12, at 137.

44. Kansas City Term. Ry. Co.-Operate-Chicago, R.I. & P., 360 I.C.C. 289 (Oct. 1, 1979). The Kansas City Terminal Railway was required to compensate the Rock Island Trustee for the use of Rock Island locomotives, freight cars, fuel and maintenance of equipment. The order relieved Kansas City Terminal of any obligation to pay rent for the use of Rock Island track and facilities unless the directed service operation proved profitable. This latter order was held not to be a taking of Rock Island's property in violation of the eminent domain clause of the Fifth Amendment. *Gibbons v. United States*, 660 F. 2d 1227, 1236-39 (7th Cir. 1981).

45. Kansas City Term. Ry. Co.-Operate-Chicago, R.I. & P., 360 I.C.C. 478 (Dec. 10, 1979); *Id.* at 360 I.C.C. 718 (Jan. 8, 1980).

46. Interstate Commerce Commission, Annual Report, 1980, 34.

47. Various Railroads-Directed Service-Chicago, Rock Island & Pacific Railroad Company, Debtor, 363 I.C.C. 72 (Mar. 28, 1980); *Id.* at 82 (April 8, 1980).

48. Gibbons v. United States, 660 F. 2d 225 (7th Cir. 1981).

49. St. Louis Southwestern Railway Company-Temporary Authority-Chicago Rock Island & Pacific Ry. Co., 363 I.C.C. 9 (March 19, 1980).

50. St. Louis S. W. Ry.-Purchase-Rock Island (Tucumcari), 363 I.C.C. 320, 328 (June 6, 1980).

51. Pub. L. 96-254, 94 Stat. 399 (1980), 45 U.S.C.A. 1001-1018 (1987). See U.S. Cong., Senate, Committee on Commerce, Science, and Transportation, *Rock Island Transition Act*, Hearing, 96th Cong., 2d Sess., 1980.

52. St. Louis S.W. Ry.-Purchase-Rock Island (Tucumcari), 363 I.C.C. at 494-495.

53. *Id.* at 344.

54. *Id.* at 357. Except for 60 route miles on the eastern end, this line was unused for 16 years. It was only in 1997, after the Southern Pacific was merged into the Union Pacific, that U.P. contracted to sell this line to a new short-line carrier, the Missouri Central Railroad. Gregory S. Johnson, *UP-SP sells a chip off old Rock (railroad)*, Journal of Commerce 1B (Feb. 11, 1997).

55. 363 I.C.C. at 494.

56. Union Pacific-Control-Missouri Pacific; Western Pacific, 366 I.C.C. 459, 585-89 (1982), affirmed Southern Pacific Transp. Co. v. I.C.C., 736 F. 2d 708 (D.C. Cir. 1984), cert. denied 469 U.S. 1208 (1985). See St. Louis Southwestern Ry. Co.-Trackage Rights Compensation, 1 I.C.C. 2d 776 (1984).

57. Chicago, R.I. & P.R. Co. Abandonment, 363 I.C.C. 150 (1980).

58. 94 Stat. 399 (1980), 45 U.S.C.A. 1001–1018 (1987).

59. *Id.*, §1017.

60. *Railway Age*, Sept. 27, 1982, 42; *Id.*, April, 1984, 62.
61. Midwestern Rail Prop., Inc.-Purchase-Rock Island, 366 I.C.C. 915 (1983).
62. *Id.* At 925.
63. *Id.*, at 924.
64. Regional Transp. Authority-Directed Service-Chicago, R.I. & P.R. Co., 360 I.C.C. 777 (1980); *Id.*, 363 I.C.C. 71 (1980).
65. U.S. Cong., Senate, Committee on Commerce, Science and Transportation, *Milwaukee Railroad and Rock Island Railroad Amendments Act*, Hearing, 97th Cong., 1st Sess., 1981, at 66. See Wall St. J., Feb. 3, 1982, at 4.
66. Bruce D. Williams, *Iowa Interstate: The Railroad with the Highway Name*, Pacific Rail News, Feb. 1989, at 20, 23-24. See Wall St. J., Oct. 16, 1984, at 55.
67. Illinois Department of Transportation, *Illinois Rail Plan: 1991-92*, 29.
68. *Id.*, at 30.
69. Railway Age, Mar. 28, 1977, at 10.
70. Richard B. Ogilive, Trustee, Chicago, Mil., St. P. & P.R. Co.-Purchase (Portion)-Chicago, R.I. & P.R. Co., F. D. No. 29917 (Sub-No. 1)(1982); I.C.C. Annual Report 28 (1982). See Railway Age, Sept. 27, 1982, at 44.
71. Union Pacific-Control-Missouri Pacific; Texas Pacific, 366 I.C.C. 460, 572-89 (1982).
72. *Milwaukee Railroad and Rock Island Railroad Amendments Act, supra*, note 65, at 81–83.
73. See Michael W. Babcock, Marvin Prater, and John Morrill, *A Profile of Short Line Railroad Success*, 34 Transportation Journal 22, 24 (1994).
74. I.C.C. Annual Report 29 (1982). See Railway Age, Sept. 27, 1982, at 43.
75. *Id.* See J. David Ingles, *Whatever Happened to the Rock Island?*, Trains, March, 1983, at 31, 33.
76. Missouri-Kansas-Texas Railroad participated in the sale of the Rock Island lines from Kansas into Texas only to purchase a freight-service easement between Dallas and Fort Worth. Acquisition of Rail Line of Chicago, R.I.&P.R.Co. Between Fort Worth and Dallas, TX, F.D. No. 29923 (1982).
77. See Railway Age, Sept. 27, 1982, at 43.

3. MILWAUKEE ROAD BANKRUPTCY

The Chicago, Milwaukee, St. Paul and Pacific Railroad filed bankruptcy on December 19, 1977. From 1977 through 1982, its aggregate net railway operating loss was $534,691,000. This exceeded the total shareholder investment on December 31, 1977. The Milwaukee Road went from being a 10,000-mile railroad in 1977 to a 3,100 mile railroad at the end of 1983. Its abandonment or sale of lines from Minneapolis to Seattle and its main line across Iowa left it a core line from Chicago to Minneapolis, Chicago to Kansas City, Chicago to Louisville and a few profitable branch lines. The Milwaukee Road was another midwest railroad in an area of excess capacity and was burdened with low-density branch lines that were 70% of its 10,000 mile total. Like the Rock Island Railroad, the Milwaukee Road was a doomed carrier. The core that remained was sold in February, 1985 to the subsidiary of the Canadian Pacific, the Soo Line Railroad.

HISTORICAL BACKGROUND

The background of the decline of the Milwaukee Road is found in its financial history. Founded in 1847, it was a thriving and expanding enterprise into the first decade of this century. Its three main routes operated from Chicago to Minneapolis, from Chicago to Omaha, and from Chicago to Kansas City. In 1905, a major investment decision was made which financial historians call "the great mistake."[1] The directors decided to extend the line westward from Minneapolis to Seattle, roughly parallel to the established Northern Pacific. The extension was completed in 1909. Although income statements by sectors are not published, most industry analysts believe this 1,771-mile line, together with its branches, had never secured sufficient density to earn a market rate of return on investment. This western extension was originally estimated to cost $60 million, while its actual completed cost was $257 million, including electrification.[2] The financing extended all the way to 1918. From June 30, 1909, to December 31, 1917, the funded debt of the Milwaukee Road increased by $266 million.[3]

After World War I, the expansion of intercity motor carriers resulted in continuing diversion of LCL traffic to them and caused many branch lines on railroads to become unprofitable. To some, like the Milwaukee Road, with extensive branches and few high-density main lines, this meant financial disaster. The Milwaukee Road had by lease acquired the Chicago, Terre Haute & Southeastern Railway, another low-density line, in 1921. Thereafter, its financial troubles worsened. By 1925, it was unable to refund its debt, and it filed the first of two bankruptcies. The receivership of 1925 resulted in sale of the properties to the present Milwaukee Road at the end of 1927.[4] In the depression of 1930s, the Milwaukee Road, like many other carriers, was again unable to meet its debts. A petition for reorganization was filed in 1935.[5] The reorganization plan was contested, and it required a Supreme Court decision in 1943 approving a plan which excluded the stockholders.[6] The Milwaukee Road finally emerged from reorganization in 1945.

After World War II, all railroads were affected by loss of traffic to motor carriers as larger trucks became more efficient and the interstate highway system was completed. More of the high-value commodities with higher rates were diverted to the motor carriers, and more railroad branch lines became unprofitable. The Milwaukee Road declined even though, in 1970, it had acquired trackage rights from the end of its line in southern Indiana into Louisville, giving it a direct connection with Southern Railway.[7]

Traffic on the Milwaukee Road increased from 16,958 million revenue ton-miles in 1947 to 18,744 million revenue ton-miles in 1974, an increase of 10.5%, and freight revenues increased from $187 million in 1947 to $363 million, an increase of 94%.[8] But costs increased more rapidly. Consequently, net railway operating income dropped from $16.8 million in 1949 to $–239,000 in 1974. The 1974 operating loss after provision for deferred income tax was $2 million. Of this loss, $208,000 was attributed to freight service, $1,616,000 was attributed to passenger commutation service, and the remainder was not related to either. As noted below, these figures are not random results but are part of a secular decline in the earning power of the railroad's operating assets.

EXCESS CAPACITY

The Milwaukee Road is an outstanding example of a carrier overburdened with low-density branch lines and with many low-density main lines. At the end of 1977, the Milwaukee Road operated 3,048 miles of main line and 7,031 miles of branch line, for a total of 10,079 miles. Branch line was 70% of the total. Compare this with the parallel Burlington Northern whose branch lines were only 46% of its total route miles. Comparative density statistics were similar. The available computations, for the year 1976, showed the Milwaukee Road with 3.1 freight trains per mile of road per day.[9] The Burlington Northern average was 4.9 and the bankrupt Rock Island was 3.4. The gross ton-miles, freight and passenger, per mile of road per day were 13,661 for the Milwaukee Road, 24,947 for the Burlington Northern, and 12,926 for the Rock Island.

The 1976 average densities for lines owned by the Milwaukee Road are listed in Table 3.1. Of the 9,274 miles in total, 3,382 miles or 36.5% have densities of less than one million gross ton-miles per mile per year. All of these are branch lines. If Milwaukee Road's average size trains of 3,473 tons were run on these branches, it would have been equivalent to one train every other day or less in both directions or approximately 4% of the practical capacity of a single-track line.[10] Given 1976 operating and maintenance costs, a reasonable estimate is that all of these lines operated at a loss or would have been loss lines if adequate maintenance were done.

Another 2,108 miles of the Milwaukee Road lines, or 22.7%, had densities from one to five million gross tons per mile per year. These were also branch lines. At the maximum of five million gross tons per mile, this would have meant 20% of single-track capacity. In this category also, any lines which were not net-loss operations, the rate of return on net salvage value was probably far below the market rate of interest. Thus for the two lowest density categories combined, or 59% of the lines, the Milwaukee Road had investment in plant which, if it were adequately maintained, would be uneconomic.

Most of the lines with densities of over five million gross tons per mile per year were main lines. For example, the lines from central Montana to Seattle

Table 3.1. Milwaukee Road Line Densities, 1976.

Density Range (millions of gross tons per mile per year)	Approximate Route Miles	Percentage in Range[b]
Lessthan 1	3,382	36.5
1 but less than 5	2,108	22.7
5 but less than 10	765	8.2
10 but less than 20	2,615	28.2
20 but less than 30	404	4.4
30 or more	0	0 0
Totals	9,274[a]	100.00

Source: U.S. Dept. of Transportation, *Final Standards, Classification, and Designation of Lines of Class 1 Railroads in the United States*, Vol. 2, 165–167 (1977), and company data.

[a] Total excludes 865 route miles owned by other carriers over which the Milwaukee Road had operating rights.

[b] The total of 67.4% with less than 10 million gross ton-miles differs from Chapter 1, Table 1.2 because this table is based on entire line averages between major cities, not each small segment of line.

were of five to 10 million gross ton densities, but the costs of operating through mountain ranges resulted in net losses. Most of the line between central Montana and Minneapolis had between 10 and 20 million gross tons per mile per year. In comparing the mileage and densities of the Milwaukee Road and its rivals on midwest main lines, statistics show that on two of these three routes, Chicago to Omaha and Chicago to Kansas City, the Milwaukee Road had the lowest average density. In part, this reflected the absence of long-term connections with western railroads for exchange of traffic and in part the fewer firms on its line and thus a lesser ability to solicit traffic in Chicago for the West. From Chicago to Minneapolis, the Milwaukee Road had its greatest main-line density of 20 million gross tons per mile per year. The parallel North Western was 19 million gross tons per mile and the more indirect Burlington Northern was 38 million gross tons per mile. From Chicago to Kansas City, the Milwaukee Road density was 11 million gross tons per mile, while the much longer North Western was 33 million gross tons and the shorter Santa Fe, with its long-haul through-route to California, was 40 million gross tons.

The Chicago to Omaha route was reviewed in the previous Chapter, Table 2.2. The Milwaukee Road had an average density in 1975 of only 12 million gross tons per mile of road. The North Western, in contrast, was most efficient with 404 miles or 89% double-tracked, and its capacity on this segment was 140 million gross tons per mile. The North Western, whose 1975 density on this line was 45 million gross tons per mile, could have carried with ease at least half of the traffic between Chicago and Omaha.

SEARCH FOR MERGER

The search of the Milwaukee Road for a merger partner goes back before World War II, when the ICC denied a petition to join the parallel North Western.[11] In the postwar period, there were a number of attempts to merge with other midwestern carriers. In 1955, the Milwaukee Road and the North Western began merger negotiations and employed consultants to make valuation studies.[12] In early 1956, the consultants reported large deferred maintenance of branch lines of the North Western, and further studies were discontinued. In late 1959, the Milwaukee Road began discussion with the Rock Island on a proposed consolidation.[13] Again, consultants were hired to make valuation studies which indicated a prospective annual savings of $30 million before abandonments. In February 1961, the negotiations over exchange of shares broke down and were terminated.[14] The Milwaukee Road then entered renewed merger discussions with the North Western. In opposition to this attempt, five Milwaukee Road directors threatened a proxy fight for control in a dispute over the proposed terms.[15] As a result, the negotiations ceased.

In 1964 the Milwaukee Road and North Western again began merger negotiations. The steps are recorded in detail to demonstrate how six years of market fluctuations in share prices, combined with numerous regulatory barriers, can lead to ultimate failure. In September 1964, agreement was reached that the North Western would convey 0.7 of a share of its common stock for each share of Milwaukee common.[16] The plan was approved by the shareholders of the two corporations in May 1965 and submitted to the ICC in May 1966. The examiner concluded hearings in January 1968, but in May, the ICC ordered them to reopen since the North Western had been conveyed to a holding company, Northwest Industries. In July 1968, new exchange terms were reached. The approval of the hearing examiner in December estimated annual savings at from $29 million to $36 million.[17] In 1969, the share price for Northwest Industries dropped much more than did the price of Milwaukee Road shares, and some Milwaukee Road shareholders withdrew their approval. In January 1970, the ICC ordered the carriers to reopen merger talks to amend the exchange terms. In February, Northwest Industries terminated its offer to merge the Milwaukee Road and offered to sell its railroad assets to the Milwaukee.[18] In April 1970, the ICC canceled the 1966 merger application upon request of the parties, and the Milwaukee Road rejected the new offer of the Northwest Industries to sell its railroads assets. Subsequently, in 1972 Northwest Industries sold the North Western Railroad to its employees.[19]

The Milwaukee Road also sought consolidation with more profitable railroads by intervening in two ICC merger proceedings of other carriers and requesting as a condition to approval that the unwanted Milwaukee be included. In the Union Pacific Railroad's application to acquire the Rock Island Railroad, the Milwaukee Road first intervened to oppose the merger.[20] Later it petitioned the ICC to require the Union Pacific to merge the Milwaukee Road as a condition to granting the main application. When the ICC finally approved the merger, the Milwaukee Road petition to join was denied.[21] Since the merger was never executed, the Milwaukee Road suffered no injury. Traffic conditions in the decision to protect the Milwaukee Road, the North Western and other carriers were so onerous that the Union Pacific decided not to go through with the merger.[22] In the meantime the Rock Island had filed bankruptcy.

The Milwaukee Road also intervened in the *Northern Lines* merger cases.[23] The merger of the Great Northern, Northern Pacific and Chicago, Burlington & Quincy would mean that the two financially stronger rivals of the Milwaukee Road in the northern tier of states would combine into an even stronger rival. The Milwaukee Road first intervened in this proceeding in 1961 and requested six conditions to its approval which would give Milwaukee new gateways in the West and trackage rights into Portland.[24] The ICC's original report disapproved the merger, largely because the plan gave inadequate protection to the Milwaukee Road and the North Western. Upon reconsideration, the applicants agreed to accept all protective conditions demanded by the Milwaukee Road and the North Western and the ICC granted the application. The merger became effective on March 2, 1970.

The published evidence does not support attribution of the growing losses of the Milwaukee Road to diversion of traffic resulting from creation of the Burlington Northern. In its initial report in the *Northern Lines* merger case, the ICC estimated that consummation of that merger would result in a loss of annual gross revenue by the Milwaukee Road of $5,147,000.[25] It further estimated that the imposition of conditions favoring the Milwaukee Road would produce gains in gross revenue to it of about $19,964,000.[26] The net increase in gross revenues to the Milwaukee Road was thus estimated at about $14.8 million. Given an estimated incremental cost of handling the increased traffic of $33\frac{1}{3}\%$, the estimated increase in net railway operating revenues was $9.8 million. There is some evidence that the Milwaukee gained traffic, at least on the eastern half of the Minneapolis to Seattle line. The 1964 average density tables showed this sector to have a total of 8.6 million gross tons per mile.[27] The 1975 densities on this sector were over 10 million gross tons per mile.[28]

On April 2, 1973, the Milwaukee Road filed a petition with the ICC for inclusion in the Burlington Northern system. This was possible because of condition 33 of the final ICC decision in the *Northern Lines* case.[29] It provided that the ICC would retain jurisdiction over the proceedings for five years following consummation of the merger so that any railroad in the territory could request inclusion. In effect the ICC retained the power to set a price for exchange of shares if it required the subsequent inclusion and the two carriers could not voluntarily agree on a price. The negotiations between the Milwaukee Road and the Burlington Northern broke down in late 1975. In 1976, the ICC held that the Milwaukee Road had effectively engaged the Commission's reserved jurisdiction under condition 33 and that the Milwaukee Road could file a formal application for inclusion under Section 5(2) (g) of the Interstate Commerce Act as amended by the Railroad Revitalization and Regulatory Reform Act of 1976.[30] On February 16, 1977, however, the Milwaukee Road's petition for inclusion was denied.[31] Without holding a full-scale hearing on the merits, the ICC found from the pleadings that the Milwaukee Road failed to show that any financial or operational difficulties it faced stemmed from the *Northern Lines* merger. Its second basis for denial was found in the rationale for the *Northern Lines* merger decision itself. The monopoly and competition issues were disposed of "largely upon the continued presence of a 'substantially strengthened Milwaukee' as the sole remaining competitive rail carrier in the Northern corridor. 331 ICC at 371-6."[32]

FINANCIAL ANALYSIS

Throughout the 1960s the net income of the rail sector of the Milwaukee Road, as distinguished from the timber and real estate activities, was under $4,025,000. This meant that even in the best year, earnings on investment in net railroad assets were under 1% and in the worst years there were losses. A significant part of the losses in the 1960s was attributed to intercity passenger service. Even in 1970, before the National Railroad Passenger Corp. became operative and took over intercity train service, the Milwaukee Road with only $9.5 million in passenger revenues assigned $10.3 million losses to passenger service.[33] This would include intercity and commuter trains. In 1971, with only $4.3 million in passenger revenue, the passenger losses dropped, to $5.1 million. In 1972, when Amtrak had taken over all intercity trains, Milwaukee Road had $1.4 million in commuter passenger revenues and $1.9 million of passenger losses.[34]

As noted in Table 3.2, the net railway operating income of the Milwaukee Road from 1969 to 1974 was either very small or a loss. But in 1975 the net railway operating loss increased to $25.4 million and by 1979 it was $144 million.[35] Starting in 1976, there are separate accounting reports of transfers from governments that offset some of the net operating losses. A 1976 transfer of $5.5 million and a 1977 transfer of $6.9 million were from the Chicago Regional Transportation Authority to subsidize commuter service.[36] The bulk of those funds originated in the federal Urban Mass Transportation Administration.[37] Part of the 1978 federal funding was a loan of $5.1 million under the Emergency Rail Services Act[38] for which the bankruptcy court approved issuance of trustee's certificates.[39] Under the Milwaukee Road Restructuring Act of 1979, the Secretary of Transportation was given power to guarantee trust certificates of the Milwaukee Road in an amount equal to the difference between the total expanses attributable to maintenance and continuation of service and the revenues of the railroad.[40] At the end of 1982, the Milwaukee Road owed federal financing agencies $182.5 million.[41]

The very low income and many years of loss from 1960 to the 1977 bankruptcy of the Milwaukee Road and thereafter resulted in great deferred maintenance of way. As Federal Railroad Administrator Sullivan observed, "The deferred maintenance problem on the Milwaukee Railroad is not limited to its branch lines. The Milwaukee mainline routes across the Northern tier to the Pacific Northwest and south from Chicago to Louisville, Kentucky, suffered

Table 3.2. Chicago, Milwaukee, St. Paul & Pacific Railroad Comparative Profit and Loss Data (Thousands of Dollars).

Year	Railway Operating Revenues	Net Railway Operating Income	Transfers From Government	Interest on Debt	Net Income
1969	269,108	−10,182		10,575	11,583
1970	277,540	−7,867		10,116	−11,772[a]
1971	295,751	2,560		9,479	−22,196[b]
1972	312,832	−6,783		6,685	−8,643
1973	355,390	2,001		7,596	3,405
1974	394,676	−2,006		5,708	11,402
1975	381,092	−25,444		8,116	−21,067
1976	440,233	−19,346	5,501	4,534	−12,079
1977	448,106	−41,638	15,980	16,685	−38,269
1978	428,781	−84,820	10,420	17,071	−65,167
1979	430,363	−143,998	25,083	21,708	−105,178
1980	371,434	−117,560	18,523	35,303	−78,405[c]
1981	390,950	−95,804	13,409	42,820	7,088[d]
1982	351,616	−50,871	11,931	42,383	−21,595
1983	367,700	7,097	1,611	39,991	8,859
1984	415,819	2,254	493	38,317	−40,853

Source: U.S. Interstate Commerce Commission, *Transport Statistics in the United States* (1969–1984).

[a] Includes $3,608,791 loss sustained in joining National Railroad Passenger Corp.
[b] Includes $18,252,842 loss sustained in joining National Railroad Passenger Corp.
[c] Excluding restructuring expense of $127,175,000.
[d] Excluding equity in undistributed earnings of $166,058,000.

from considerable deferred maintenance with numerous slow orders that reduce operating speeds to 10 miles per hour. These slow speeds rendered the company unable to offer adequate, reliable, competitive service to shippers, causing yet further erosion of their traffic base, further reducing already insufficient revenues, and increasing operating expenses."[42] By December 31, 1978, deferred maintenance of way had reached $587 million.[43] Rehabilitation of only the 3,700 miles of main line tracks was estimated to cost $482 million. But the actual rehabilitation was extremely limited by lack of funds. In 1977, the $9.1 million in preference share financing from the Federal Railroad Administration was used to rehabilitate the Chicago-to-Milwaukee corridor.[44]

The investing public did not calculate the financial results of the railroad sector separated from nonrail activities. The total net income did not become negative until 1969, and it showed a recovery to net profits in 1973 and 1974. Investors who did not check the ICC reports might have relied on the published annual reports of the holding company, Chicago Milwaukee Corporation. Since its creation in 1971 in order to diversify the investment in the railroad, the holding company acquired firms in other industries. By 1975, only 86.1% of its revenues were from transportation. The Chicago Milwaukee Corporation reported profits of $2,096,000 in 1971, $559,000 in 1972, $11,399,000 in 1973, and $11,274,000 in 1974. It reported a loss of $19,595,000 in 1975.[45] Up to 1975, the unwary investor might have considered the firm to be relatively secure from financial failure. The fact that the railroad, its main asset, had been and continued to be in bad financial condition was hidden in consolidated reporting. Only in June 1975 did *Forbes* magazine publish an article about the Milwaukee Road entitled "No Visible Means of Support."[46] The corporation's 1975 annual report showed that the railroad had a negative cash flow from operations of $10,684,000.

BANRUPTCY AND SALE OF LINES

The trustee in bankruptcy was appointed in January, 1978, and he soon thereafter employed an independent consulting firm to evaluate the separate lines of the Milwaukee Road in order to estimate which ones had a significant probability of operating profitably. On August 3, 1978, trustee Stanley Hillman stated "There are portions of the railroad's light-density main lines which are not being operated and which cannot be operated to make a positive contribution to earnings, at least to any reorganized Milwaukee Road.... The principal main line which, I have determined, represents a drain on the railroad is the extension from Minneapolis-St. Paul to the Pacific North Coast. The Milwaukee Road can no longer operate as a transcontinental carrier."[47] It was essential for the Milwaukee to abandon its line crossing three mountain ranges, lines very expensive to maintain yet producing little revenue.

The Milwaukee Road survived from early 1978 to Spring of 1979 by investing $100 million in maintaining line and repairing equipment. These funds came from not paying taxes and interest and deferring some wages, from dividends and loans from its profitable land company, and from federal aid.[48] The latter was $55.2 million from the Department of Transportation in financial assistance under Title V of the Railroad Revitalization and Regulation Reform Act of 1976.[49] Of this fund $33.8 million was made available to finance track rehabilitation between Milwaukee and Minneapolis. There were not adequate funds to maintain the light-density main lines and branch lines. Milwaukee Road President Smith asserted in May 1979, "To operate the entire 9800-mile Milwaukee Road for the next eight months would require $80 to $90 million more cash than the railroad can itself generate."[50]

On April 23, 1979, the trustee requested the Bankruptcy Court to order him to embargo all but 2,500 route miles of the Milwaukee Road and to reduce employment to what would be required to operate that smaller railroad. The remaining road would connect Louisville, Chicago, Milwaukee, Minneapolis and Duluth; Chicago, Rockford to Madison and Portage, Wis.; Milwaukee, Green Bay, Wis. and Menominee, Mich.; and Twin Cities to Miles City, Mont.[51] The last was included because of assistance from the state of South Dakota.

The request of April 23 to the Court also asked for power to borrow $20 million additional funds to continue service while the courts considered the future of the carrier. On June 1, the Court granted the request to borrow funds but it held that it had no power to order an embargo.[52] On Oct. 2, 1979, the Court of Appeals affirmed the borrowing but reversed the lower court on the second issue and vacated the order of June 1 denying the embargo.[53]

On August 8, 1979 the trustee filed an application with the ICC to abandon all lines west of Miles City, Mont. But, before this application could be decided, the Milwaukee Road Restructuring Act became law on Nov. 4, 1979, transferring the abandonment jurisdiction to the bankruptcy court.[54] The ICC retained only an advisory role for Milwaukee Road abandonments. However, the trustee had filed his reorganization plan with the court on August 10, 1979 and for a second time requested an embargo for all lines outside a 3,200-mile the Midwest core. Noting the precarious cash position of the Milwaukee Road, the court granted the trustee's second embargo request on September 27, 1979, effective November 1, 1979.[55] The Congress passed the restructuring act in an attempt to provide funds for short-term continued service over the entire system. But funds were not available on November 1, and the Milwaukee Road ceased operations outside the Midwest core. Under Section 906 of the restructuring act the Secretary was given authority to guarantee trustee certificates of the Milwaukee Road for 60 days.[56] When these funds became available, the embargo outside the core was lifted. On February 25, 1980, the court authorized a third embargo request of the trustee, and on March 1, 1980 the embargo was reinstated. It became completely effective on April 1, 1980.

The trustee's 3,200-mile Midwest core system (Milwaukee II) had evolved from a comprehensive evaluation of rehabilitation requirements by Booz, Allen & Hamilton to determine which parts of the Milwaukee Road might became viable.[57] This three-volume study was supported by the U.S. Department of Transportation, Federal Railroad Administration, which estimated that the Midwest core should produce positive net railway operating income. FRA concluded:

> USDOT believes that, once stabilized, Milwaukee II would be an attractive merger candidate for a larger rail system. The agency states that, because prospects for success of

Milwaukee II are tied to the use of proceeds of sales of nonoperating properties and assets and revenues of the Milwaukee Land Company, those proceeds, assets and revenues must be dedicated to the support of Milwaukee II, as a condition of further USDOT financial assistance.[58]

Trustees for creditors filed a joint statement opposing the Midwest core plan, contending it would violate the constitutional rights of creditors and that the core railroad could not be made economically viable.[59]

The reorganization plans to create a possibly viable Milwaukee Road based on the midwest core or on full rebuilding were disapproved by the ICC on March 19, 1980.[60] Both the trustee's plan and the alternate plan of employees and shippers that hoped to reopen the western line to Seattle were found to be based on overoptimistic predictions of increased carloadings.[61] The disapproval was without prejudice to the submission of new or revised plans.

The Milwaukee Road proceeded with its plans to abandon or sell about 7,000 miles of its lines. On January 29, 1980, the ICC recommended to the bankruptcy court that Milwaukee lines in Montana, Idaho, Washington and Oregon be abandoned, but that actual abandonment be postponed until sale of segments could be considered.[62] On August 21, 1980, the ICC approved the sale of about 400 miles of the Western line to the Burlington Northern for $21 million.[63] Most of this consisted of terminal trackage or portions of Milwaukee branch lines connecting to the Burlington lines. However, the purchase included 57 miles of Milwaukee main line. The Union Pacific was permitted to purchase about 100 miles of Milwaukee line in Washington and Idaho for $19 million that would increase its efficiency, especially in Spokane, Seattle and Tacoma.[64] Another segment of the western line was preserved in 1982 when the South Dakota Railroad Authority purchased the 480-mile Milwaukee line from Ortonville, Minn. to Terry, Mont. for $30.4 million plus $7.3 million for track rehabilitation.[65] In 1983, it was reported that the state of South Dakota had purchased a total of 936 miles of the Milwaukee Road, financed by a one-cent increase in sales tax, in order to assure the marketing of the state's farm products.[66] The Burlington Northern was appointed operator of these lines.

Some other lines were also sold to state and local agencies. In January, 1980, the State of Wisconsin purchased 278 miles of Milwaukee Road branch lines.[67] Under the agreement, the state filed condemnation proceedings of the lines after they were abandoned and no longer under ICC jurisdiction.[68] In October, 1982, the Chicago Regional Transportation Authority leased the trackage of the Chicago commuter service of the Milwaukee Road.[69]

By August of 1981, the Milwaukee Road had received permission to abandon or sell 5,900 miles of track and another 1000 miles were targeted for disposal.[70] This cut the work force by 3,000 workers and reduced annual payroll by $70 million. Pursuant to Section 908 of the Milwaukee Road Restructuring Act, the railroad and the unions agreed to severance pay for released workers equal to 80% of each worker's pay for three years.[71] This accounts largely for the 1980 restructuring expense of $127,175,000. Retained workers agreed to defer 10% of their wages in the last five months of 1980 plus an additional 7% in 1981. The savings of $16 million to the railroad were to be repaid to the workers in stock. By the end of 1981, the Milwaukee Road was expected to have $113.9 million from the sale of lines in escrow accounts.[72]

In addition to the abandonments of branch lines, the Milwaukee Road abandoned low-density main lines. Most of the 1561 miles west of Butte, Montana were abandoned. In the mountain ranges from Montana to Washington, many of the lines where tracks were removed became hiking trails. The line from Chicago to Louisville was replaced. The longer portion from Chicago to Terre Haute, IN, was abandoned in 1980 as the Milwaukee Road secured trackage rights over parallel lines of Consolidated Rail Corp. and the Chessie System.[73]

The main line from the Mississippi River to Omaha was abandoned as it became clear that the Milwaukee could not compete with the rehabilitated Chicago and North Western to exchange traffic with the Union Pacific. In contrast, the line from Davenport to Kansas City was scheduled for rehabilitation as the parallel Rock Island line was abandoned and removed.[74]

MILWAUKEE CORE SOLD TO SOO LINE

Three Class I carriers bid to purchase the Milwaukee Road. In 1982, the Grand Trunk Corporation, a subsidiary of Canadian National Railways, reached agreement that the Grand Trunk should acquire stock control of the Milwaukee Road. The two carriers also signed a voluntary coordination agreement to run through freight service to destinations on the Milwaukee Road. The Milwaukee Road and the Grand Trunk filed a plan of reorganization for the Grand Trunk to acquire stock control of the Milwaukee.[75] This plan as amended was accepted for consideration by the ICC in April, 1983. In July, 1983, the Chicago and North Western filed an alternate plan for its subsidiary to acquire the Milwaukee Road. The Chicago Milwaukee Corp., parent of the Milwaukee Road filed an alternate plan for the carrier to be reorganize as an independent railroad. In January, 1984, six months after the deadline, the Soo Line Railroad sought Court permission to file an asset acquisition proposal for the Milwaukee Road under section 5(b) of the Milwaukee Road Restructuring Act.[76] The motion was granted and later upheld on appeal.[77]

The Grand Trunk proposal for the Milwaukee Road core assets was to assume $410 million in Milwaukee liabilities and to meet other offers up to approximately

$80 million.[78] The trustee valued the North Western proposal, including debt assumption, to be $569.9 million and the similar Soo Line proposal to be $570.6 million.[79] As of December 31, 1984, when the Milwaukee Road owned only 2,305 miles of the 3,023 miles of line it operated, the book value of this core that was about to be sold was $574.7 million.[80] The key element of this was the physical properties whose stated value was $554.9 million.

In its September, 1984 opinion, the ICC first rejected the proposal of the Chicago Milwaukee Corp. that the Milwaukee Road core should continue as an independent carrier. The ICC found that the voluntary coordination agreement with the Grand Trunk was the key factor predicting net profit operations of the Milwaukee Road. But there was no assurance that the voluntary coordination agreement would continue.[81] Chicago Milwaukee Corp.'s earnings projections were held to be unacceptably speculative.[82]

The proposal of Grand Trunk Corporation was also rejected as failing to meet the statutory requirements regarding the Milwaukee Road shareholders. Since Grand Trunk made a firm offer only to assume the liabilities of the Milwaukee, Road, there was no clear offer of compensation for the core assets.[83] Grand Trunk also had suffered substantial losses over the recent years, undermining its financial stability. Grand Trunk's announcement that it had entered a voluntary coordination agreement with the Burlington Northern indicated a lack of commitment to the Milwaukee.

The ICC did not reach a majority on North Western's Alternative Plan and Acquisition proposals.[84] It did find that this parallel merger would have a significant adverse competitive effect on rail transportation in three corridors.[85] In the Chicago-Milwaukee corridor, the combined carriers would have 98% of the total rail tonnage. In the Chicago-Green Bay corridor, the combined tonnage would be 97.2%. In the Duluth-Kansas City and Twin Cities-Kansas City corridors the respective combined tonnage would be 76.3% and 73.4%.

The ICC approved the Soo Line's Alternative Plan to acquire the Milwaukee Road core as compatible with the public interest, was fair and equitable and protected the interests of the creditors and stockholders.[86] In the corridors between Chicago and Milwaukee, Chicago and Twin Cities, and Chicago and Duluth, the merger was held not to significantly reduce potential competition. Either the North Western or the Burlington Northern or both were significant rivals in these key corridors.

Following the September, 1984 opinion of the ICC, the North Western filed an amended acquisition proposal under the Milwaukee Railroad Restructuring Act on October 9, 1984. The North Western offered $210 million in additional consideration for the net-loss Milwaukee Road core.[87] The Reorganization Court authorized the trustee to request modification of the plan approved in September relating to North Western's acquisition of the Milwaukee core. The Court asked the ICC to state a preference for the Soo or the North Western if the ICC approved the North Western's modified proposal.

The Chicago Milwaukee Corporation was for the first time willing to accept an offer of purchase for the Milwaukee Road core. It reversed its view that the carrier should remain independent because most of the benefit of the increased sale price would go to its shareholders.[88] The Soo Line, of course, opposed the North Western modified proposal, arguing that its primary purpose was to acquire a monopoly. Soo officials maintained that potential North Western line abandonments would hurt shippers.[89] The Wisconsin Department of Transportation also opposed the North Western modified proposal and questioned the financial viability of the carrier.[90] The optimistic projections of economic growth and increased carloadings did not have a great likelihood of being realized.

The ICC found that the modified proposal of the North Western to pay $786.6 million for the Milwaukee core met the public interest criteria of the statutes.[91] The North Western reiterated its earlier prediction of operational savings of $123.1 million and asserted that these savings were not dependent on the abandonment of any railroad lines. The ICC indicated that in 1985 the North Western was unlikely to be able to cover its fixed charges by the minimum ratio of 2.0, but the longer run outlook was more favorable.[92]

The ICC held that there was no issue about the fairness and equity of the consideration in the modified offer of the North Western. Both the trustee and the Chicago Milwaukee Corp. were willing to accept the offer. The public interest conclusion of the ICC favoring the North Western accepted the estimated $123 million annual savings and only noted that line abandonments to achieve the savings would have to be approved by the Commission. The ICC found the price financially sound and the projected revenue sufficient to cover fixed charges as well as significant benefits to the stockholders and protection for discharged employees. It found that the public benefits outweighed the potential competitive harm of the combination, and part of the latter was ameliorated by trackage rights for railroad rivals.[93]

The final conclusion of the ICC was to state a preference for one of the two approved carriers. The conclusion was that the benefits offered by the Soo Line proposal outweighed those of the North Western.[94] The original offers of the Soo Line and the North Western were comparable. The ICC concluded that the extra $210 million offered by the North Western did not change the factors of evaluation of the Milwaukee Road core properties but only a change in North Western's business judgment. The increase would not affect the rights of creditors but would inure solely to the Milwaukee stockholders and to displaced workers. The parallel unification of the North Western and the Milwaukee Road would mean large shifts of traffic to most efficient lines and downgrading of less efficient to the possible detriment of shippers on these low density lines. The greatest concern of the ICC was the alleged monopolistic effects of North Western's proposal. Given the substantial deregulation of ratemaking in the recent statutes, encouragement of competition was a primary policy issue.

The ICC decision against the North Western offer was not based on sound economics. The alleged competition in rates or innovations of financially weak railroads is unproven. Furthermore, rivalry of the strong Burlington Northern between the Chicago area and Minneapolis was the most important railroad economic factor in the area. Within Wisconsin, the new Wisconsin Central Railroad and motor carriers were and could continue as rivals to a larger North Western to transport farm products. The ICC policy of maintaining excess capacity in parallel rail lines such as the Milwaukee Road and the North Western prevented the most efficient use of key rail lines in Wisconsin. The Milwaukee Road line from Milwaukee to Minneapolis with a capacity of 135 million gross ton-miles per mile of road was a prime example. The policy of ICC prevented abandonment of the least efficient of parallel lines, a necessary element of railroad efficiency.

The reorganization judge announced on February 5, 1985 that he favored the ICC recommendation that the Soo Line purchase the Milwaukee Road core.[95] After oral argument, he so ruled, adopting the reasoning in the ICC report, and he refused to stay his order.[96] Over the objection of the trustee and Chicago Milwaukee Corp., the sale transaction of the Milwaukee Road core was completed on February 20, 1985.[97] The North Western immediately withdrew its higher offer, thus removing a key basis of appeal. Nonetheless, the Chicago Milwaukee Corporation and the unions filed an appeal, which they lost.[98] The Milwaukee Road Restructuring Act made adequate compensation for assets a condition of any sale. The ICC and the reorganization court found the Soo Line's offer of $570 million to match fair market value. On appeal, Judge Easterbrook concluded: "It is unsettling to contemplate the prospect of $210 million gone without redress – without even full appellate review of the decision to sell to the Soo. But we cannot undo the sale now, and to treat judicial error as a 'taking' has no support in the history of the Constitution or the first 200 years of its interpretation."[99]

SOO LINE FINANCIAL IMPACT AND SALE OF LINES

The Soo Line had operated 4,628 route miles in 1984, of which it owned 4,179 miles. It expanded its operated mileage by the merger in 1985 to 7,975, of which 6,383 miles were owned.[100] The 1985 Soo Line had 3,447 miles of main line and 4,528 miles of branch lines.[101] Thus 56.8% of the expanded railroad was branch lines. Expenditures on maintenance of way and structures increased from $61.6 million in 1984 to $124.7 million in 1985, the acquired Milwaukee main line from Chicago to Kansas City receiving priority for track improvement work.[102] The Soo Line assumption of debt of the Milwaukee Road meant that Soo Line long-term debt rose from $95.6 million in 1984 to $252.1 million in 1986 and to $298.3 million in 1986.[103] Consequently, fixed charges rose from $8 million in 1984 to $24.6 million in 1985.

The Soo Line's estimated economic benefits to be realized from merger of the Milwaukee Road were $35.3 million per year.[104] There is no evidence that these savings were actually realized. The predictions of the Soo Line management and the actual economic results of the merger in 1985 through 1987 are reported in Table 3.3. In 1984, the year prior to merger, the combined railway operating revenues of the Soo Line and the Milwaukee Road core were $738.6 million. The net revenue from railway operations was $23.2 million for the Soo Line and $4.7 million for the Milwaukee Road core for a total of $27.9 million. Of the total fixed charges of $50.9 million, $41.8 million were from the Milwaukee Road because of its large borrowings from the national government. So that the 1984 net income before taxes for the Soo Line was $28.6 million while the net loss for the Milwaukee Road core was $26.3 million.

It is doubtful that the expected savings could have been realized in 1985 because the Soo Line held the acquired Milwaukee Road assets in a separate company which was not merged into the Soo Line until January 1, 1986.[105] Even if some of the expected savings in costs were realized in 1985, an unpredicted drop in demand resulted in a significant drop in freight revenues. In second quarter 1985, carloadings of farm products were down 22% from that of the previous year.[106] As noted in Table 3.3, predicted 1985 revenues for the merged Soo/Milwaukee were $766.3 million and actual revenues were $600.4 million, a difference of 22%. Instead of its 1985 predicted net income of $2.1 million, the carrier suffered a loss of $11.6 million. Results for 1986 were worse. The predicted operating revenues were $819.7 million and the actual revenues were $606.3 million, a difference of 26%. Instead of a predicted 1986 profit of $25.9 million, the loss was $73.7 million. However, this loss was reported to include an $82 million restructuring charge.[107] Even with higher predicted operating revenues for 1987 of $874.2 million, the actual revenues were $589.4 million. The difference was 33%. Instead of predicted 1987 profits of $26.1 million, the 1987 loss was $3.9 million.

It became clear that a significant amount of the pre-merger Soo Line routes had become low density lines. The key example was the Soo Line route from

Wisconsin to Chicago. Having purchased the high-capacity, rehabilitated Milwaukee route from Chicago to Milwaukee and on to Minneapolis, it made economic sense for the Soo Line to transfer its traffic to this line. Since low-density lines could not be operated at a profit by a Class I railroad with union wage and work rule burdens, it made sense to sell some lines. In October 1987, the ICC approved the sale of Soo Line's Lake States Division, 1,801 miles of line in Wisconsin, Michigan, Minnesota, and Illinois to the Wisconsin Central Ltd..[108] This was a new railroad, created by a group of Chicago investors. The sale also included trackage rights, so the total route miles were 1960. The Soo Line indicated that it would use the $131 million in proceeds primarily to reduce long-term debt.[109]

The Wisconsin Central, with about 1,350 miles of its line in Wisconsin, would be a non-union carrier, operating at lower costs per mile than the Soo. The policy of the ICC not to attach protective conditions for rail workers losing jobs in sales of routes to new carriers made possible the sale of such lines.[110] Absent this policy, the sales would not occur and the Class I carriers would have to petition the ICC to permit abandonment.

In 1991, the Soo Line sold its 102-mile line from Superior to Ladysmith, Wisconsin to the Wisconsin Central.[111] In 1991, Soo Line also sold its 145-mile line from Hopkins to Appleton, Minnesota to the Twin Cities and Western Railroad. By 1992, Soo Line had reduced its route mileage to 5,033, of which 1,533 miles were trackage rights over other carriers.[112] Its mileage in Wisconsin had dropped to 381, a distant third in size behind the North Western. In contrast, Wisconsin Central had became the longest carrier in Wisconsin with 1460 route miles, 35% of the state's total.[113]

As early as 1990, the Soo Line officers determined that its 532-mile route from Chicago directly west to the Mississippi River and then south to Kansas City could not compete successfully with the Burlington Northern and the Santa Fe. The BN route was 455 miles and the Santa Fe was 448 miles. In 1990, the Soo Line had won ICC approval to sell this line to the Southern Pacific Railroad for $140 million, but the sale required transfer to S.P. of 42 miles of trackage rights over the Chicago & North Western between Polo, Missouri and Kansas City.[114] The North Western challenged the transfer and an arbitration panel ruled in its favor.[115] The Southern Pacific then was able to secure a less costly alternative, trackage rights over the Burlington Northern between Kansas City and Chicago.[116] Its new through route from the west coast to Chicago would greatly reduce the incentive of the Southern Pacific to interchange traffic with other parallel carriers at Kansas City. Soo Line President Edwin V. Dodge commented, "The business reasons which initially prompted us to sell the line have not changed. This is a highly competitive corridor with excess capacity."[117]

Table 3.3. Financial Results and Predictions for Combined Soo/Milwaukee[a] (Millions of Dollars).

	1984	1985		1986		1987	
	Combined Actual	Prediction	Actual	Prediction	Actual	Prediction	Actual
Railway Operating Revenue	$738.6	$766.3	$600.4	$819.7	$606.3	$874.2	$589.4
Operating Expanses	710.7	726.0	597.9	769.3	674.4	808.7	583.8
Net Revenue from Railway Operations	27.9	40.3	2.5	50.4	(68.1)	66.1	5.6
Other income-net	25.5	8.4	12.0	26.0	19.4	10.0	17.8
Total income	53.4	48.7	14.5	76.4	(48.7)	76.1	23 4
Miscellaneous Deductions	0.2		0.6		0.7		0.9
Available for Fixed Charges	53.2	48.7	13.9	76.4	(49 4)	76.1	22.5
Fixed Charges	50.9	46.6	25.5	50.5	24.3	50.0	26.4
Net income betore taxes	2.3	2.1	(11.6)	25.9	(73 7)	26.1	(3.9)

Sources: Milwaukee-Reorganization-Acquisition by GTC, 2 I.C.C. 2d 161, 403, Tab 618; Chicago, M., St. P. & P. R. Co., Report to S. E. C. 30 (1984); Moody's Transportation Manual 222 (1991).
[a] The predictions use the pro-forma statements presented by the Soo Line adjusted by the ICC for loss of the former voluntary coordination agreement of the Milwaukee Road and the Grand Trunk and for added interest costs. The 1984 actual financial results occurred before merger and are the sum of the two separate carrier reports to the ICC and the SEC.

In 1997, the Soo Line was finally able to sell the line from Chicago to Kansas City as part of a large sale of lines to a new regional carrier, I&M. Rail Link, LLC.[118] The total sale was for 1,109 miles of rail line and 262 miles of trackage rights in Iowa, Illinois, Minnesota, Missouri, Wisconsin and Kansas. This included the "Corn Lines" from Sabula on the Mississippi into Northern Iowa and in Southern Minnesota. The Surface Transportation Board allowed an acquisition exemption to-become effective on April 4, 1997.

CONCLUSION

The Milwaukee Road, like the Rock Island, was a carrier with almost no high density rail lines. In fact, in 1976 the Milwaukee Road had 59.2% of its lines with less than five million gross tons per mile per year. The amount of maintenance of way expenditures on these clearly net loss lines is not available. However, by the end of 1978, deferred maintenance of way on all Milwaukee

Road lines was $587 million. The reasonable inference is that the few profitable lines would not have sufficient earnings to cross-subsidize the net loss ones.

Like the Rock Island lines, the attempts of the Milwaukee Road to solve its financial distress was to search for a merger with another railroad. But, unlike the Rock Island, the Milwaukee Road could find no profitable Class 1 railroad whose management saw a financial advantage in considering a merger. Starting before World War II and extending into the 1970s, the Milwaukee Road entered a series of negotiations for merger with the Chicago & North Western. But the North Western was another financially weak carrier with 79% of its lines carrying less than 10 million gross tons per mile per year. As the relative shares prices of the two railroads fluctuated unevenly, the merger negotiations failed. Even if they had succeeded in a merger, the financial remedy would still have depended upon convincing the ICC to permit abandonment of their many duplicate parallel lines. Wisconsin was the prime example of this problem.

Like the Rock Island, the bankruptcy of the Milwaukee Road became inevitable. The result was the necessity of dismembering the railroad with abandonment of all but 3,200 miles of line. The key abandonment example was the line from Minnesota to the Pacific coast, the expansion line that critics assert should never have been built. The segment from Montana through the mountains to Seattle was clearly a long-term net loss burden on the carrier. The ICC should have encouraged abandonment of this line long before. Instead the ICC made the false assumption that the weak Milwaukee Road would be a significant rival to the Burlington Northern. Unfortunately, the policy of the ICC was to preserve weak railroads.

The ICC rejected the proposal of the core-size Milwaukee Road to remain independent. The highest bid for the Milwaukee Road was its long-time suitor, the Chicago & North Western. The ICC rejected this bid and ruled in favor of the bid of the Soo Line. Once again the ICC ruled in favor of preserving alleged inter-railroad competition and against reducing excess capacity in parallel rail lines.

NOTES

1. Max Lowenthal, *The Investor Pays*, ch. 2 (New York: Alfred A. Knopf, 1933).
2. August Derleth, *The Milwaukee Road: Its First Hundred Years*, 198 (N. Y.: Creative Age Press, 1948).
3. Ibid., 199.
4. Chicago, Milwaukee & St. Paul Reorganization, 131 I.C.C. 673 (1928), 138 I.C.C. 291 (1928), 154 I.C.C. 586 (1929).
5. Chicago, Milwaukee, St. P. & P. Co. Reorganization, 212 I.C.C. 150 (1935), 239 I.C.C. 484 (1940), 254 I.C.C. 707 (1943), 257 I.C.C. 223 (1944).

6. Group of Inst. Investors v. Chicago, M., St. P. & P. R. R., 318 U.S. 523 (1943). See In re Chicago, M., St. P. & P. R. R., 145 F.2d 299 (7th Cir. 1944).

7. Louisville & N. R.Co.-Merger-Monon Railroad, 338 I.C.C. 134, 158, 199 (1970). See Chicago, M., St. P. & P. R. Co. – Trackage Rights, 342 I.C.C. 578 (1973), aff'd sub nom., Louisville and Nashville Railroad Co. v. United States, 369 F. Supp. 621 (W. D. Ky. 1973), aff'd mem., 414 U.S. 1105 (1973).

8. Figures for 1947 are from U.S., I.C.C., *Statistics of Railways in the United States* (1947). Figures for 1974 are from U.S., I.C.C., *Transport Statistics in the United States* (1974).

9. Compiled from reports to the Interstate Commerce Commission in Association of American Railroads, *Operating and Traffic Statistics*, Series No. 218 (1977).

10. The theoretical capacity of a single-track line with block signals under optimum operating conditions is 40 trains per day. The practical capacity estimated by those in the industry is 20 to 25 trains per day. See U.S. Dept. of Transportation, *Rail Service in the Midwest and Northeast Region*, Vol. 1, 5 (1974).

11. See Chicago & North Western Railway Co. Reorganization, 230 I.C.C. 548 (1939).

12. Chicago, Milwaukee, St. Paul & Pacific R. Co., *Annual Report* 17 (1955).

13. Chicago, Milwaukee, St. Paul & Pacific R. Co., *Annual Report* 3 (1959); *Id.* 4 (1960). See Railway Age 34 (Nov. 16, 1959).

14. See Wall Street Journal 20 (Feb. 13, 1961); *Id.* 2 (Feb. 24, 1961).

15. See Railway Age 40 (March 6, 1961); Wall Street Journal 26 (Feb. 27, 1961); *Id.* 6 (March 17, 1961).

16. Chicago, Milwaukee, St. Paul & P. R. Co., *Annual Report* 6 (1964). See Railway Age 11–12 (March 29, 1965).

17. Chicago, Milwaukee and North Western Transportation Co., F. D. 24182, Examiner's Report 60 (Dec. 18, 1968). See Dudley F. Pegrum, *The Chicago and North Western-Chicago, Milwaukee, St. Paul and Pacific Merger: A Case Study in Transport Economics*, 9 Transp. J. 43 (1969).

18. Chicago, Milwaukee, St. Paul & P. R. Co., *Annual Report* 5 (1969). See Wall Street Journal 2 (Jan. 29, 1970); ibid. 11 (Feb. 26, 1970); *Id.* 9 (April 2, 1970); *Id.* 11 (April 3, 1970).

19. North Western Employees-Purchase-Chicago & N. W. Ry., Co., 342 I.C.C. 58 (1972); Chicago & N. W. Trans. Co. Stock, 342 I.C.C. 839 (1973).

20. Chicago, Milwaukee, St. Paul & P. R. Co., *Annual Report* 6 (1965).

21. Chicago & North Western R. Co.-Control-Chicago, Rock Island and Pacific R. Co., 347 I.C.C. 556, 615 (1974).

22. Union Pacific Corp., *Annual Report* 9 (1975).

23. Great Northern Pac.-Merger-Great Northern, 328 I.C.C. 460 (1966), 331 I.C.C. 228 (1967), aff'd in United States v. United States and Interstate Commerce Commission, 296 F. Supp. 853 (D.C. D.C. 1968), aff'd in Northern Lines Merger Cases, 396 U.S. 491 (1970).

24. Chicago, Milwaukee, St. Paul & P. R. Co., *Annual Report* 9 (1961). See Railway Age 33 (May 8, 1961).

25. 328 I.C.C. 460, 483 (1966).

26. 328 I.C.C. at 497.

27. Chicago, Milwaukee and North Western Transportation Company, F. D. 24182, Examiner's Report, Appendix D-1, p. 5 (1968).

28. U.S. Dept. of Transportation, *Final Standards, Classification and Designation of Lines of Class 1 Railroads in the United States*, Vol. II (Interim) 65, 73, 113 (1977).
29. Great Northern Pac.-Merger- Great Northern, 331 I.C.C. at 359 and 879.
30. 90 Stat. 61-66, 49 U.S.C. 1654 (1976).
31. Great Northern Pac.-Merger-Great Northern, 348 I.C.C. 821 (1977).
32. 348 I.C.C. at 830.
33. U.S., I.C.C., *Transport Statistics in the United States* 149 (1970).
34. *Id.* 151 (1971); *Id.*, 153 (1972).
35. Contrary to railroad accounting, net railway operating income should not include transfers from government, which are listed separately in Table 2.
36. *Moody's Transportation Manual* 682 (1978).
37. Frank Malone, *Chicago RTA: Keeping Up With the Commuter Influx*, Railway Age, Feb. 11, 1980, 46, 48.
38. 84 Stat. 1975 (1970), 45 U.S.C.A. §661 et seq. (1987).
39. *Railway Age*, April 24, 1978, 12.
40. Milwaukee Road Restructuring Act, 93 Stat. 740 (1979), 45 U.S.C.A. §906 (1987).
41. Chicago, Milwaukee, St. Paul & Pacific Railroad Co., *Annual Report to S.E.C.* 44 (1982).
42. U.S. Cong., House, Committee on Interstate and Foreign Commerce, *Milwaukee Road Bankruptcy*, Hearing, 95th Cong., 2d Sess., 1978, 10.
43. Chicago, M., St. Paul & P. R. Co. Reorganization, 363 I.C.C. 17, 25 (1980).
44. *Milwaukee Road Bankruptcy, supra* note 42, at 31 (testimony of A. Daniel O'Neal, Chairman, Interstate Commerce Commission).
45. *Moody's Transportation Manual* 199 (1974); *Id.* 35 (1976).
46. Forbes, June 15, 1975, 19. See *Mal-waukee Road?*, Forbes, July 1, 1975, 23.
47. Statement of trustee Stanley E. G. Hillman, reported in *Railway Age*, Aug. 14, 1978, 10.
48. Statement of W. L. Smith, President of the Milwaukee Road, in U.S. Cong., House, Committee on Interstate and Foreign Commerce, *Reorganization of the Milwaukee Railroad*, 96th Cong., 1st Sess., 1979, 59.
49. Statement of Robert E. Gallamore, Federal Railroad Administration, in *Id.*, 90.
50. *Id.*, at 58.
51. *Id.* At 60.
52. Matter of Chicago, M., St. P. & P.R. Co., 471 F. Supp. 964 (N. D.Ill., 1979).
53. Matter of Chicago, Milwaukee, Etc., 611 F. 2d 662, 670 (7th Cir. 1979). Citing Brooks-Scanlon Co. v. Railroad Commission, 251 U.S. 396, 399 (1920), the Court apllied an eminent domain principle: "It is settled that a railroad that is cashless cannot be required to continue operating to serve the public interest." *Id.*, at 669.
54. 93 Stat. 737 (1979), 45 U.S.C.A. §904 (1987).
55. Chicago, M., St. Paul & P. R. Co. Reorganization, 363 I.C.C. 17, 20 (1980).
56. 45 U.S.C.A. §906 (1979).
57. Chicago, M., St. Paul & P. R. Co. Reorganization, 363 I.C.C. 19 (1980).
58. *Id.* at 35–36.
59. *Id.* at 36.
60. *Id.* at 41–46.
61. For the statutory rights of employees and shippers to submit alternative plans, see Milwaukee Road Restructuring Act, 45 U.S.C.A. §905 (1979).
62. Burlington Northern Inc.-Pur.-Chicago, M., St. P., 363 I.C.C. 298, 300 (1980).

63. *Id.*, at 306. As to valid preliminary approval by the court before the railroad filed an application to I.C.C for approval of purchase, see Matter of Chicago, M., St. P. & P.R. Co., 641 F. 2d 482 (7th Cir. 1981).
64. 363 I.C.C., at 307–308.
65. Chicago, Milwaukee, St. Paul & Pacific R. Co., Report to the Securities and Exchange Commission 31 (1982). See *Wall St. Journal*, Feb. 23, 1982, 14; *Id.*, Mar. 17, 1982, 46.
66. I.C.C. Annual Report 28 (1982); John Merwin, *Lets Make a Deal*, Forbes, Nov. 21, 1983, 86.
67. Traffic World, Jan. 28, 1980, 18.
68. Matter of Chicago, M., St. Paul & P.R. Co., 739 F. 2d 1169 (7th Cir. 1984).
69. Report to S. E. C., *supra*, note 62, at 34. See Wall St. Journal, Aug. 23, 1982, 27.
70. Business Week, Aug. 10, 1981, 96.
71. Matter of Chicago, Milwaukee, St. Paul & P. R.Co., 713 F. 2d 274, 278 (7th Cir. 1983), cert. denied 465 U.S. 1100 (1984).
72. Railway Age, Sept. 28, 1981, 12.
73. F. D. 29186 (Sub-No. 1), Chicago, Milwuakee, St. Paul & P. R. Co., debtor-Trackage Rights-over Indiana Harbor Belt R. Co. between North Harvey, IL. and Gibson, IN., and over Consolidated Rail Corp. between Gibson, IN and Terre Haute, IN. (April 15, 1980); Docket No. AB7 (Sub-No. 87) Chicago, M. St. P. & P. R. Co.-Abandonment between Chicago Heights, IL and Fayette, IN (April 16, 1980). Abandonment was authorized by the reorganization Court Order No. 328 (May 5, 1980).
74. Railway Age, Sept. 27, 1982, 42, 44. See chapter 2, notes 69 and 70 and accompanying text.
75. Milwaukee-Reorganization-Acquisition by GTC, 2 I.C.C. 2d 161, 170 (1984).
76. *Id.*, at 17 1.
77. Matter of Chicago, Milwaukee, St. Paul & P. R. Co., 756 F. 2d 508, 513 (7th Cir. 1985).
78. Milwaukee-Reorganization-Acquisition by GTC, 2 I.C.C. 2d at 177.
79. *Id.*, at 392.
80. Chicago, Milwaukee, St. Paul & Pacific Railroad Co., Report to the Securities and Exchange Commission 33 (1984).
81. Milwaukee-Reorganization-Acquisition by GTC, 2 I.C.C. 2d at 216–17.
82. *Id.*, at 259.
83. *Id.*, at 257.
84. *Id.*, at 272.
85. *Id.*, at 225-26, 236.
86. *Id.*, at 271–72.
87. Milwaukee-Reorganization-Acquisition by GTC, 2 I.C.C. 2d 427, 429 (1985).
88. *Id.*, at 430.
89. *Id.*, at 431.
90. *Id.*, at 434.
91. *Id.*, at 438.
92. *Id.*, at 440.
93. *Id.*, at 449.
94. *Id.*, at 460–63.
95. Wall St. Journal, Feb. 6, 1985, 19.

96. Wall St. Journal, Feb. 11, 1985, 16.
97. Wall St. Journal, Feb. 21, 1985, 44.
98. Matter of Chicago, Milwaukee, St. Paul and Pacific, 779 F. 2d 217 (7th Cir. 1986), cert. denied 481 U.S. 1068 (1987).
99. *Id.*, at 328.
100. U.S., I.C.C., *Transport Statistics in the United States* 105 (1984); *Id.*, 75 (1985).
101. *Moody's Transportation Manual* 632 (1986).
102. *Id.*
103. *Moody's Transportation Manual* 222 (1991).
104. Milwaukee-Reorganization-Acquisition by GTC, 2 I.C.C. 2d at 389.
105. *Moody's Transportation Manual* 632 (1986).
106. *Railway Age,* Aug. 1985, 37.
107. Wall St. Journal, Oct. 9, 1987, 10.
108. Wisconsin Central Ltd.-Exemption, Acquisition and Operation-Certain Lines of Soo Line Railroad Co., F. D. 31102 (1988).
109. Wall St. Journal, Oct. 13, 1987, 60.
110. Class Exemption for the Acquisition and Operation of Rail Lines Under 49 U.S. C. 10901, 1 I.C.C. 2d 810, 814 (1985), *affirmed sub nom.* Illinois Commerce Commission v. ICC, 817 F. 2d 145 (D.C. Cir. 1987).
111. *Moody's Transportation Manual* 215 (1996).
112. *Moody's Transportation Manual* 234 (1993).
113. Steve Glischinski and J. David Ingles, *A Time of Transformation,* Trains, May, 1994, 51.
114. Rio Grande Ind., Inc.-Purchase & Trackage-Soo Line R. Co., 6 I.C.C. 2d 854, 902 (1990).
115. *Traffic World,* July 2, 1990, 13.
116. *Traffic World* Aug. 6, 1990, 13.
117. *Id.*
118. I&M Rail Link, LLC-Acquisition and Operation Exemption-Certain Lines of Soo Railroad Co. D/B/A Canadian Pacific Railway, 2 S. T. B. 167 (1997).

4. ILLINOIS CENTRAL MERGER AND SALES OF LINES

The Illinois Central Railroad merger of the Gulf, Mobile and Ohio Railroad was an example of a parallel merger designed to increase the traffic density on the key rail route from Chicago to New Orleans. A high level of maintenance of way expenditures was needed to enable the I.C. to outperform rival water and highway carriers. Under its contract with AMTRAK, I.C. was also required to maintain track at the highest level to accommodate high-speed passenger trains. As a consequence of the merger, I.C. obtained a large number of low-density lines that could not be operated at a profit under the labor contracts of a Class 1 railroad. The merger reduced most main lines of the G.M.&O. to low-density lines and thus aggravated the problem of net-loss lines. The result was the I.C. policy to sell low-density lines to short-line railroads, which were not bound by national Class 1 Railroad labor contracts. The I.C. managers expected these short-line railroads would become feeder lines to the I.C. However, some of these shortline railroads were eventually acquired by the Kansas City Southern Railway over opposition of the I.C.

MERGER AGREEMENT

The Interstate Commerce Commission in August, 1972 approved the Illinois Central Railroad merger of the Gulf, Mobile and Ohio Railroad to form the Illinois Central Gulf. In 1971, the Illinois Central reported 6,760 miles of road.[1] Its primary main line was between Chicago and New Orleans, but other main lines connected the primary line to St. Louis, Louisville, Indianapolis and Birmingham. Another main line extending West from Chicago reached Omaha, Council Bluffs, Sioux City, Sioux Falls and cities to the North.

The Gulf, Mobile & Ohio Railroad had been created in 1940 through merger of the Mobile and Ohio Railroad with the Gulf Mobile & Northern. It was a carrier from St. Louis south to Mobile and to New Orleans with concentration of lines in Mississippi.[2] It became a single-line rival of the Illinois Central for traffic between Chicago and New Orleans in 1947, when it bought the Chicago

& Alton Railroad.[3] The 959 mile Alton had extended from Chicago south to St. Louis with a main branch west from Springfield to Kansas City. In 1971, the Gulf, Mobile & Ohio had 2,734 miles of road of which 2,290 miles were owned by the carrier.[4]

The merger agreement between the I.C. and the G.M.&O. was reached in 1968. In 1968, the I.C. freight revenue train miles were 13.3 million while those of G.M.&O. were 3.3 million or 25% of I.C. Total freight revenue for the I.C. in 1968 was $264.1 million while that of G.M.&O. was $89.0 million or 34% of I.C. Passenger revenues presented a different picture because the I.C. had both intercity and commuter service. I.C. passenger revenues in 1968 were $23.7 million while those of the G.M.&O. were just $2 million. As a result, the I.C. stated passenger deficit for 1968 was $17 million while that for the G.M.&O. was $3.7 million. The effect of this was that the net railway operating income of the I.C. in 1968 was $15.9 million while that of the G.M.&O. was $10.4 million. The 1968 I.C. rate of return on depreciated value of physical property used in transportation plus cash and cost of materials and supplies was 2.10%. The G.M.&O. rate of return was 4.55%.

These facts clearly affected the exchange ratio for shares. Both I.C. stock and G.M.&O. stock were to be exchanged for stock in the holding company, I.C. Industries, Inc. Each share of G.M.&O. common stock was exchanged for 0.75 share of I.C. Industries new $6 cumulative preferred with the stipulation that each share of preferred could be converted at any time into three shares of I.C. Industries common stock. In effect, this meant that each share of G.M.&O. common could be exchanged for 2.25 shares of I.C. Industries common stock. Each share I.C. Railroad common stock would be exchanged for two shares of I.C. Industries common stock. So that the valuation ratio of G.M.&O. common stock to I.C. railroad common stock was 1.125 to 1.

The financial results of the I.C. and G.M.&O. in 1971, the year before the merger was implemented, are presented in Table 1. The I.C. railway operating revenues from freight service were $324.9 million or 3.2 times the $101.5 million of the G.M.&O. The I.C. freight train miles needed to earn these revenues were 4.3 times those of the G.M.&O. while the total ton miles of the I.C. were only 2.8 times that of G.M.&O.

The 1971 net railway operating income of the I.C. was $26 million while that of the G.M.&O. was $10 million. The relative deficiency of the I.C. is directly attributable to the passenger deficit of $12.7 million. Amtrak took over the intercity passenger service on May 1, 1971, so that the passenger deficit for intercity services reflects four months of loss. The major part of the I.C. passenger deficit must have been incurred by the Chicago commuter service. The 1971 net income of the I.C. was $14.2 million. But the I.C. allocated $28.3

Table 4.1. Financial Results of The I.C. and G.M.&O., 1971 and I.C.G., 1973 (Thousands of Dollars).

	Illinois Central 1971	Gulf, Mobile & Ohio 1971	I.C.G. 1973
Railway Operating Revenue	352,377	106,127	525,993
Freight Service	338,446	105,204	514,103
Passenger Service	13,931	924	11,890
Railway Operating Expenses	274,702	81,047	395,442
Rent of Cars and Equipment	−19,591	−6,572	−35,196
Net RailwayOperating Income	26,003	9,935	42,757
Freight Service	38,716	12,392	56,345
Passenger Service	−12,713	−2,457	−13,588
Other Income	14,696	3,393	25,066
Income Available for Fixed Charges	37,407	12,233	67,430
Fixed Charges	11,585	3,501	20,223
Extraordinary Items	−11,654	−2,151	0
Net Income	14,168	4,463	45,132

Source: U.S., *I.C.C., Transport Statistics in the United States*, 1971 and 1973.

million for expenses relating to Amtrak's assumption of intercity passenger operations.[5]

The carriers estimated their minimum annual merger savings at $12.1 million and the ICC examiner concluded the savings would approximate $10.8 million.[6] In 1967, the carriers had interchanged 80,847 cars at 26 terminals. These included 35,340 revenue loads. Savings would occur in eliminating switching costs and in accounting between firms.[7] Major savings were anticipated from consolidation of offices, agencies and yard operations. Consolidated freight train service was expected to save $1.2 million per year as some lines were downgraded or abandoned. Furthermore, service was estimated to be more direct and faster between Chicago and main southern cities.

The Antitrust Division of the Department of Justice had intervened to oppose the merger of I.C. and G.M.&O.[8] The Justice position was argued in spite of the fact that the merger application was heard years before the rate deregulation in the transportation acts of 1976 and 1980. In this earlier period, rail rates were set by cartel in rate bureaus so that there was almost no interrailroad rate competition. Service competition was largely prevented by geography. Industries located on sidings of the I.C. or the G.M.&O. were almost sure to choose those carriers in order to avoid the time lost in an additional switching. Industries in the Chicago area on other rail sidings were more likely to choose the I.C. for shipments south because it was faster. The G.M.&O. line went through the congested East St. Louis switching yards where cars could be left or added, but this could add 24 hours to the trip from Chicago to Mobile or New Orleans.

Justice ignored the geographic constraints and the cartel rate-making to argue that these two direct routes between Chicago and the Gulf were in vigorous competition with each other. The less direct route of Louisville and Nashville Railroad from Chicago to Nashville and on to the Gulf was not considered competitive by Justice. Justice discounted the rivalry of water carriers on the Mississippi for bulk commodities and the rivalry of motor carriers for manufactured goods. Justice further argued that the potential economic benefits of the merger did not justify approval because I.C. and G.M.&O. were two financially healthy carriers. But this ignored railroad cost structures. A key objective of the merger was to reduce the maintenance of way for high-speed freight lines from two routes to one. The ability to keep a high level of maintenance of way was firstly structural, but even when there was a cyclical drop in demand for transport service, a single high density line would assure that there would be no slow orders, a key element in the market rivalry with motor carriers. Thus one can understand the overwhelming shipper support for the merger.

The ICC rejected the arguments of the Justice Department. Of the 13 stations that would be left no rival railroad to the I.C.G., the only city of significant size was Jackson, Miss. The aggregate revenues of I.C.G. from the 13 stations would be less the 0.5% of total revenues. The ICC accepted the examiner's report that gave significant weight to the presence of rival carriers to the proposed I.C.G., namely Southern Railway, the Missouri Pacific, and the Louisville and Nashville.[9]

In approving the merger as meeting the statutory public interest standard, the ICC emphasized the national transportation policy of the Transportation Act of 1940 among whose objectives was avoidance of injurious waste and development of a more efficient transportation system.[10] A key finding was that improved service to shippers would be provided, substantial improvements in operations could be achieved, and a more effective use of capital and equipment would be realized.[11] As to diversion of traffic from other carriers to the more efficient I.C.G., the commission found that no single railroad would suffer substantial injury. Neither the applicants nor the commission noted that the promotion of efficiency in one railroad and the prevention of diversion of traffic from less direct rival railroads are inconsistent concepts.

Upon petition of three short-line railroads in Mississippi that feared substantial loss of traffic to the merged carriers, the ICC conditioned its approval upon their inclusion in he Illinois Central Gulf.[12] The short-line roads reached agreements with ICC to exchange their assets for I.C. Industries common stock. The 27-mile Bonhomie & Hattiesburg Southern Railroad received shares worth

$888,278 and became a key connection between the I.C. and the southern 69 miles of one G.M.&O. line into Mobile. The 44-mile Fernwood, Columbia and Gulf Railroad received shares worth $661,164, but this line was later abandoned by the I.C.G.[13] The Columbus and Greenville Railway, with 168 miles; received $5 million in shares, but area shippers found I.C.G. service unsatisfactory. Consequently, in October, 1975, the line was sold back to local business interests for $1.2 million.[14]

Subsequent appeals of the ICC decision by the Missouri Pacific Railroad and the Kansas City Southern Railway were rejected by the courts.[15] The Missouri Pacific case centered on alleged control of I.C. by the Union Pacific which owned 16% of the I.C. stock. The commission had allowed Union Pacific ten years to divest itself of the stock, but the U.P. had transferred its I.C. stock to an independent trustee, giving up control. Consequently, the Kansas City Southern had sought a condition to the merger that would have allowed it to purchase I.C. lines enabling it to reach Chicago and East St. Louis. The commission had rejected this condition that would have extended the Kansas City Southern into new territory and would have created a great windfall to the Kansas City Southern to the detriment of the I.C.G.

MERGER EFFECTS AND SALES OF LINES

The early aggregate results of the merger of the two railroads into the new Illinois Central Gulf Railroad are recorded in Table 1, but freight revenues were the test of success. The first full year of operations of I.C.G. was 1973. The freight revenues of the I.C.G. in 1973 were $492.4 million as compared with the 1971 combined freight revenue of the two separate railroads of $426.5. The increase was $65.9 million or 15.45%.

In 1973 the I.C.G. net railway operating income from freight service was $56.3 million as compared with that of the 1971 combined railroads of $51.1, an increase of 10.2%. The results in passenger service were still negative. With the takeover of intercity passenger service by Amtrak on May 1, 1971, the passenger deficit should have decreased, but the I.C.G. passenger deficit increased to $–13.6 million. This reflects the increased costs of operation of commuter service and that significant intercity passenger service costs were not truly avoidable when the service was taken over by Amtrak.

The apparent success of the merger in 1973 was deceiving. The financial decline of Illinois Central Gulf Railroad is demonstrated in Table 4.2. The net railway operating income of I.C.G. in 1974 was $24.1 million, half that in 1973, and, for the next eight years, it was all downhill. In 1975, net railway operating income dropped to $9 million, and for the next three years it was minimal. In

Table 4.2. Illinois Central Gulf Railroad Route Miles and Financial Results.

year	Route Miles Operated	Operating Revenue (in $000)	Transfers from Government (in $000)	Net Railway Operating Income[a] (in $000)	Net Income (in $000)
1974	9568	577,843		24,095	29,474
1975	9463	547,449		9,028	1,080
1976	9260	614,724		2,727	13,859
1977	9330	671,871		1,174	3,339
1978	8866	733,132	15,530	2,558	–1,972
1979	8704	833,851	19,445	–29,850	–32,072
1980	8366	947,914	25,352	–9,833	–27,227
1981	7963	1,011,349	21,418	–18,439	–5,921
1982	7518	870,125	25,737	–88,242	–24,859
1983	7086	852,860	21,307	8,399	–7,396
1984	6676	932,666	22,022	62,586	62,353
1985	4772	861,783	18,735	43,771	29,968
1986	3788	658,018	21,470	62,862[b]	–171,674
1987	3205	541,417	7,219	35,659	1,510
1988	2900	556,386		52,931[c]	14,300
1989	2887	547,043		85,249	9,692
1990	2773	544,174		133,853	46,179
1991	2766	549,728		145,097	65,292
1992	2732	547,436		150,343	97,004
1993	2717	564,651		177,600	68,500
1994	2665	595,300		192,400	112,700
1995	2642	645,300		221,900	119,800
1996	2623	617,264		219,500	126,600
1997	2600	622,500		227,900	136,200

Source: U.S., I.C.C., *Transport Statistics in the United States, 1974–1998.*
[a] Including transfers from government.
[b] Excludes $412 million special charge for restructuring.
[c] Excludes $35 million special charge for restructuring.

1979, the net railway operating income was $–29.85 million in spite of a transfer from government of $19.4 million. The operating losses continued for three more years. This was true in spite of substantial increases in operating revenues until 1981.

By 1976, it was clearly understood by I.C.G. management that over two thirds of its lines that were low density could earn only minimal operating income or operating losses. While maintenance-of-way expenses rose from $65.4 million in 1973 to $93.5 million in 1976, the largest part had to be concentrated on the main lines from Chicago to the Gulf of Mexico. And for the carrier as a whole, the ICC asserted that the I.C.G. had a decline in the quality of freight service. The ICC stated that this was "the result of a combination of factors: substantial amount of delayed capital expenditures for roadway improvements, deferred maintenance-of-way-and-structures, and increase in the miles of slow-order track, and an increase in the number of derailments caused by defective track."[16] In fact, the complaints of Amtrak officials about the condition of main lines resulted in arbitration that lead to a 1974 settlement concerning the upgrading of lines.[17]

The 1977 Report by the Secretary of Transportation designated only one I.C.G. line as a high-density main line.[18] The 921-mile route from Chicago to New Orleans had in excess of 30 million gross ton miles per mile of road per year for lines in Illinois, Kentucky and Tennessee. This main line in Mississippi and Louisiana had between 20 and 30 million gross ton miles. The 289-mile former G.M.&O. route from Chicago to East St. Louis was designated a secondary main line with more than 10 million gross ton miles per mile over most of the route. The 515-mile line from Chicago to Omaha was also designated a secondary main line. The eastern half had more than 10 million gross tons per mile, but the western half had between five and 10 million gross tons. The Federal Railroad Administration estimated the deferred maintenance of way of the I.C.G. to be $238 million, mostly attributable to secondary main lines and branch lines.[19]

The problem of low-density lines was most severe in Mississippi where in 1973 I.C.G. had 3,064 miles of line, 32% of its total routes. Once the former G.M.&O. lines became part of I.C.G. and were reduced in status to local traffic, they could not be maintained and still earn a profit given the crew requirements and work restrictions of unionized Class I railroads. It became clear to management that net-loss lines had to be abandoned or sold. Before the Staggers Act, between 1974 and 1980, I.C.G. sold only two lines, the largest being the Columbus to Greenville of 168 miles. After the 1980 Staggers Act but before ICC and court rulings denying compensation to discharged workers on Class 1 railroads, few lines were sold. From 1980 to 1984, I.C.G. sold 470 miles of line in eleven line segments after receiving ICC approval to abandon ten of the eleven.[20] Only one segment of this group was in Mississippi.

After the courts ruled against compensation to workers on Class 1 railroads selling lines to new, short-line railroads, sales increased greatly. The largest sale of Mississippi lines by I.C.G. took place in 1985 and 1986. The Gulf & Mississippi Railroad paid $22.5 million for 713 miles of lines.[21] These included the bulk of the two former North-South main lines of the former G.M.&O. and some former I.C. lines. In 1986, the Mid-South Rail Corp., a new railroad, paid $123.5 million for 421 miles of line.[22] The largest segment was the former I.C.

East-West line of 314 miles from Meridian, Mississippi to Shreveport, Louisiana. The price may reflect the substantial investment that I.C.G. had made to upgrade the track and roadbed of the line.[23] It may also reflect the fact that the Mid-South price no longer had to be discounted for taking I.C.G. union worker off the I.C.G. payrolls. In 1988, the Mid-South Corp. acquired the Gulf & Mississippi Railroad Corp. in an exchange of shares.[24]

A separate chapter concerns the disposition of I.C.G. lines west from Chicago to Omaha, Sioux City, Iowa and Sioux Falls, South Dakota. It began in 1980 with ICC grant of permission to abandon the 97-mile branch line from Cherokee, Iowa to Sioux Falls.[25] In 1981, I.C.G. sold the 59 mile branch from Freeport, Il. to Madison Wis. to the Central Wisconsin Railroad for $2.9 million.[26] In 1984, the I.C.G. sold the 107-mile branch line from near Waterloo, Iowa to Albert Lea, Minn. to the Cedar Valley Railroad for $3 million.[27] In 1985, Jack Haley, the entrepreneur who had created the Cedar Valley Railroad, bought the 686 mile I.C.G. lines from Chicago to Omaha and Sioux City for $75 million and named the carrier Chicago Central & Pacific Railroad.[28] Haley borrowed $75 million from General Electric Credit Corp. (G.E.C.C.) to finance the purchase, and when the railroad could not meet its debts as they came due, G.E.C.C. in 1987 removed him and placed its agent in charge of the carrier.[29] In 1991, Haley's Cedar Valley Railroad failed and shut down, followed by an ICC order to the Chicago Central & Pacific Railroad to operate as directed service carrier on the line.[30]

The totally unexpected event was the 1996 repurchase by the Illinois Central Corp., parent of I.C. Railroad, of the Chicago Central & Pacific Railroad and the Cedar Valley Railroad.[31] The I.C. Corp. paid $125 million in cash and assumed $14 million in debt and $18 million in capitalized lease obligations. After G.E.C.C. had taken control of the Chicago, Central & Pacific in 1987 and supplied additional short-term financing, the carrier became solvent. Its 1995 operating revenue was $76 million and its operating ratio was under 70%.[32] The carrier had reduced crew size on each train from four workers to two and work district distances were doubled so that trainmen all had to work full days.

Two additional major branch lines were sold by I.C.G. in 1986. The 117-mile line from Indianapolis to Sullivan, Indiana was sold to the Indiana Rail Road Co. for $5.3 million.[33] The 304-mile line from Paducah to Louisville and Clayton, Kentucky was sold to the Paducah & Louisville Railway for $70 million.[34] This transaction included the Paducah locomotive shop complex and 97 locomotives.[35] Total sales of lines by I.C.G. in 1985 and 1986 were $318.9 million. As a result, as noted in Table 2, the I.C.G. accounts report a special charge for restructuring of $412 million for severance pay to employees, disposition and write down of excess equipment, and other costs related to reducing the size of the carrier.[36] In the railroad's annual report to the ICC, this charge is not reported separately but is buried in other railway operating expenses, such as $83.9 million for locomotives, $317 million for freight cars, $110 million for lease rentals of cars, $128 million for depreciation, and $161 million for other general administrative expenses.[37] The total for these railway operating expenses for 1986 was $800 million compared to the 1987 total for the same items of $200 million.[38] Since no earlier restructuring expenses were reported, the 1986 special expense could possibly apply to the three years, 1984 through 1986 when the I.C.G. sold 2663 miles of line and structures thereon. Sales of lines plus abandonments of lines in the three years were 3298 route miles or a 46.5% decrease. The number of I.C.G. employees dropped from 9,848 in March, 1984 to 4,334 in September, 1987, a drop of 56%.[39]

The largest sale of I.C.G. lines in 1987 was the routes of the former Alton Railroad that the former G.M.&O. had acquired in 1947 and had became part of I.C.G. in 1972. These included lines from Joliet to East St. Louis, Il. with trackage rights over I.C.G. from Joliet to Chicago and the line from Springfield, Il. to Kansas City, together with branch lines.[40] The sale of 631 miles of lines for $81 million was to Venango River Corp. which created the Chicago, Missouri & Western Railroad.[41] The purchase price and working capital were financed by Citicorp North America and by Heller Financial Corp. for a total of $108 million.[42] The carrier operated one year with positive net operating income but was unable to meet its monthly interest payments of over $1 million. It filed for protection under Chapter 11 of the bankruptcy laws in April, 1988.[43] Chicago, Missouri & Western then sued I.C.G. for fraud relating to the sale and the diversion of traffic that had formerly moved on the sale lines to I.C.G.'s other lines. Under settlement, I.C.G. refunded $26.5 million of the purchase price.[44]

In 1989, the Southern Pacific purchased the Chicago, Missouri & Western line from Joliet to East St. Louis, Il. and the trackage rights over I.C.G. from Joliet to Chicago. The price was $22 million in cash plus the assumption of $7 million in debt.[45] The line had significant deferred maintenance of way since it had not been part of I.C.G.'s main line to New Orleans, and I.C.G. owned an alternate route from Chicago to St. Louis. The Chicago, Missouri & Western had not been financially able to rehabilitate the roadway. The fate of the Chicago-St. Louis corridor was of great concern to the Illinois Department of Transportation and to Amtrak, whose trains used the line. State bond funds and federal grants were assembled to loan the Southern Pacific $36 million for a three-year program to rehabilitate the line.[46]

The remaining 361 route miles of the Chicago, Missouri & Western, from Kansas City to Springfield and E. St. Louis, Il., was sold by the trustee in January, 1990 to a new carrier, Gateway Western Railway.[47] The Gateway Western and the Southern Pacific jointly owned track in the East St. Louis

Terminal area. The physical condition of the Gateway Western track and roadbed was so deteriorated that the carrier needed $26 million over the following few years for upgrading. Gateway Western applied to the Illinois Department of Transportation for financial aid in rehabilitating the line from Springfield to the Mississippi River.[48]

The Gateway Western also applied to the Illinois Department of Transportation for financial assistance to rehabilitate its rail yard in East St. Louis.[49] When the Illinois Central Gulf sold its lines into East St. Louis, it had retained trackage rights from Springfield to East St. Louis. The obligations of Chicago, Missouri & Western to I.C.G. to maintain these yards became the obligation of Gateway Western. In order to meet its contractual obligation to provide switching service to I.C.G. and to its shippers, the Gateway Western was in need of about $700,000.[50]

In 1997 Kansas City Southern Industries (KCSI), parent of Kansas City Southern Railway, purchased the shares of the Gateway Western Railway Co.[51] In early 1996, KSCI had contracted with Gateway to assist Gateway to obtain a loan to refinance existing debt and additional operating capital. As part of the agreement, KSCI was able to acquire the stock of Gateway. Since the purchase was by a Class 1 rail carrier, the Surface Transportation Board was required to make a finding whether any anticompetitive effects of the transaction outweighed the public interest in meeting significant transportation needs.[52] Since the common control was in effect an end-to-end merger, the STB found nothing in the record showing any anticompetitive effect. On the contrary, the merger would open new single line routes for shippers and especially improve shipper access to the Mexican market. The price for the Gateway stock was $10 million.[53] When this market price is added to the $29 million total that Southern Pacific paid for the Joliet to E. St. Louis line, the total market value of the former Chicago, Missouri and Western was $39 million. This is in comparison to the original amount Venango River Corp. paid for the lines after the $26.5 million refund, which was $54.5 million.

The other major sale of I.C.G. in 1987 was the 10-mile commuter line, from Chicago downtown to the southern suburbs. The sale was to the Metropolitan Transportation Authority (METRA) for $28 million.[54] This brought to an end the ten years of subsidies from METRA to the I.C.G. that are noted in Table 4.2 as transfers from government.

The final large sale of I.C.G. line was to Norfolk Southern Corporation in 1988. The lines from Fulton, Ky. To Haleyville, AL. were 224 miles and sold for $38 million.[55] As part of the agreement, the Norfolk Southern received trackage rights of 154 miles over the Illinois Central from Fulton, Ky. to Centralia, Il. where a Norfolk Southern line ran west to St. Louis.[56] This enabled

Norfolk Southern to run through trains from Birmingham to St. Louis and to exchange cars at Corinth, Miss. with the MidSouth lines that were the former G.M.&O. lines from Mobile.

The reduction in lines operated by Illinois Central Gulf Railroad from 1973 to 1996 are tabulated in Table 4.3. In 1973, Illinois Central Gulf operated 9626 miles of road and owned 9,008 miles of this road.[57] In 1996, the Illinois Central operated 2,623 miles of road and owned 2,431 miles of this road.[58] This does not include the Chicago, Central & Pacific and the Cedar Valley lines which returned to control of the Illinois Central in 1996. Between 1974 and 1988, the Illinois Central Gulf sold to other railroads 4,183 miles of road that it had owned.[59] In that time, Illinois Central abandoned an additional 1,925 miles of road. It also reduced lines leased or operated under trackage rights from 612 in 1974 to 189 in 1988.

As noted in Table 4.3, Mississippi with the greatest reduction in I.C.G. lines operated from 3,064 in 1974 to 868 in 1996, had a drop of 71.7%. The reduction in Illinois of 1,642 miles was 57.7%. The large reduction of lines in Kentucky, Tennessee and Alabama resulted from disposal of routes to Louisville, Nashville and Birmingham. Abandonment of a main line from Memphis to Baton Rouge accounts for much of the reduction in Louisiana. The sale of lines between Illinois and Kansas City to the Chicago, Missouri & Western terminated Illinois Central service in Missouri.

The remarkable financial results of contracting the routes of the Illinois Central were reported in Table 4.2. Once the expenses of restructuring the railroad were reported in the financial statements of 1986 and 1988, the carrier

Table 4.3. Illinois Central Gulf Milage Operated By States in 1973 and 1996[a.]

State	1973	1996
Illinois	2848	1206
Indiana	183	0
Kentucky	690	143
Tennessee	659	142
Mississippi	3064	868
Louisiana	742	229
Alabama	441	35
Missouri	245	0
Total	8872	2623

Sources: *Moody's Transportation Manual* 616(1973) and 19(1998).
[a] Excluding the lines, mainly 685 miles in Iowa, that were sold to the Chicago Central & Pacific Railroad in 1985 and again came under control of Illinois Central in 1996.

could receive the benefits of a primarily high-density railroad, operating under the freedoms of the Staggers Act. Contract rates and reduced train crews were significant. From 1989 onward, the net railway operating income had a significant rise. While the ton-miles of freight carried increased by 27.7% from 1989 to 1996 and freight train miles increased 33% in that period, net railway operating income increased 157%. The sale and abandonment of net-loss lines and low-income lines, together with relaxed regulation of rates enabled the I.C. to rise progressively to $227.9 million net railway operating income in 1997 and a net income of $136.2 million.

The great financial success of the Illinois Central in the 1990s as low-density lines were sold or abandoned is demonstrated by the high-density in traffic on the remaining lines. The revenue freight density, the member of tons of revenue freight density, the number of tons of revenue freight carried one mile per mile of road, increased greatly after restructuring. In the ten years before the 1972 merger, the Illinois Central revenue freight density never exceeded 3.7 million tons.[60] By the end of 1985, when 50% of the lines had been sold or abandoned, the I.C.G. revenue freight density was 4.2 million tons. By 1990, when 71% of the lines had been sold or abandoned, the I.C.G. revenue freight density was 6.3 million tons.[61] By 1995, when 73% of the lines had been sold and rail traffic had greatly increased, the I.C. revenue freight density reached 9.7 million tons.[62]

This level of traffic on high-speed freight trains could not have been reached without great investment in track and signaling systems. The major investment began with $559 million capital expenditures on road from 1977 through 1982.[63]

In that period, I.C.G. installed 879 miles of new continuous welded rail, 603 miles of used crossties.[64] The Federal Railroad Administration aided this rehabilitation of main lines with a $152.5 million 30-year loan.

The capital expenditures on track and structures from 1983 to 1990 were $441.6 million, and from 1991 to 1997 the expenditures were $445.4 million.[65] Part of the funds were used to complete the installation of centralized traffic control on the main line from Chicago to New Orleans. This permitted reducing some lines from double track to single track, thereby reducing maintenance costs. Some funds were allocated to construct new or expanded intermodal facilities in Chicago and Memphis. In 1996, $20.1 million was expended to construct an intermodal terminal for the Canadian National Railway.[66]

CANADIAN NATIONAL RAILWAY CONTROL OF THE ILLINOIS CENTRAL

On May 25, 1999, the Surface Transportation Board approved the acquisition of control of the Illinois Central Railroad by the Canadian National Railway.[67]

The Canadian National operated 14,150 miles of line from Halifax, N.S. in the East to Prince Rupert and Vancouver, B.C. in the West. The Canadian National subsidiary, Grand Trunk Western Railroad operated 1,150 route miles in the United States connecting the Canadian lines with Chicago, Detroit and Buffalo. The Illinois Central operated 3,370 route miles, including the Chicago, Central & Pacific from Chicago to Omaha and Sioux City. Since the Canadian National was an East-West system and the Illinois Central primarily a North-South system, they were joined at a single point, Chicago.

By June, 1998, Canadian National Railway had acquired indirect beneficial ownership of 100% of the common stock of I.C. Corp., the holding company of the railroad. The stock was held by a voting trustee pending approval of the control.[68] The cost of these shares was approximately $1,821 million. The 1997 consolidated balance sheet of I.C. Railroad Co. showed current assets of cash, receivables and supplies of $149 million and net properties after depreciation of $1,362.9 million, for a total of $1,511.9 million.[69] The $309 million excess of the price paid for the stock over the book value must be attributed to the earning power of the assets in recent years, as noted in Table 4.2 and to expected earnings increased of the merged companies.

A key complementary aspect of the Canadian National control of Illinois Central is an Alliance Agreement with Kansas City Southern Railway.[70] The three carriers contemplate coordination of marketing, operating, investment and other functions. They seek to improve service by single-transaction, through priced movements of shipments and expanded routing options. This will facilitate through train service by the allied carriers to U.S. markets reached only by Kansas City Southern and, via its affiliates, to the Mexican market. The carriers took the position that the Alliance Agreement was a voluntary coordination agreement that did not require STB approval under the Interstate Commerce Act, as amended.

The STB found that the Alliance Agreement did not constitute legal control or actual control of the Kansas City Southern by the CN-IC.[71] The Alliance Agreement fostered independent rivalry in the few areas, mainly in Louisiana, where the IC and KCS both served the same shippers. The STB concluded that the Alliance would not result in common control or pooling, and that was not likely to reduce competition between applicants and KCS. Many such cooperative agreements are regularly entered by railroads without need of STB approval.

The merging carriers estimated the resulting cost savings of over $137 million per year.[72] The major items were crew reductions of $46 million, reduction of over 6,200 freight cars of about $33 million, and reduction in general and administrative expenses of over $30 million per year. There would also be a reduction of 120 locomotives, saving 7.7 million per year, and consolidation of purchasing, saving $9.5 million per year. It is clear that these large savings could not be achieved by mere coordination agreements because there must be a new managerial structure to execute operations of the merged firm. This new structure would be needed to make the Alliance Agreement with KCS successful and take full advantage of moving freight from Canada and the U.S. to and from Mexico.

The financial condition of the newly expanded Canadian National is estimated to be sound in spite of greatly increased debt. In order to purchase 75% of IC stock at $39 per share, Canadian National undertook $1.8 billion in new debt.[73] The other 25% was acquired by an exchange of shares. In spite of the new debt, the CN expects to improve its financial condition by about $216 million per year, including the estimated $137 million in cost savings. The estimate is that after 2 years there will be $90 million per year in net revenue gains. These are expected to arise from diversion of traffic from other rail carriers, diversion of intermodal traffic from truck to rail, and intermodal port diversions.

The optimistic estimates are based on the fact that the IC has become the best performing Class 1 railroad in the United States. The IC has had significantly better financial ratios than other carriers. Consequently, Canadian National should be even stronger financially after the merger. The transactions were thus approved by the Surface Transportation Board as consistent with the public interest.[74]

CONCLUSION

The merger approval for the Illinois Central of the Gulf, Mobile and Ohio was a remarkable example of ranking railroad efficiency ahead of alleged inter-railroad competition. The ICC correctly rejected the negative arguments of the intervening Antitrust Division of the U.S. Justice Department that assumed that parallel railroads engaged in rate competition and also had discounted the competition of water carriers on the Mississippi River and of motor carriers.

The Illinois Central Gulf Railroad is a prime example of a carrier determined under deregulation to dispose of net loss branch lines. This was facilitated by the court rulings that sales of branch lines to new short line railroads did not require the Class I selling railroad to pay special compensation to discharged workers. The route miles of the Illinois Central Gulf decreased from 9,568 in 1974 to 2,600 in 1997.

In contrast to gross ton-miles, which includes both the contents and all the equipment to move it, the revenue freight density is defined as the number of tons of freight carried one mile per mile of road. The Illinois Central revenue freight density, which had never exceeded 3.7 million tons before 1972, reached 9.7 million tons in 1995. Net Railway operating income rose from $24 million in 1974 to $192 million in 1995, a multiple of 8. Thus, by the key measures, the Illinois Central Gulf Railroad, and its long run income improvements were mostly due to reductions in costs of operation.

The sale of the Illinois Central to the Canadian National Railway in 1999, together with its Alliance Agreement with the Kansas City Southern, created a true international railroad. Shippers were offered what was in effect single line service from much of Canada, through the Midwest, to the Mexican border. The advantages to shippers in the movement of goods was matched by the expected savings in costs by the combined carriers

NOTES

1. U.S., I.C.C., *Transport Statistics in the United States* 207 (1971). The founding and expansion of the carrier is treated in detail in John F. Stover, *History of the Illinois Central Railroad* (New York: Macmillan Publishing, 1975).

2. See James H. Lemly, *Gulf, Mobile and Ohio: A Railroad that had to Expand or Expire* (Homewoed, Il.: Richard D. Irwin, 1953).

3. Gulf, M.&O. R.Co. Purchase Securities, 261 I.C.C. 405 (1945), 267 I.C.C. 145 (1947), 267 I.C.C. 201 (1947), 267 I.C.C. 265 (1947). See Michael Conant, *Railroad Mergers and Abandonments* 71–73 (Berkeley: University of California Press, 1964).

4. *Moody's Transportation Manual* 297 (1972).

5. Stover, *History of the Illinois Central Railroad, supra* note 1, at 499.

6. Illinois Cent. Gulf R.-Acquisition-G.M.&O., Et AL, 338 I.C.C. 805, 818 (1971).

7. *Id.,* at 885.

8. *Id.,* at 830 to 842.

9. *Id.,* at 838 to 840.

10. *Id.,* at 874.

11. *Id.*

12. *Id.,* at 852–53.

13. See J. David Ingles, *ICG's Garage Sale,* Trains, March 1988, at 34, 35.

14. See Gary W. Dolzall, *The Railroad that Came Home to the People,* Trains, Oct. 1982, at 27.

15. Missouri Pacific Railroad Co v. United States, 346 F. Supp., 1193 (E. D.Mo. 1972), *aff'd* 409 U.S. 1094 (1973); Kansas City Southern Railway Co. v. United States, 346 F. Supp. 1211 (W. D.Mo. 1972), *aff'd* 409 U.S. 1094 (1973).

16. *Railway Age,* March 14, 1977, 30.

17. *Id.*

18. U.S. Dept. of Transportation, *Final Standards,Classification, and Designation of Lines of Class 1 Railroads in the United States,* Vol. 2, 156–159 (1977).

19. *Railway Age,* May 28, 1979, 14.

20. U.S. Cong., House, Committee on Energy and Commerce, *Rapid Growth of Short-Line and Regional Railroads,* Hearing, 100th Cong., 1st Sess., 1987, 253.

21. Gulf & Miss. R. R. Corp.-Purchase Exemption-I.C.G. R.R., F. D.No. 30439 (1985).
22. MidSouth Rail Corp.-Purchase Exemption-I.C.G. R.R., F.D.No. 30807 (1986).
23. See *Railway Age,* March 14, 1977, 30.
24. *Moody's Transportation Manual* 437 (1997).
25. Illinois Central Gulf R. Co.-Abandonment, 363 I.C.C. 93 (1980) (Labor costs of line plus real property taxes on roadbed sold are avoidable costs.) The Court of Appeals finally upheld the I.C.C. recognition of opportunity costs as a factor supporting abandonment. *City of Cherokee* v. *I.C.C.* 727 F. 2d 748 (8th Cir. 1984).
26. *Rapid Growth of Short Line and Regional Railroads, supra,* note 20, at 267. The entire 275-mile line south from Freeport, Il. To Centralia was abandoned except one 18 mile segment just south of Decatur that was sold in 1986 to Central Illinois Shippers for $450,000. *Id.,* at 268. See People of the State of Ill. v. I.C.C., 698 F. 2d 868 (7th Cir. 1983).
27. *Rapid Growth of Short-Line and Regional Railroads, supra,* note 20, at 267.
28. Chicago, Cent. & Pac. R.R. Co.-Purchase (Portions), Trackage Rights and Securities
Exemption (Chicago), F.D. No. 30663 (1985). See *Wall St. Journal,* April 3, 1985, 36.
29. *Wall St. Journal,* Sept. 18, 1987, 42; *Railway Age,* Nov. 1987, 42.
30. *Traffic World,* June 10, 1991, 33.
31. Illinois Central Corp. and Illinois Central R. Co.-Control-Chicago Central & P.R. Co. and Cedar River R. Co., STB Finance Docket 32858 (May 14, 1996). See *Moody's Transportation Manual* 28 (1996).
32. *Traffic World,* Jan. 22, 1996, 33. See Mark W. Bailey, *IC's Iowa Division Rebounds,* Trains 24 (July, 1997).
33. Indiana Rail Road Co.-Exemption-Acquisition and Operation-Illinois Central R. Co., F.D. No. 30789 (1986). In 1990, the I.C.C. approved purchase by Indiana R. R.Co. of connecting lines from Sullivan, Ind. to Newton, Il. and on to Browns, Il. Indiana R. Co.-Acq. & Oper.-Illinois Central R. Co. 6 I.C.C. 2d 1004 (1990).
34. Paducah & Louisville Railway, Inc.-Exemption-Acquisition and Operation-Illinois Central Gulf R. Co., F.D. No. 30891 (1987).
35. See *Trains,* March 1988, 34.
36. Illinois Central Gulf Railroad, *Annual Report to S.E.C.* 19, 23 (1988). See *Moody's Transportation Manual* 56 (1987).
37. U.S., I.C.C., *Transport Statistics in the United States* 44, 48 (1986).
38. *Id.,* at 44, 48 (1987).
39. *Moody's Transportation Manual*(1985); *Id.*(1987).
40. Chicago, Missouri & Western Railway Co.-Exemption Acquisition and Operation-Illinois Central Gulf R. Co., F.D. No. 30911 (1986). See notice, 51 Fed. Reg. 37,665 (1986).
41. *Traffic World,* May 23, 1988, 6.
42. *Traffic World,* Aug. 14, 1989, 17.
43. In Re Chicago, Missouri & Western Ry. Co., 109 B.R. 308, 309 (N.D. Ill. 1989), appeal dismissed 899 F. 2d 17 (7th Cir. 1990). See *Traffic World,* May 23, 1988, 6.
44. *Traffic World,* Aug. 14, 1989, 17.
45. Rio Grande-Purchase-Trackage Rights-Chicago, Missouri & Western between St. Louis and Chicago, 5 I.C.C. 2d 952 (1989).
46. Illinois Department of Transportation, *Illinois Rail Plan: 1991–92 Update* 4–6 (1992).

47. *Id.*, at A-14.
48. *Id.*, at A-13 to A-19.
49. *Id.*, at A-55.
50. *Id.*, at A-59.
51. Kansas City Southern Industries-Control-Gateway Western Railway Co., STB Finance Docket No. 33311 (May 5, 1997).
52. 49 U.S.C. § 11324 (d).
53. Kansas City Southern Industries, *supra* note 51, at 5.
54. *Rapid Growth of Short-Line and Regional Railroads, supra* note 20, at 268.
55. *Id.*
56. See *Wall St. Journal*, June 9, 1987, 65.
57. U.S., I.C.C., *Transport Statistics in the United States* 183 (1973).
58. *Moody's Transportation Manual* 19 (1998).
59. *Rapid Growth of Short-Line and Regional Railroads, supra* note 20, at 268.
60. *Moody's Transportation Manual* 281 (1972).
61. *Moody's Transportation Manual* 19 (1998).
62. *Id.*
63. *Moody's Transportation Manual* 50 (1987).
64. *Railway Age*, Aug. 1984, 62.
65. *Moody's Transportation Manual* 47 (1989), 31 (1990), 28 (1996), 16 (1998).
66. *Id.*
67. Canadian National R. Co. et. al.-Control-Illinois Central Corp., STB Finance Docket No. 33556 (May 25, 1999).
68. *Id.*, at 8.
69. *Moody's Transportation Manual* 18-19 (1998).
70. Canadian National R. Co. et. al.-Control-Illinois Central Corp., *supra* note 67, at 9.
71. *Id.*, at 14.
72. *Id.*, at 28.
73. *Id.*, at 29.
74. *Id.*, at 31.

5. UNION PACIFIC MERGERS: 1982 AND 1988

Union Pacific Railroad engaged in two major acquisitions in the 1980s. The first was in 1982 to acquire the Missouri Pacific Railroad and the Western Pacific Railroad.[1] The second was in 1988 to acquire the Missouri-Kansas-Texas-Railroad, known as the Katy.[2] The result was to turn a highly efficient, well maintained, dominant carrier in the central corridor that had eastern termini in Omaha and Kansas City into a railroad that connected with eastern carriers in Chicago, St. Louis and Memphis. It also acquired lines south to Texas and the Gulf of Mexico.

As noted in Chapter 1, these mergers occurred after the enactment of the Railroad Revitalization and Regulatory Reform Act of 1976[3] and the Staggers Act of 1980[4] which favored economic rationalization of railroad plant, including mergers. In mergers of Class 1 railroads, the ICC was required to consider the effects on competition in making a decision, but the ICC was free to remedy negative effects on competition by granting trackage rights over specific lines of the merged system to intervening carriers.

UNION PACIFIC CONTROL OF THE MISSOURI PACIFIC AND WESTERN PACIFIC

The ICC approved the Union Pacific control of the Missouri Pacific and Western Pacific on September 24, 1982. The Union Pacific operated from Kansas City and Omaha west to Ogden, Utah with main lines from Ogden north to Portland and south to Los Angeles. In 1982, Union Pacific operated 9,082 miles of road but owned only 8,432 miles, of which 4,556 miles or 54% was labeled main line. This percentage of main lines, as reported to the ICC, is not consistent with the 1975 U.S. Department of Transportation network study, which reported UP as having a total 3,451 miles of road or 41.3% of its lines in medium plus high densities (over 10 million gross ton-miles per mile of road). These lines carried 88.4% of UP gross ton-miles, equal to 28.7 million gross ton-miles per mile of road.[5] As noted in Table 5.1, Union Pacific Railway Operating Revenues in 1981 were $2,100.8 million. Net Railway Operating Revenue was $292.35 million, and the operating ratio was 86.08%.

The Missouri Pacific had acquired the Chicago & Eastern Illinois rail route from St. Louis to Chicago in 1967.[6] MP was mainly a North-South carrier, extending from Chicago and St. Louis south to New Orleans, Dallas, Houston and Laredo. Another line extended south from Omaha to Kansas City to Dallas. The Texas and Pacific Railway division of MP extended from El Paso to Fort Worth, Dallas and Shreveport and on to New Orleans. MP's one line to the west extended from Kansas City to Pueblo, Colorado where it exchanged traffic with the Denver & Rio Grande Western. This line paralleled the Union Pacific and the Santa Fe, but only the UP went directly to Denver. All three of these lines were of medium density, class B-main lines. In contrast, the UP line from the West to Fremont and Omaha was high density.

In 1982, MP operated 11,167 miles of road. MP owned 10,042 miles, of which 6,730 miles or 67% were labeled main line. This company labeling of main lines is inconsistent with the 1975 U.S. Department of Transportation study which showed MP to have a total of 38.9% of its lines in medium plus high densities. These lines carried 80.7% of MP gross ton-miles, equal to 21.7 million gross ton-miles per mile of road.[7] As noted in Table 5.1, the Missouri Pacific Railway Operating Revenues in 1981 were $1,887.7 million. Net Railway Operating Revenue was $227.5 million and the Operating Ratio was 87.95%.

The Western Pacific key main line ran from Salt Lake City to San Francisco, a distance of 924 miles. One main line extended north in California from Keddie to Bieber, a distance of 112 miles, to connect with the Burlington-Northern. The total lines owned by Western Pacific, including branches in the San

Table 5.1. Financial Results of Applicant Railroads, 1981 (Thousands of Dollars).

	Union Pacific	Missouri Pacific	Western Pacific
Railway Operating Revenues	$2,100,793	$1,887,660	$188,250
Railway Operating Expenses	1,808,443	1,660,169	193,917
Net Railway Operating Revenues	292,350	227,491	−5,667
Income Available for Fixed Charges	310,022	293,178	24,057
Fixed Charges	64,431	86,272	10,091
Income Taxes	−40,567	−74,551	249
Provision for Deferred Income Taxes	118,790	123,756	4,464
Net Income	167,368	148,323	9,132

Source: Union Pacific-Control Missouri Pacific; Western Pacific, 366 *ICC* 459, 808–810 (1982).

Francisco and San Jose area, were 1,332 miles. As noted in Table 5.1, the Western Pacific in 1981 had a net railway operating loss of $5,667,000, and its operating ratio was 103%. Since it had a gain on property sold of $20.8 million, the net income was $9.1 million.

The Union Pacific control of the Missouri Pacific and the Western Pacific was primarily an end-to-end merger designed to move through trains from the West Coast to Chicago, St. Louis, Dallas and New Orleans. It could thus rival the Santa Fe through trains from California to Chicago. Union Pacific was already the dominant carrier in the central corridor, east from the Utah gateways of Ogden and Salt Lake City. It carried 77% of the freight traffic moving east of Denver to and from Omaha and Kansas City.[8] This included 65.9% of the tonnage originating in Northern California for the Central Corridor, delivered to Union Pacific by the Western Pacific and the Southern Pacific.

Given the Union Pacific dominance in the Central Corridor, the ICC was concerned with the effects of the merger on competition. Union Pacific had been the major carrier exchanging traffic with the Southern Pacific at Ogden equal to 50% of the tonnage moving in the central corridor. Once the rival Western Pacific became part of the Union Pacific, the exchange with the Southern Pacific line from northern California could be expected to drop greatly. Offsetting this diversion was the fact that Southern Pacific served exclusively 12,800 shippers in Northern California and Southern Oregon compared to about 200 shippers served exclusively by Western Pacific.[9] Furthermore, the Southern Pacific route between the San Francisco Bay area and Utah was approximately 180 miles shorter than the Western Pacific and S.P. generally had more favorable grades and less curvature.[10]

The solution of the ICC was to prescribe an alternative through route in the central corridor based on the Southern Pacific and the Denver Rio Grande Western. The DRGW, carrying freight from Salt Lake City to Pueblo, Colorado had depended on Missouri Pacific as its neutral connection at Pueblo. In order to preserve DRGW independence, the ICC conditioned this merger on a grant of trackage rights to DRGW by M. P. on its 619-mile route from Pueblo to Kansas City.[11] In order to create a fully independent rival to U.P., it would have been better if this line had been sold to DRGW, but the ICC did not have statutory authority to order the sale of a line. The ICC also conditioned the merger on Southern Pacific receiving trackage rights over M.P. from Kansas City to St. Louis.[12] The effect was a coordinated through route to the connections with the eastern carriers in St. Louis with Southern Pacific operating the segments west of Salt Lake City and east of Kansas City and DRGW running the trains in between.

Missouri-Kansas-Texas Railroad was granted trackage rights over the Missouri Pacific lines from Kansas City to Topeka and north to Omaha and Lincoln, Nebraska, and to Council Bluffs, Iowa.[13] This was designed to offset the loss of the Union Pacific as a friendly connection to MKT at Kansas City. The MKT direct access to grain shippers at those points preserved potential competitive rail services in those areas. MKT became a long-haul alternative from those points to Galveston on the Gulf of Mexico.

The public interest evaluation of the ICC centered on direct efficiencies resulting from cost reductions and improved service. The economic comment was clear and correct:

> Cost reductions resulting from more efficient operations benefit the public directly to the extent they are passed on to shippers through reduced rates and deferred rate increases. Savings generated by cost reductions reflect the amount of resources freed for other productive uses . . ..
>
> Efficiency-related cost reductions also benefit the public by creating a stronger, more financially viable, responsive and competitive railroad industry, enhancing its capital base by ensuring that resources are available for the maintenance of transportation equipment and facilities.[14]

The efficiency-related cost reductions per year from this merger were estimated by the carriers to be $64 million, but the ICC reduced the public benefits from cost reductions and service improvements to $47 million.[15] The operating efficiencies of through trains on the combined lines and from reorganizing car and engine maintenance were added to expected administrative efficiencies. The key cost reductions were in the coordination of the Union Pacific and Missouri Pacific. A prime example was moving trains with preclassified destinations that arrived from the West via Union Pacific at Kansas City and avoiding reclassification in the congested Kansas City rail yards. A day or more in transit time could be saved as these shipments moved to the South and gulf ports.[16] The consolidation of Union Pacific yards at Kansas City with those of Missouri Pacific made Kansas City the hub of the combined system.[17]

Union Pacific and Missouri Pacific estimated annual net revenue gains as a result of diversion of traffic from other railroads of $32.5 million plus gain in estimated annual net revenue from motor carriers of $7.5 million. This total of $40.4 million was reduced by the ICC to an estimated total of $38 million.

CRITIQUE OF ACQUISITION OF WESTERN PACIFIC

While the merger of Union Pacific and Missouri Pacific had significant potential for operating efficiencies, the acquisition of the Western Pacific did not. The

Western Pacific was not a highly profitable railroad and management lacked the funds for adequate maintenance of way.[18] The maintenance of way expenditures of the Western Pacific per mile of road were approximately half of that for the Union Pacific.[19] Table 5.2 uses the Union Pacific maintenance of way expenditures before the merger as the standard for first-rate maintenance.[20] If Western Pacific had made the maintenance expenditures per mile that U.P. made, it would not have had its reported profits from railway operations from 1978 through 1980. Rather, it would have had losses from railway operations rising from $8.2 million in 1978 to $27.7 million in 1981.

Upon acquisition of Western Pacific, Union Pacific undertook a massive five-year rehabilitation on the road costing $90 million.[21] Western Pacific had 257 miles of mainline track that in 1980 had been in place for an average of 28 years.[22] The main line had 894 curves, totaling 182 miles, equaling about 20% of the main line, and 65% of those curves were in excess of two degrees.[23] As it became a U.P. main line into northern California, it had an expected maximum increase of 3.5 million gross tons over what had been carried by the W.P.[24]

The critical issue is whether the Union Pacific should have acquired a net-loss railroad in which it would have to invest another $90 million or instead should have continued its prior practice of delivering through trains to the Southern Pacific and receiving through trains from the Southern Pacific.

Table 5.2. Western Pacific Railroad Before Merger
Financial Results and Estimated Losses if Maintenance of Way and Structures Had Been at High Standard[a] (Thousands of Dollars).

	Operating Revenues	Operating Expenses	Net Revenue from Railway Operations	Estimated Operating Expenses if Maintenance Were at U.P. Level[b]	Estimated Net Revenue from Railway Operations if Maintenance Were at U.P. Level
1978	$144,228	$135,407	$8,821	$152,470	$-8,242
1979	166,955	163,430	3,525	185,970	-19,015
1980	185,013	181,094	3,919	205,060	-20,047
1981	188,250	193,917	-5,667	215,970	-27,720

Source: *Union Pacific-Control-Missouri Pacific; Western Pacific*, 366 I.C.C. 462, 810 (1982); *Moody's Transportation Manual* 878 (1982), 162 (1984).

[a] High standard of maintenance of way and structures per mile of road is estimated by Union Pacific expenditures.

[b] The additional maintenance of way and structures expenditures per mile of road for Western Pacific to equal that of Union Pacific were $11,506 in 1978, $15,199 in 1979, $17,079 in 1980, and $15,368 in 1981.

In fact, it can be argued that Union Pacific paid much too high a price for a net-loss railroad. But, for the year of 1979, just before the purchase offer, Western Pacific deferred maintenance enough to report a small profit of $3 million. This equaled a return on net investment in rail property of 3.4%.[25] Prior to the U.P. tender offer of January 23, 1980 to Western Pacific shareholders to pay $20 per share, U.P. had acquired 139,800 shares of Western Pacific Class A common stock in the market for $1,734,000. This equaled $12.40 per average share.

The last reported sale price on the exchange on the day before U.P. made its tender offer to the Western Pacific shareholders was $14.50.[26] Since no dividends had been paid after 1978, this last sale price was surely a maximum based on rumors concerning merger negotiations. The inference is that the market expected a U.P. offer of $15 per share. Instead, the U.P. tender offer the following day of $20 represented a 38% premium over the $14.50 market price. Union Pacific paid a total of $27.1 million for Western Pacific shares and assumed Western Pacific debt of $150 million.[27] Nonetheless, the Interstate Commerce Commission concluded that the terms of the transaction were just and reasonable based on the expected merger benefit to Western Pacific.[28] But U.P. would pay for the merger benefits. The $90 million capital investment to rehabilitate the Western Pacific roadbed and rail came from U.P. as would the funds to raise the level of regular maintenance of way.

While the Western Pacific Railroad was reported merged into the Union Pacific Railroad shortly after the ICC approval in September, 1982, Western Pacific financial results were reported separately to the ICC through 1985. As noted in Table 5.3, Western Pacific had net loss from railway operations for the year 1982 of $11.3 million, during the first nine months of which it was still an independent carrier. After the merger, in 1983 net loss from railway

Table 5.3. Western Pacific Railroad Financial Results (Thousands of Dollars).

	1982	1983	1984	1985
Railway Operating Revenues	$171,797	$147,362	$146,740	$156,815
Railway Operating Expenses	183,117	177,344	163,315	184,325
Net Revenue from Railway Operations	−11,320	−29,982	−16,575	−27,510
Other Income	17,427	14,802	16,579	21,543
Miscellaneous Deductions	2,321	1,037	2,103	1,716
Fixed Charges	10,891	11,771	21,523	26,122
Net Iincome	−4,050	−11,078	−6,820	−12,744

Source: Transportation Statistics in the United States, 1982–1986.

operations rose to $30 million. In 1984 this loss was $16.6 million, and in 1985 it again rose to $27.5 million. These losses were not offset by the carrier's other income, so that net losses occurred in all four years. This evidence refutes the ICC 1982 prediction that the merger benefits would result in growing profits to the new Western Pacific sector of U.P.

UNION PACIFIC FINANICAL RESULTS AFTER MERGER

The financial gains of the Union Pacific subsequent to the merger have been remarkable. The combined effects of the efficiencies accomplished and the increased traffic on the expanded single-line service resulted in large increases in income. As noted in Table 5.4, in 1983 the combined net revenue from railway operations of the Union Pacific and Missouri Pacific was $375 million, and in 1988 the total was $799 million. Combined net profits rose from $197 million in 1983 to $497 million in 1988. Only in 1986 was there a sharp drop in net income as Union Pacific took a special charge of $659.7 million against earnings to recognize the diminished value of certain assets and large costs incurred in severance pay to reduce the number of employees.

Table 5.4. Union Pacific Railroad and Missouri Pacific Railroad Financial Results After Merger (Dollar figures in Thousands).

Year	Union Pacific[a]			Missouri Pacific		
	Milage	Net Revenue From Rail Operations	Net Income	Milage	Net Revenue From Rail Operations	Net Income
1983	9,081	$193,468	$110,434	11,056	$181,516	$86,730
1984	8,932	194,920	122,690	10,992	186,623	129,910
1985	8,783	257,855	187,145	10,920	117,613	71,017
1986	21,416	681,702	4,697[b]			
1987	20,944	651,244	421,955			
1988	22,653	799,327	496,995			

Sources: Transport Statistics in the United States, 1983–1989; Moody's Transportation Manual 100 (1990).

[a] Union Pacific data for 1986, 1987, and 1988 includes the merged Missouri Pacific and the Western Pacific.

[b] In 1986, Union Pacific made a special charge against earnings of $659,734,000 to recognize the diminished value of certain assets and to pay costs associated with reductions in number of employees.

In the five years, 1983 to 1988, the number of workers was reduced from 41,721 to 30,120, a drop of 27.8%.[29] As a result, the gross ton-miles of freight service per employee nearly doubled. In addition to reducing the operating employees, management reorganization resulted in discharge of mid-level managers. A key example was the Missouri Pacific investment of $40 million in a highly advanced shop for heavy repair of locomotives in Little Rock.[30] This led to the closing of the 100-year-old Union Pacific shops in Omaha, forcing 800 workers either to move to Little Rock or to find other employment.[31]

Increasing intermodal transport services is another area where Union Pacific has concentrated sales efforts. Railroads had previously lost significant traffic to long-haul truckers. With reduced train crews, labor costs per ton-mile were lowered enough to allow railroads to compete to haul trailers and containers on their new extended routes.

UNION PACIFIC ACQUISITION OF MISSOURI-KANSAS-TEXAS

On May 13, 1988, the ICC approved Union Pacific control of the Missouri-Kansas-Texas Railroad.[32] The combined Union Pacific and Missouri Pacific operated 23,816 miles of road, of which 16,441 miles or 69% was labeled main lines.[33] The MKT operated over 3,130 miles of road, of which 2,250 miles or 72% was labeled main lines. The MKT main line routes ran south from Omaha, Kansas City and St. Louis to Dallas, Fort Worth, San Antonio, Houston and Galveston.[34] Of the total miles of road operated by MKT, 1,688 miles were owned by MKT, 503 miles were leased, primarily from the State of Oklahoma, and 939 miles were trackage rights over other carriers.[35] A significant part of the trackage rights was the coordination between MKT and the parallel Missouri Pacific. The MKT had been a 2,140-mile railroad in 1982 when it acquired from the bankrupt Rock Island lines the road from Salina, Kansas south to Forth Worth Texas. This line, known as the Oklahoma-Kansas-Texas Railroad, had increased the MKT total road to 3,071 miles.

The petition for Union Pacific to acquire MKT had been filed in 1986, the year MKT had an operating ratio of 97.74%, and the operating ratio from 1981 forward had been over 92%.[36] The facts were that the MKT was not a successful rival to the two main carriers with single-line service from the far West to Kansas City and south to the Gulf of Mexico. These were the Burlington Northern-Frisco and the Union Pacific-Missouri Pacific combine. Merger with the UP-MP lines would enable MKT to be part of single-line service from the West and from Chicago and St. Louis directly to the Gulf.

The negative financial condition of the MKT is illustrated by its deferred expenditures on maintenance of way and structures. In 1984, the MKT expenditures on way and structure per mile of road was $17,096, which was only 72% of those on the Missouri Pacific.[37] By 1986, MKT expenditures were lowered to $12,990 per mile of road, and in 1987 they were $12,342 per mile of road. These figures were 55% and 50%, respectively, of the combined Missouri Pacific-Union Pacific maintenance per mile of road, the only comparable data available.[38] The estimated income results of this deferred MKT maintenance is shown in Table 5.5. The reported MKT net revenue from railway operations is in column 3 and is positive from 1983 to 1987. The estimated net revenue from railway operations if MKT had made maintenance of way and structures expenditures per mile of road equal to the Missouri Pacific is estimated in column 5. The losses from railway operations would have risen from $9.76 million in 1983 to $28.9 million in 1986, the year the sale of MKT to Union Pacific was negotiated.

The MKT road was closely parallel to the Missouri Pacific on most of its lines. From an efficiency calculation, this meant merger would allow concentration of through traffic on the most efficient lines and either conversion of parallel lines to branch status or their abandonment. On the other hand, under the Staggers Rail Act of 1980[39], one of the factors to be considered by the ICC in approving a merger was whether the proposed transaction would have adverse effect on competition between rail carriers in the affected region. The ICC made a detailed analysis of the major commodities being moved by railroads in MKT service area.[40] As to the trackage rights over Union Pacific from the Omaha area to Kansas City which MKT would no longer use as an independent rival, the ICC ordered the U.P. to negotiate to grant trackage rights to any one of three carriers. These were Santa Fe, Southern Pacific, or Kansas City Southern.[41] The trackage contract was awarded to Kansas City Southern.[42]

The ICC denied the requests of other major carriers for trackage rights over Union Pacific lines as conditions to the MKT merger. Prime examples were denial of trackage rights to Santa Fe between Kansas City and St. Louis and denial of trackage rights to Southern Pacific to Chicago.[43]

Denial of trackage right was usually based on the view that there were sufficient rival railroads to Union Pacific in those corridors concerned. The ICC did approve a settlement agreement between Union Pacific and Southern Pacific for the latter to have trackage rights on small subsidiary railroads and a major industrial park in Texas.[44]

The public benefits from the U.P.-MKT. merger in terms of cost reductions and service improvements resulting from new operating efficiencies were estimated to be $60.9 million per year.[45] Of this total, about $48.2 million were

Table 5.5. Missouri-Kansas-Texas Railroad Before Merger Financial Results and Estimated Losses If Maintenance of Way and Structures Had Been at Missouri Pacific Standard (Thousands of Dollars).

	1	2	3	4	5
Year	Operating Revenues	Operating Expenses	Net Revenue from Railway Operations	Estimated Operating Expenses if Maintenance Were at M.P. Level	Estimated Net Revenue from Railway Operations if Maintenance Were at M.P. Level
1982	230,048	212,915	17,133	226,346	3,702
1983	248,515	232,956	15,559	258,279	−9,764
1984	275,565	259,401	16,164	280,425	−4,860
1985	263,102	251,483	11,619	269,840	−6,738
1986	232,695	227,435	5,260	261,478[a]	−28,873
1987	241,770	220,777	20,993	262,088[a]	−20,318

Source: Transportation Statistics in the United States, 1982–1987; Moody's Transportation Manual 137–142 (1988).

[a] Maintenance standard for 1986 and 1987 is the combined maintenance per mile of road of the Missouri Pacific and the Union Pacific.

estimated operational savings and $12.7 million were estimated administrative savings. The operating efficiencies would be implemented by consolidation of mechanical, engineering and terminal facilities and the rerouting of traffic on the shortest, best maintained lines. For example, traffic between St. Louis and Dallas would save almost a full day over previous MKT routes. Likewise expedited services between Kansas City and Dallas over the MKT route would provide faster service for all UP Dallas traffic.

The line abandonments granted by the ICC in this proceeding illustrate a key area of cost reduction. MKT petitioned to abandon 83.8 track miles in Texas, 33.6 miles in Missouri and 44.5 miles in Kansas.[46] OKT petitioned to abandon 7.5 miles in Kansas. MP petitioned to abandon 34.1 miles in Kansas and 123.6 miles in Oklahoma. The latter line from Henryetta, OK south to Durant was a circuitous MP route.[47] The small local traffic on the MP route with 1986 revenue of only $4,237 had avoidable costs of $709,695, meaning the operating loss was $705,438. This calculation was valid because MP already had trackage rights over MKT for through trains.

The extreme financial weakness of the MKT is shown in the 1986 Balance Sheet where the common stock was valued at $11.6 million and the accumulated deficit was $19.5 million, so that the shareholders equity was negative, −$7.9 millions.[48] Nevertheless, Missouri Pacific paid $98 million for the MKT shares and assumed MKT debt obligations totaling $256.9 million.[49] An expert witness valued MKT properties not required for railroad operations at an estimated market value of $54.4 million and rail properties at a market value of $46.6 million.[50] Since these properties were pledged as collateral for MKT debt transactions, it is difficult to understand how they could have been a basis for share evaluation. This is especially difficult since MKT had not paid a dividend on its common stock since 1930, and restrictions against dividends in MKT debt indentures made it highly unlikely that MKT could pay any dividends in the foreseeable future. Nevertheless, the ICC found the stock valuation to be reasonable.

CONCLUSION

Some of the railroad mergers in the period of deregulation following the passage of the Staggers Act appear to be responses to earlier ones. The Union Pacific acquisition of the Missouri Pacific in 1982 appears to be a reaction to the Burlington Northern acquisition of the St. Louis-San Francisco Railway in 1980. The application for the latter merger was filed in 1977. At that time, the Union Pacific executives could assume that a BN end-to-end merger had a high likelihood of being approved, and they had to review the possible rail service impact of such a merger.

As the ICC later found, the direct service rivalry of UP and BN came into play. The BN acquisition of the St. Louis-San Francisco gave it single line service from the Pacific Northwest through its Kansas City yards to the Gulf of Mexico. The BN lines from Kansas City and from St. Louis met in Memphis and terminated in Mobile and Pensacola. The best way for Union Pacific to meet the service-time efficiencies of this rivalry was to acquire a carrier in the same territory. The Missouri pacific became the ideal partner.

The Union Pacific acquisition of the Missouri Pacific enabled many cost reductions as had been estimated for the ICC. Combined net profits in 1988 were more than twice those in 1983. The carriers were also able to negotiate reductions in the size of train crews so that total employment dropped, and the gross ton-miles of freight service per employee nearly doubled. In contrast, the Union Pacific acquisition of the Western Pacific was a net loss venture.

The Union Pacific acquisition of the Missouri-Kansas-Texas Railroad was a move to reduce excess capacity of rail lines in the area from Kansas City south to Dallas and to the Gulf of Mexico. The MKT and the Missouri Pacific already had some coordination of routes, and merger would enable greater concentration of high density lines. This would also foster abandonment of the least efficient lines.

The key issue was the valuation of the equity interest in MKT. On the MKT balance sheet, the shareholders equity was negative, proof of the extreme financial weakness of the carrier. The best argument is that Missouri Pacific paid $98 million for the shares in order to secure the vote of MKT shareholders to approve the merger.

NOTES

1. Union Pacific-Control-Missouri Pacific; Western Pacific, 366 I.C.C. 462 (1982), *affirmed*, Southern Pacific Transp. Co. v. I.C.C., 736 F. 2d 708 (D.C. Cir. 1984), *cert. Denied* 469 U.S. 1208 (1985)(cited hereafter as Union Pacific Control). See Curtis M. Grimm, *An Evaluation of Economic Issues in the UP-MP-WP Railroad Merger*, 20 Logistics and Transportation Rev. 239 (1984).

2. Union Pacific Corp. et al.–Control-Mo-Ks-Tx Co. et al., 4 I.C.C. 2d 409 (1988).

3. 90 Stat. 31 (1976).

4. 94 Stat. 1897 (1980).

5. See Chapter 1, Table 1.2. In the 1975 network study, the 4905 miles of low density line, 58.7% of UP total route miles, carried only 11.6% of its gross ton-miles. This averaged 2.7 million gross ton-miles per mile of road.

6. Missouri Pacific-Control-Chicago & Eastern Illinois, 327 I.C.C. 279 (1965), *affirmed*, Illinois Central R. Co. v. United States, 263 F. Supp. 421 (N. D.Ill. 1966), *affirmed per curium*, 385 U.S. 457 (1967). MP merged the C&EI in 1976. Missouri Pacific-Merger-Texas & Pacific and Chicago & Eastern Illinois, 348 I.C.C. 414 (1976), *affirmed in part*, City of Palestine, Texas v. United States, 559 F. 2d 408 (5th Cir. 1977), *cert. denied*, 435 U.S. 950 (1978). See Richard Saunders, *Merging Lines: American Railroads 1900–1970*, 309–312 (Dekalb: Northern Illinois University Press, 2001).

7. See Chapter 1, Table 1.2. The 1975 network study reported that MP low-density lines were 61.1% of its total lines and these averaged only 3.3 million gross ton-miles per mile of road.

8. Union Pacific Control, 366 I.C.C., at 511.

9. *Id.* at 515.

10. *Id.*

11. *Id.* at 572. In the only available data, from 1975, the average density on this line was 13 million gross tons per mile while its line capacity was 46 million gross tons per mile. U.S. Department of Transportation, *Final Standards, Classification, and Designation of Lines of Class 1 Railroads in the United States*, Vol. 1, Appendix 3–16 (1977).

12. Union Pacific Control, 366 I.C.C., at 585–586. This would allow Southern Pacific to forego rehabilitating its former Rock Island Kansas City-St. Louis line, which by 1982 was anticipated to cost $100 million. Id. At 586. The Southern Pacific did propose to upgrade the 27 miles of its Missouri line between Kansas City and Pleasant Hill, which paralleled the Missouri Pacific, if necessary to eliminate congestion. Id. at 585.

13. Union Pacific Control, 366 I.C.C. at 566–570.

14. *Id.* at 488.

15. *Id.* at 488–489; Appendix H, *Cost and Benefit Analysis, Id.* at 764–777. See favorable comments of the Court of Appeals. Southern Pacific Transp. Co. v. I.C.C., 736 F.2d at 720.

16. Union Pacific Control, 366 I.C.C. at 490.

17. *Id.* at 496–498. Net annual operating benefits at Kansas City were estimated at over $1.5 million. *Id.*, at 766–767. See statement of John C. Kenefick, CEO of Union Pacific, in *Railway Age* 36 (April, 1984).

18. See *Railway Age* 43 (July 1983).

19. The maintenance of way expenditures per mile of road for four years before the merger were as follows:

Year	Union Pacific $	Western Pacific $
1978	25,392	13,886
1979	30,215	15,016
1980	34,121	17,042
1981	36,320	20,952

20. See *Railway Age* 19 (Aug. 9, 1982).

21. *Union Pacific Control*, 366 I.C.C. at 491.

22. See *Railway Age* 22 (Aug. 9, 1982).

23. *Railway Age* 44 (July, 1983).

24. *Id.*

25. Union Pacific Control, 366 I.C.C. at 810.

26. *Id.* at 637.

27. *Id.* at 633 and 810.

28. *Id.* at 636–38.

29. See Jack Willoughby, The Rebuilding of Uncle Pete, *Forbes* 183 (Nov. 14, 1988).

30. See *Railway Age* 67 (Aug. 1984).

31. See *Forbes* 183 (Nov. 14, 1988).

32. Union Pacific Corp. et. al.–Control-Mo-Ks-Tx Co. et. al., 4 I.C.C. 2d 409 (1988) (cited hereafter as UP-Control-MKT).

33. As explained in notes 5 and 7, *supra*, this asserted percentage of main line, as opposed to low-density lines, seem too high. In the 1975 network study, UP had 58.7% of its lines with low density and MP had 61.1% of its lines with low density.

34. *Id.* at 420.

35. *Moody's Transportation Manual* 137 (1988).

36. *Id.*, at 142.

37. *Id.* at 141–142.

38. *Moody's Transportation Manual* 92 (1990).

39. Staggers Rail Act of 1980, Pub. L. 96-448, 49 U.S. C. § 11344 (b)(1).

40. UP-Control-MKT, 4 I.C.C. 438–448.

41. *Id.* 452–458.

42. *Moody's Transportation Manual* 46 (1994).

43. UP-Control-MKT, 4 I.C.C. 2d 474-75.

44. *Id.* at 521, 569–571.

45. *Id.* at 428–431.
46. *Id.* at 486.
47. *Id.* at 490–492.
48. *Id.* at 544.
49. *Id.* at 515–516.
50. *Id.*

6. BURLINGTON NORTHERN – SANTA FE MERGER

On August 16, 1995, the Interstate Commerce Commission approved the merger of the Burlington Northern Railroad and the Atchison, Topeka and Santa Fe Railway.[1] The BN had operated 22,189 miles of road in 1994 including lines from Chicago to Minneapolis and west to Portland and Seattle, from Chicago to Kansas City and to Denver, and from Lincoln, Nebraska across Wyoming to Billings, Montana. Two BN merged subsidiaries, the Colorado and Southern and the Fort Worth and Denver, connected the northwest routes with Denver, Dallas, Houston and Galveston. By virtue of its acquisition of the St. Louis and San Francisco in 1980, the BN had lines running from Kansas City and St. Louis through Memphis to Mobile and Pensacola.[2] It also had lines running south from Kansas City to Dallas and to West Texas. In 1994, BN owned 20,060 miles of the road on which it operated.

The Santa Fe had operated 8,362 miles of road in 1994, including a main line from Chicago to Kansas City and south through Texas, New Mexico and Arizona to Los Angeles and north to San Francisco, a line from Kansas City to Colorado, and lines from Kansas City south to Fort Worth and Houston with branches into east Texas and Louisiana. In 1994, Santa Fe owned 7,043 miles of road.

The essential background information to this merger is the 1980 Burlington Northern acquisition of the St. Louis-San Francisco Railway. This merger is treated first in this chapter.

BACKGROUND MERGER
BURLINGTON NORTHERN – ST. LOUIS SAN FRANCISCO

The Burlington Northern and the St. Louis San Francisco applied to the ICC in 1977 to merge their lines, and the merger was approved on March 25, 1980. Upon denial of an appeal, merged operations began on December 1, 1980. In 1979, the Burlington Northern had operated 22,798 miles of road and the St. Louis San Francisco had operated 4,488 miles of road.[3] At the end of 1980, the merged BN reported that it operated 27,361 miles of road.[4] The lines owned by BN were 25,326 miles, divided into 15,316 miles of main lines (60.5%) and 10,010 miles of branch lines (39.5%). The remainder were leased lines and trackage rights. This was an end-to-end merger, since in the midwest BN's southern most terminals were Kansas City and St. Louis and these two cities were the northern most terminals of SLSF. Thus new single line service was established from the Pacific Northwest through Kansas City to cities on the SLSF route to Dallas and through St. Louis to Memphis, Birmingham, Mobile and Pensacola.

The SLSF had only two lines, totaling 1,157 miles of road, with over 20 million gross tons annually of trains plus freight per mile of road.[5] These were from St. Louis to Tulsa and from Kansas City to Birmingham. Another 391 miles of line had between 10 and 15 million gross tons per mile of road. These combined 1,548 miles of road, or 35% of SLSF total miles, carried 80.4% of the gross ton-miles on the railroad in 1975.[6] The least-used line of 184 miles from Oklahoma City to Quanah, Texas, had only 1 million gross tons per mile of road. The 117-mile Class II subsidiary from Quanah to Floydada, whose tonnage is not reported, must have had similar light traffic. In 1975, the 65% of SLSF lines with low density averaged 2.67 million gross tons of traffic per mile of road.[7]

The net revenue freight density measures the number of tons of revenue freight carried one mile per mile of road. It is calculated by dividing the total ton-miles of freight by the miles of road. From 1974 to 1979, Moody's reported the SLSF freight density ranged from 2.8 million to 3.6 million.[8] These averages combining low-density and high-density lines, are not useful to financial analysts. The estimated revenue freight density on the 1,548 miles of SLSF main lines was over 9.0 million and comparable to that of BN on its main lines.[9] Consequently, the SLSF was a net-profit carrier with an operating ratio of 90.07 in 1978 and 91.64 in 1979.[10]

The expected public interest benefits of the BN after the acquisition of SLSF were estimated net reduction in costs of operating the joint carriers and the significantly, improved service to shippers in new single-line service, reduced transit times, more frequent service, and improved car utilization.[11] In addition, on some routes SLSF had excess line capacity that BN could utilize.

Single-line services would allow preblocked trains to move over much longer distances from the Northwest to the Southeast and the Gulf. Eliminating interchange at congested yards such as Kansas City and St. Louis would create valuable saving of shipping time for customers. For example, the expected reduction in transit time from Chicago to Tulsa was 19 hours or 43%. A scheduled service for containers and trailers on flat car from Chicago to Houston was 58 hours, an reduction in time of 36%. The longest new run was from Portland, Oregon to Birmingham, Alabama of over 3,000 miles, the longest through freight in the United States.[12]

The estimated net annual savings in costs by the third year were over $20.3 million.[13] Rail yard consolidation at St. Louis and Kansas City was estimated to save $3.75 million.[14] Use of shorter routes and reduced interchange costs would save $1.1 million. Car utilization would save $5 million and overhead would be reduced by $15 million. On the other hand, equipment costs for the added train schedules would increase by $5.5 million.

The Burlington Northern made estimates of the expected diversion of traffic from other railroads to its new through routes from the Northwest into the South. The Missouri-Kansas-Texas was the only carrier expected to have a significant loss of traffic to BN, estimated at 6.8% of M-K-T revenues.[15] When the ICC refused to condition the merger with indemnification by BN to M-K-T, the latter filed an appeal in the Fifth Circuit.[16] Noting that the Department of Justice had found no significant anticompetitive effects of the merger, the Court affirmed the ICC approval.[17] In 1978, the ICC had adopted a new policy favoring railroad mergers, and this was reaffirmed in its General Policy Statement of 1981.[18] The public interest standard was redefined. So long as essential rail services by some other railroad would not be terminated, the merger was to be approved. In this case, even if the M-K-T lost so much revenue that it was forced into bankruptcy, other carriers would immediately bid to purchase M-K-T main lines and keep its essential services in operation.[19]

BURLINGTON NORTHERN – SANTA FE MERGER

The two carriers filed their application in 1994 with the ICC to merge and create a carrier with over 30,500 miles of road. The approval by the ICC in August, 1995, was its last major decision before the ICC was eliminated by Congress and its functions were taken over by the new Surface Transportation Board of the Department of Transportation. The acquisition was preceded by a bidding war as the Union Pacific also tried to acquire the Santa Fe. The original agreement, approved by the Boards of Directors of the two carriers, had been for an exchange of BN stock for Santa Fe stock at a total price of $2.7 billion.[20] At the end of the bidding war, U.P. offered $18.50 cash for each Santa Fe share for a total of $3.6 Billion. The total amount paid by BN for a tax-free exchange of shares was about $4 billion. In order to block U.P., the Santa Fe became burdened with about $1.1 billion of new debt and the Burlington had undertaken $500 million in debt.[21]

Table 6.1. Financial Results of Burlington Northern and Santa Fe, 1994 (Thousands of Dollars).

	Burlington Northern	Santa Fe
Railway Operating Revenue	4,995,371	2,680,936
Railway Operating Expenses	4,163,232	2,252,035
Net Revenue: Railway Operations	831,431	428,901
Other Income	32,198	75,888
Miscellaneous Deductions	15,489	27,460
Income Available for Fixed Charged	848,140	477,329
Fixed Charges	79,296	64,951
Income Taxes	299,307	162,245
Net Income	459,138	249,167

Source: Transport Statistics in the United States 64–66 (1994).

The financial results in 1994 for the Burlington Northern and the Santa Fe are reported in Table 6.1. The railway operating revenues of the Burlington Northern were nearly $5 billion while those of the Santa Fe were near $2.7 billion. But the route miles of the Santa Fe were only 37.7% of that on the Burlington. So that in 1994, the freight revenue per mile of road on the Burlington was $220,122 while that on the Santa Fe was $315,606. Both carriers were among the most profitable, with operating ratios of 83.3 on the Burlington and 84.0 on the Santa Fe. The 1994 net income of the Burlington was $459 million and that of the Santa Fe was $249 million. Nevertheless, the ICC in its annual determination of railroad revenue adequacy, having found the cost of capital to railroads in 1994 to be 12.2%, rated both these carriers to have inadequate earnings.[22] The Burlington return on investment was 11.8% and the Santa Fe return was 7.4%.

COMMON CONTROL IN THE PUBLIC INTEREST

The BN-Santa Fe merger was found to be in the public interest because most of their routes were in different areas of the country and thus were not competitive. The BN was mostly in the Northwest, the northern Midwest, and in the Southeast. The Santa Fe was mostly in the Southwest and from Colorado and Kansas into Chicago. The main parallel routes were Denver to Chicago and Kansas City to Chicago. The two railroads were also complementary in their specializations. The BN was the largest carrier of grain in the nation and received about one-third of its revenues from carrying coal from the Powder

River Basin in Wyoming. The Santa Fe received 47% of its revenues from intermodal transport.[23]

It is significant to note that this merger could not complete lines connecting the Northwest and Southwest because the Santa Fe's northern most point in California was in Sacramento while the BN's most southern line in California ended 250 miles farther north in Bieber. This line connecting Sacramento and Bieber had been a Western Pacific route. The Santa Fe had sought to acquire the Western Pacific in 1960 with the latter's consent. While the ICC hearing examiner recommend approval of this end-to-end merger, the ICC in 1965 finally found it not to be in the public interest.[24] The ICC concluded that both SP and Santa Fe had incentive to direct traffic away from the main Western Pacific route from San Francisco to Salt Lake City in favor of their longer southern routes to the midwest.

The ICC held that the evidence demonstrated that the B. N.-Santa Fe merger would be largely pro-competitive, that it would stimulate price and service competition in markets served by the merged carrier, and shippers would experience lower rates and improved service over many routes.[25] In the routes from the Southwest to the Southeast the BN-Santa Fe could offer single-line rail service linking California and the other southwestern states with Mississippi, Alabama and Florida. One of the most significant through routes created by the merger would be from Los Angeles to St. Louis over Santa Fe lines to Avard, Oklahoma and over the BN Frisco lines to St. Louis. In addition to avoiding Kansas City rail yard congestion, this became the shortest route from Los Angeles to St. Louis.[26] It also reversed the policy of a 1965 ICC denial of Santa Fe entry into St. Louis from Kansas City that had been based on the economic fallacy of protecting less efficient rival railroads.[27]

Another area for more efficient service would be new through routes from the upper Midwest to the southwest.[28] Single-line service from Minneapolis to Los Angeles would become available. This would also facilitate rail service from Canada to California and to Mexico. Common control of the two railroads would mean access for all their shippers to ports on the Gulf of Mexico and on the Pacific coast. This expanded access to ports was expected to increase significantly the railroads intermodal service of containers on flat cars and thereby offer more effective competition to the Union Pacific and the Southern Pacific.

In order to secure ICC approval of the merger, BN and Santa Fe entered settlement agreements with rival carriers designed to lessen anticompetitive effccts of the merger.[29] Union Pacific received trackage rights over Santa Fe lines from Abilene, KS to Superior, NE. This branch line completed a connection between the UP main line from Ogden, Utah to Omaha and the UP main line from Denver to Kansas City. It would provide competition for grain moving from the area of Superior, NE. A second extended trackage right was to Southern Pacific from Pueblo, CO to Fort Worth, TX, a distance of 683 miles, with access to industries in Amarillo and to Plainview and Lubbock, TX. A third action of the ICC was an exemption proceeding to confirm Southern Pacific trackage rights over BN between Kansas City and Chicago which had been initiated by agreement of the carriers in August, 1990. The exemption included the parallel line of the former Santa Fe.[30]

A unique part of the settlement agreements was one for reciprocity. The Southern Pacific granted the new Burlington Northern Santa Fe trackage rights between El Paso, TX and Topeka, KS, a distance of 876 miles.[31] Southern Pacific also agreed to provide haulage services for BN-Santa Fe freight cars between Caldwell, TX and the Mexican gateway at Eagle Pass, TX and between Caldwell and Elmendorf, TX. It would seem that Southern Pacific was able to bargain for trackage over BN lines from Colorado to Ft. Worth only by reciprocating and giving BN-Santa Fe the trackage from El Paso to Topeka. The Southern Pacific route was about 200 miles shorter than the old Santa Fe route from Topeka to El Paso.

Two unsuccessful appeals were brought to challenge the ICC approval of the BN-Santa Fe merger. In *Western Resources, Inc.* v. *Surface Transp. Bd.*,[32] four electric utilities complained that the merger would harm their ability to ship coal from various mines to their power plants. They urged that the ICC erred in denying their requests for trackage rights and rate caps. The disputed aspects of the merger involved almost exclusively vertical integration. The Santa Fe had a monopoly on rail delivery of coal to most of the utilities bringing this appeal.[33] Burlington Northern, as original carrier of the coal, had merely delivered it to Santa Fe. The controversy here centered on the "one-lump theory," in economics that there is only one monopoly rent to be gained from the sale of the end-product which here was transport service. Where the final seller to the user of the product has a monopoly, the monopolist's upstream vertical integration can not create more monopoly power. Hence, the final buyer of the good or service will not be adversely affected. The ICC findings concerning lack of competitive harm were held by the Court of Appeals to be supported by substantial evidence.[34]

The second unsuccessful appeal was *Grainbelt Corp.* v *Surface Transp. Bd.*[35] Grainbelt Corp. and Farmrail Corp. are two affiliated short line rail carriers that transported wheat.[36] Through their connections with Class 1 railroads, Grainbelt and Farmrail provided wheat shippers in western Oklahoma with rail access to Texas Gulf ports. Before the BN-Santa Fe merger, Grainbelt and Farmrail had, directly or indirectly, three Class 1 rail connections: BN, Santa Fe and Union

Pacific. Under lease of its line from BN, Grainbelt was under a blocking provision that required it to pay additional rental payments if it handled shipments in conjunction with a carrier other than BN if the shipment was to points served by BN. The ICC conditioned the BN-Santa Fe merger on the blocking provision not being extended to points on the Santa Fe.[37] ICC also imposed a condition that Grainbelt be allowed to interchange at Quanah with Southern Pacific, a new alternative. Given these constraints, the Appeal Court held that petitioners had provided no evidence of a reduction of competition.[38] Union Pacific and BN-Santa Fe would provide two independent Class 1 railroad connections for Farmrail, and Southern Pacific would be available to Farmrail as an alternative to the lost Santa Fe connection resulting from the merger.

FINANCIAL ANALYSIS

The projected annual cost savings from the Burlington Northern-Santa Fe merger, as tabulated in Table 6.2, were $453 million. Annual operational savings were projected at $107 million. The first element was $26.6 million savings from common point and route consolidations. While Chicago and Kansas City were major rail yard examples, there were others. At Denver, the Burlington and its subsidiary, Colorado & Southern, met the Santa Fe. At Amarillo, the Santa Fe crossed the Burlington subsidiary, Fort Worth & Denver. Between Dallas and Houston, the Santa Fe and the Fort Worth & Denver had parallel lines. On their parallel lines from Kansas City to Chicago, both Burlington and Santa Fe had yards at Galesburg, IL. The ICC granted an exemption for construction of connecting tracks so that Santa Fe trains could gain access to Burlington yards, which would become a key switching point for the combined railroads.[39]

The mechanical savings of $45.7 million annually would in part be from combining the specialized facilities for the repair and rebuilding of locomotives and freight cars. The engineering-maintenance of way savings of $12.7 million annually would in part arise from reduced maximum speed of trains on one of two parallel lines. This would not apply if increased traffic required increased capacity. If, for example, the BN Santa Fe used its new trackage rights over Southern Pacific from Vaughn, NM to Topeka, KS for some through trains, the BN-SF former Santa Fe route through Amarillo would still need a high level of maintenance of way. The purchasing and materials annual saving of $13.3 million would arise from merger of those departments on the two carriers and the merged firm's ability to deal more successfully with suppliers. Merger of intermodal facilities in key markets such as Chicago, Kansas City and Denver were expected to save $8.7 million annually.

Table 6.2. Burlington Northern-Santa Fe Projected Annual Cost Savings (Millions of Dollars).

Operational Savings	
Operations: Common Point and Route Consolidations	$26.6
Mechanical	45.7
Engineering: Maintenance of Way	12.7
Purchasing & Materials	13.3
Intermodal Operations	3.7
Subtotal	107.0
Support Function Savings	
Chairman's Office	$9.4
Transportation Overhead	18.8
Maintenance of Way	12.3
Maintenance of Equipment	6.2
Purchasing	32.4
Operating Support	24.2
Management Information Systems	45.1
Business Unit Overheads	86.8
Other General and Administrative	110.8
Subtotal	$346.0
Total Annual Savings	$453.0

Source: Burlington Northern et. al. – Merger – Santa Fe Pacific Et. Al., 10 ICC 2d. 661, 740–41 (1995).

The annual support functions savings, as noted in Table 6.2, were expected to be $346 million. Most of these savings must arise from reduction in employment. The Chairman's Office alone was expected to save $9.4 million annually. Transportation overhead would be reduced in part by no longer having to account and bill for rail cars interchanged by the merging railroads. One combined management information system would be adequate for the merged firm. All local sales and service offices across the nation could be combined. At the corporate offices, merger of marketing, finance and law departments would lower overhead costs significantly.

IMPACT OF MERGER

Following the BN-Santa Fe merger there was continuous growth in revenue ton-miles and in revenue, but a significant part of this growth was due to the expanding economy. The revenue ton-miles of the two carriers in 1994 before merger totaled 360,605 million.[40] The revenue ton-miles of the BN-Santa Fe in

2000 were 491,959 million, an increase of 39%. As noted in Table 6.1, before merger the combined 1994 railway operating revenues of the BN and the Santa Fe were $7,676 million and the combined railway operating incomes were $1,260 million. The financial results after the merger are compiled in Table 6.3. By 1999, railway operating revenues had reached $9,183 million and railway operating income had increased by 75%. The drop in operating income and net income in 2000 was due primarily to the effect of a $232 million increase in fuel costs.

The revenue information by commodities for the year 2000 shows intermodal (containers or trailers on flatcars) at $2,654 millions or 29% of the total.[41] But the revenue per flatcar was half of that for freight in boxcars, so that intermodal cars were 42% of the total cars hauled. Carload freight was $2,572 million or 28% of freight revenue. Coal was $2,131 million or 23% of freight revenue. Agricultural commodities were $1,257 millions or 14% of freight revenues. Automobiles and trucks were $493 million or 6% of the total.

The key factor enabling the large growth in traffic on the BN-Santa Fe was a significant expansion in capital expenditures. In 1995, before the merger completion, capital expenditures for the two carriers was $1,215 millions. In the five years, 1996 to 2000, BN-Santa Fe had capital expenditures totaling $9,748 million.[42] Maintenance of Way, as capitalized, accounted for $4,272 million of the expenditures. The largest maintenance element was for replacement or addition of rail in the amount of $1,178 millions for 4,861 track miles of rail laid. A lead element was completion of the double-tracking of the Santa Fe transcontinental line from Chicago to Los Angeles. The final sector was 656 miles between Wellington, Kan. and Belen, New Mexico.[43] Completion of the

Table 6.3. Burlington Northern-Santa Fe Railway Co. Financial Results (Millions of Dollars).

Year ended Dec. 31	2000	1999	1998	1997	1996
Operating Revenues	9,200	9,183	9,049	8,366	8,187
Operating Expenses	7,096	6 981	6,894	6.600	6,485
Operating Income	2,104	2,202	2,155	1,766	1,702
Interest Expense	287	291	293	281	133
Other Income	−5	39	77	5	3
Income Before Income Taxes	1,812	1,950	1,939	1,490	1,640
Income Taxes	694	721	733	561	628
Net Income	1,118	1,229	1,206	929	1,012

Sources: Burlington Northern & Santa Fe Railroad Co., 10K Reports to Securities and Exchange Commission, Disclosure Page 25 (1996); *Id.* at 27 (1999), *Id.* at 20 (2000).

double-tracking on the Chicago-Los Angeles route was expected to increase its line capacity by 15 trains per day.[44]

New rail yard efficiency is demonstrated by the reconfiguration of the yards at Kansas City. The former Santa Fe Argentine Yard was reworked to install one single efficient hump as a replacement for two older humps and to install new state-of-the-art switching and retarders.[45] The work required laying 74.5 miles of track. This enabled the Argentine Yard to handle its own merchandise traffic plus that of the former BN Murray Yard. The hump in the Murray Yard was flattened and the yard was transformed into a long-track operation for coal and grain trains in order to increase efficiency of moving those trains through the Kansas City terminal. The amount spent on terminal and line expansion from 1996 through 2000 was $1,694 million.[46]

Another prominent factor increasing productivity in the BN-Santa Fe merger has been the accelerated replacement of locomotives. The two carriers had 4,277 diesel locomotives at the time of merger in 1995.[47] By the end of 1999 BN-Santa Fe had 5,095 diesel locomotives.[48] But this increase in the total does not explain the replacement of locomotives. BN-Santa Fe acquired 1,400 new locomotives in the 4 years, 1996–1999.[49] Of these, 400 were delivered in 1998 and 470 were delivered in 1999.[50] The latter purchase at a cost of $750 million was the largest order by a carrier in U.S. railroad history. This enabled the replacement of old, failing locomotives so that 25% of the units at the end of 1999 were less than five years old.[51] One effect was to restore freight service on the Chicago-Los Angeles route to its previous fastest time.

In order to obtain additional intermodal capacity through the state of Washington, in 1996 BN-Santa Fe reopened the long-closed former Northern Pacific route through Stampede Pass.[52] This 229 mile line was between Pasco and Auburn, Washington. This third route linking Central Washington and the Pacific Coast required 47 miles of new and relay rail, placement of 145,000 concrete crossties and 165,000 wood crossties plus other rehabilitation of structures and bridges.[53]

In order to complete the Stampede Pass Route, BN-Santa Fe had repurchased the Washington Central Railroad Company in December 1996 through exchange of BNSF common stock.[54] BN-Santa Fe reported operations over the Washington Central route of 128 miles between Kennewick and Cle Elum, Washington. The Washington Central Railroad was a regional carrier created in 1987 to purchase from Burlington Northern 413 miles of line formerly operated by Northern Pacific.[55] There was no report whether part of the line was abandoned.

Another Key element of resource reallocation of the BN-Santa Fe was the decision to sell about 75 segments of line covering 3,300 miles of line.[56] By the end of 1997 approximately 2,800 miles of line had been sold. In the corporate capital accounts, $105 million was written off net book value of the 3,300 miles of line, anticipating the amount sale proceeds would fail to realize book value. Another $89 million charge related to the costs of terminating leased facilities, a majority of which had been vacated by the end of 1997.[57] The decision to sell 3,300 miles of rail line that was or would become unprofitable to the merged carrier did not reduce BN-Santa Fe miles of road in 1996. The Union Pacific-Southern Pacific merger in 1996 resulted in that new carrier agreeing to grant trackage rights to BN-Santa Fe over more than 4000 miles of its lines.[58] In addition UP-SP sold 335 miles of line to BN-Santa Fe for $150 millions.

Efficiencies of merger also required combining office and managerial functions and thereby reducing the number of employees. Costs of $287 million related to the BN-Santa Fe Plan to centralize the majority of its clerical functions.[59] The plan included reduction of approximately 1600 union clerical workers. The company and unions entered an agreement for separation benefits in the forms of lump-sum payments or payments over several years. Costs of $190 million were recorded for salaried employees in terms of severance, pension, and other benefits. These costs reflect the elimination of about 1000 former BN employees.[60] Another $105 million was expanded for severance and other termination benefits for about 500 former salaried Santa Fe employees. The consolidated balance sheet of BN-Santa Fe for December 31, 1996 showed current and long-term liabilities for merger and separation of employees of $580 million. Part of this relates to separation of conductors and trainmen pursuant to agreements to reduce freight train crew sizes.[61]

CONCLUSION

The Burlington Northern acquisition of the St. Louis-San Francisco Railway gave the BN a second line from the Northwest to the Gulf of Mexico. BN also gained lines from Kansas City and St. Louis to the Gulf. While rail yard consolidations were substantial, the largest saving was in management, an example of economy of scale.

The Burlington Northern merger with the Santa Fe was approved by the ICC because most of their routes were in different areas of the nation and they were not market rivals. In one of the cases where the two railroad lines were parallel, from Kansas City to Chicago, it was likely that both lines would be needed to carry the large traffic on the route. Some efficiency gains were achieved, however, by the reorganization of duplicate rail yards in major cities.

The most significant aspect of this major merger was the settlement agreements with Union pacific and Southern Pacific to grant trackage rights over extended lines of the new BN-Santa Fe Railroad. The applicants anticipated major opposition from shippers at the ICC hearings if there were not at last two railroads serving major cities and industries. The trackage rights with authority in the new carrier to serve major industries on those lines were emphasized in the official ICC approval of the merger. As has been noted in other railroad mergers, shippers were aware of the railroad cost structures and did not expect active rate competition between railroads. What the shippers demanded was the service of at least two railroads as a guarantee of service. If one of the carriers was affected by service interruptions, such as strikes by workers or shortage of freight cars, hopefully the other carrier would be available.

The expected savings in costs of operation from this merger were so large because these were two of the largest railroads in the United States. However, the savings on route and yard consolidations plus mechanical savings on equipment and its maintenance was only 15% of the total. In contrast, the projected savings on support functions were 76% of the total. These were the areas of office operations and management that could be combined and significant reductions in work force that could be accomplished. Given the many factors affecting revenues and costs, especially wages, it is not possible to determine the extent to which the savings were realized. In fact annual railway operating income did rise from 1996 to 2000 by $400 million.

NOTES

1. Burlington Northern et al. – Merger – Santa Fe Pacific et al., 10 I.C.C. 2d 661 (1995). As to the creation of Burlington Northern, see Northern Lines Mergers Cases, 396 U.S. 491 (1970). See comments of Richard Saunders, *Merging Lines: American Railroads 1900-1970*, 338-342 (Dekalb: Northern Illinois University Press, 2001); Rush Loving Jr., *A Railroad Merger That Worked*, 86 Fortune 128–133 (Aug. 1972).

2. Burlington Northern-Control and Merger-St. Louis-San Francisco, 360 I.C.C. 784 (1980), *affirmed*, Missouri-Kansas-Texas R. Co. v. United States, 632 F. 2d 392 (5th Cir. 1980), cert. denied 451 U.S. 1017 (1981).

3. *Transport Statistics in the United States* 43, 94 (1979).

4. *Moody's Transportation Manual* 519 (1981).

5. 360 I.C.C. at 1178.

6. The gross-ton miles are calculated from Chapter 1, Table 1.2.

7. *Id.*

8. *Moody's Transportation Manual* 791 (1980).

9. The revenue freight densities were estimated by allocating 85% of total revenue ton-miles to main lines and dividing by the main line milage. Moody's average data on maintenance of way and structures per mile of line is also not useful. If one allows a high railroad industry average of $3,500 per mile of branch line for maintenance in 1979, the expenditure per mile of main line by both SLSF and BN is estimated at

$36,000 to $37,500. See Donald W. Larson and Robert C. Vogel, *Railroad Abandonment: Optimal Solutions and Policy Outcomes*, in Kenneth D. Boyer and William G. Shepherd, eds., *Economic Regulation: Essays in Honor of James R. Nelson* 65, 75 (E. Lansing: Michigan State University Press, 1981).

10. *Moody's Transportation Manual* 795 (1980).
11. 360 I.C.C. at 817–18.
12. Statement of T. J. Lamphier, Burlington Northern executive, in 184 *Traffic World* 31 (Oct. 20, 1980).
13. 360 I.C.C. at 819.
14. *Id.* at 1096–97.
15. See Illinois Legislative Investigating Commission, *The Burlington Northern & St. Louis-San Francisco Railway Merger* 45 (1980).
16. *Missouri-Kansas-Texas R. Co. v. United States*, 632 F. 2d 392 (5th Cir. 1980), cert. denied, 451 U.S. 1017 (1981).
17. 632 F.2d at 398.
18. Railroad Consolidation Procedures, 359 I.C.C. 195, 199 (1978), adopting the policies from I.C.C. Rail Services Planning Office, *Rail Merger Study: Final Report* (1978). See Railroad Consolidation Procedures, General Policy Statement, 363 I.C.C. 784, 786 (1981).
19. 632 F.2d at 400–404.
20. See 241 *Traffic World* 10 (Feb. 6, 1995).
21. The ICC approved a minimum exchange ratio of 0.4 shares of BN common stock for each share of Santa Fe stock, equal in value to about $20 per share. A maximum of 0.4347 shares of BN common stock for each share of Santa Fe common stock was approved if Santa Fe repurchased 10 million shares of its stock prior to merger. 10 I.C.C. 2d at 791.
22. Ex Parte 524, *Railroad Revenue Adequacy*, 10 I.C.C. 2d 657, 660 (1995).
23. *Moody's Transportation Manual* 1 (1995); *Railway Age* 36, 40 (December 1995).
24. Southern Pac. Co. – Control – Western Pac. R. Co., 327 I.C.C. 387 (1965). The rival Southern Pacific petition to acquire the Western Pacific was rejected because they were parallel carriers and merger would substantially lessen competition. See Saunders, *Merging Lines: American Railroads 1900-1970*, supra note 1, at 213-216.
25. Burlington Northern et al.-Merger-Santa Fe Pacific et al., 10 I.C.C. 2d 661, 733 (1995).
26. See Chicago, Burlington & Quincy Control, 271 I.C.C. 63, 162-63 (1948).
27. See Michael Conant, *Railroad Mergers and Abandonments* 105-06 (Berkeley: University of California Press, 1964).
28. 10 I.C.C. 2d at 735–37.
29. *Id.* at 676, 763.
30. Rio Grande Industries, Inc., Southern Pacific Transportation Company, Denver and Rio Grande Western Railroad Company, St. Louis Southwestern Railway Company, and SPCSL Corp. – Trackage Rights Exemption – Burlington Northern Railroad Company Lines Between Kansas City, MO and Chicago, IL, Finance Docket No. 31730 (Sub-No.1), noted at 10 I.C.C. 2d 767 (1995). See 223 *Traffic World* 13 (Aug. 6, 1990); 224 *Traffic World* 8 (Oct. 1, 1990).
31. 10 I.C.C. 2d at 811.
32. 109 F.3d 782 (D.C.Cir. 1997). The ICC Termination Act of 1995, 109 Stat. 803, provided that suits against the ICC were to be continued against the new Surface Transportation Board. 109 Stat. 104, 838-39.

33. 109 F.3d at 784.
34. *Id.*
35. 109 F.3d 794 (D.C.Cir. 1997).
36. Grainbelt operated 178 miles of line and had overhead trackage rights over 59 miles of BN line. Under lease from the State of Oklahoma, Farmrail operated 187 miles of rail line formerly owned by Santa Fe and sold to the state upon abandonment.
37. Burlington Northern-Merger Santa Fe et al., 10 I.C.C. 2d at 776–78.
38. 109 F.3d at 800.
39. 10 I.C.C. 2d at 674, 796. Exemption for connecting tracks at other towns are detailed at *Id.* 673 to 675.
40. Burlington Northern & Santa Fe Railway Co., 10K report to Securities and Exchange Commission, 11 (1996); *Id.* 11 (2000).
41. *Id.*, at Disclosure Page 13 (2000).
42. *Id.*, at 6 (1997); *Id.* at 6 (2000).
43. See *Railway Age* 25, 29 (June 1999).
44. *Id.*, at 31.
45. *Id.*, at 30.
46. BNSF 10K Report, *supra* note 40, at 6 (1997); *Id.*, at 6 (2000).
47. *Id.*, at 5 (1997).
48. *Id.*, at 5 (2000).
49. *Railway Age* 31 (June 1999).
50. *Id.*, at 28.
51. *Id.*, at 31.
52. BNSF 10K Report, *supra* note 40, at Disclosure Page 7 (1996). See statement of C. Hautamaki of the Port of Seattle reported in 262 *Traffic World* 27,28 (June 12, 2000).
53. *Railway Age* 29 (June 1999).
54. BNSF 10K Report, *supra* note 40, at Disclosure Page 7 (1996).
55. John F. Due and Suzanne D. Lever, *The Post-1984 Experience with New Small and Regional Railroads*, 33 Transportation Jl. 40, 41 (1993).
56. BNSF 10K Report, *supra* note 40, at Disclosure Page 37 (1997).
57. *Id.*
58. *Id.*, Disclosure Page 13 (1996).
59. *Id.*, Disclosure Page 30 (1996).
60. *Id.*, Disclosure Page 31 (1996).
61. *Id.*

7. UNION PACIFIC MERGER OF SOUTHERN PACIFIC

On August 12, 1996, the Surface Transportation Board (STB), in an opinion of 397 pages, approved the merger of the Union Pacific Railroad Co. and the Southern Pacific Transportation Corp.[1] The acquisition was consummated on September 11, 1996. The Union Pacific together with its recently acquired Chicago and North Western Railway operated 22,785 miles of road.[2] As noted in Chapter 6, the Union Pacific had acquired the Missouri Pacific and Western Pacific in 1982 and the Missouri-Kansas-Texas in 1988. The Union Pacific in 1995 extended from Chicago to the west coast with lines to Los Angeles, San Francisco, Portland and Seattle. Its Missouri Pacific acquisition gave it lines from Kansas City and St. Louis to the southeast and the Gulf of Mexico.

The Union Pacific acquisition of the Chicago and North Western Railway was finalized in 1995.[3] This end-to-end merger grew out of the long-term relationship of the two carriers in exchanging freight trains at Fremont, Nebraska.[4] In 1990, the ICC approved the Union Pacific acquisition of trackage rights over the North Western between Fremont, Neb. and Chicago.[5] However, the North Western was to act as Union Pacific's agent in hauling trains over the line and delivering them to terminals or to eastern carriers in Chicago. The primary function of this agreement seems to have been to provoke the North Western to commit to make $115 million in capital expenditures on the line. In consideration thereof, the Union Pacific agreed to invest $100 million in the parent corporation of the North Western.[6] In 1993, Union Pacific petitioned to convert its 29.5% of the shares in the North Western Holdings Corp into voting stock and take control of the firm.[7] In approving the control in 1995, the ICC stated, "We Believe that there will be no meaningful reduction in such transportation competition as exists today."[8] The ICC rejected Southern Pacific's request for trackage rights; the evidence did not indicate that this merger would impair essential Southern Pacific services. The ICC ruled that the Union Pacific Corp.'s $35 per share offer to acquire all the stock in Chicago and North Western Transportation Corp. was reasonable.[9] This price was 34% above the market price for North Western stock on the day before the offer was announced.

The Southern Pacific operated 15,581 miles of road in 1995.[10] Its southern route was from Los Angeles to New Orleans and north to St. Louis. Its northern route was from San Francisco to St. Louis over its own lines and its affiliated Denver Rio Grande Western to Colorado and over trackage rights on Missouri Pacific to Kansas City and St. Louis. From Kansas City, SP had trackage rights over Burlington Northern into Chicago and it later purchased another line from St. Louis to Chicago. The west coast line of Southern Pacific was from Los Angeles to San Francisco and Portland.

In 1988, the ICC had approved the acquisition of Southern Pacific Transportation Co. by Rio Grande Industries Inc., parent of the Denver and Rio Grande Western Railroad Co.[11] This was a result of the ICC order of divestiture against the Santa Fe in 1987 after its attempt to merge the Southern Pacific was denied as anticompetitive.[12] The Rio Grande operated 2,211 miles of road from Ogden and Salt Lake City, UT to Denver and Pueblo, Co, and from there on trackage rights over the Missouri Pacific to Kansas City. The Southern Pacific and its subsidiaries, before the Rio Grande merger, had operated 11,699 miles of road, of which 7,767 miles was main line and 3932 miles of branch lines.[13] The merged firm operated under the name of the Southern Pacific.

The Rio Grande end-to-end merger received support from the U.S. Department of Justice and the U.S. Department of Transportation.[14] The estimated public benefits of the merger in terms of cost savings in operations were $75 million per year.[15] Internal rerouting of trains was estimated to have annual savings of about $12 million. The locomotive maintenance was estimated to save $27.5 million annually. Freight car rentals were estimated to have a $12 million annual savings, and reductions in the work force were estimated to create a $17.4 million annual savings.

FINANCIAL BACKGROUND

The financial results of the Union Pacific and Southern Pacific in 1995, the year before merger, are reported in Table 7.1. The railway operating revenues of Union Pacific were $6.6 billion while those of the Southern Pacific were $2.94 billion. The freight revenues per mile of road of the Union Pacific were $264,449 while those on the Southern Pacific were $182,753. The S. P. was 69% of the UP. In 1995 the net revenues from railway operations of the Union Pacific were almost $1.4 billion while those of the Southern Pacific were a negative $21 million. Consequently, the freight operating ratio of Union Pacific was 78.7 while that of the Southern Pacific was 100.7. The 1995 net income of the Union Pacific was almost $915 million while the net loss of the Southern Pacific was $74 million.

Table 7.1. Financial Results of Union Pacific and Southern Pacific, 1995 (Thousands of Dollars).

	Union Pacific[a]	Southern Pacific
Railroad Operating Revenues	6,602,389	2,940,730
Railroad Operating Expenses	5,206 924	2 961,863
Net Revenue from Operations	1,395,465	–21,133
Other Income	290,814	105,081
Miscellaneous Deductions	–35,692	–81 440
Income Before Fixed Charges	1,650,587	2,508
Fixed Charges	244.104	114,676
Income After Fixed Charges	1,406,483	–112,168
Contingent Interest	9,615	0
Income Taxes Paid	283,109	18,500
Provision for Deferred Taxes	198,905	–56 667
Net Income	914,854	–74,001

Source: Association of American Railroads, *Analysis of Class 1 Railroads* 37, 39 (1995).
[a] Includes the Chicago and North Western Railroad.

The poor financial condition of the Southern Pacific Railroad as a rail carrier, in contrast to its non-operating income, was significant to the STB 1996 merger decision.

As will be examined, this issue is of great importance to estimating the likelihood of rate-cutting rivalry by SP. Table 7.2 demonstrates the long-run financial weakness of the SP and subsidiaries as a rail carrier. Net revenue from railway operations was negative in all years since 1982 except four. The very large operating losses in 1986 and 1991 to set up reserve for restructuring costs are detailed in the notes to Table 7.2. Many of the actual expenditures were made in subsequent years and charged against the reserves.

The non-operating income from 1982 to 1995 was clearly sufficient to offset the operating losses of the carrier so that unsophisticated investors might mistakenly think that Southern Pacific Railroad was a profitable rail carrier. By far, the largest element of non-operating profits was sale of real property from the large land holdings of the carrier. In 1991, for example, when net revenue from railroad operations was –$369.5 million, the gain from sale of property was $469.8 million.[16] The second largest non-operating revenue was from real estate and other rentals, which in 1991 was $23.6 million.

The rail sector of the Southern Pacific had been in serious financial difficulty for a long time. From the ICC adoption of the New Uniform System of Accounts

Table 7.2. Southern Pacific Transportation Co. and Subsidiaries Financial Results (Thousands of Dollars).

Year	Operating Revenues[a]	Operating Expenses	Net Revenue from Operations	Non Operating Income	Net Income
1982	2,321,971	2,389,364	−67,393	200,939	42,013
1983	2,315,969	2,327,885	−11,916	143,208	55,983
1984	2,609,204	2,567,020	42,184	202,625	181,785
1985	2,430,877	2,426,635	4,242	197,812	138,205
1986	2,256,373	2,850,238	−593,865[b]	142,068	−280,735
1987	2,286,077	2,215,783	70,294	223,949	175,582
1988	2,323,003	2,427,161	−104,158	522,780	377,834
1989	2,322,896	2,397,649	−74,753	384,222	97,943
1990	2,413,534	2,460,881	−47,347	279,107	29,138
1991	2,332,429	2,701,890	−369,461[c]	534,525	1,449
1992	2,374,657	2,407,026	−32,369	351,053	109,493
1993	2,394,233	2,438,332	−44,099	74,121	−204,838
1994	2,941,527	2,718,027	223,500	353,416	201,742
1995	2,940,730	2,961,863	−21,133	105,081	−74,001

Source: U.S., I.C.C., *Transport Statistics in the United States* (1982–1995).

[a] Excludes transfers from governmental authorities for current operations.

[b] In 1986, company reported $601 million charge for restructuring costs as follows: sale or abandonment of 3,100 miles of rail lines plus buildings and structures ($273 million); separation or relocation of 3,800 employees ($208 million); disposal of locomotives and freight cars ($120 million). *Rio Grande Industries*, 4 I.C.C. 2d 834, 985 (1988).

[c] In 1991 company reported $270 million charge for restructuring costs as follows: reduction in crew size and relocation costs ($125 million); sale or abandonment of 1,200 miles of line ($55 million); restoration and clean up of properties ($74 million); legal matters ($16 million). SEC 10K Report of Southern Pacific Transportation Co. (1993).

in 1978 to 1981, the SP operating ratio rose from 97.5 to 99.8.[17] From 1982 to 1995, the operating ratio was over 100 in all years but four. In the early 1980s, the economic recession had a severe impact on earnings. In September 1982, the ICC approved the Union Pacific acquisition of the Missouri Pacific and the Western Pacific.[18] The long-term exchange of trains between Union Pacific and Southern Pacific at Ogden, Utah went into decline. The number of carloads exchanged dropped from 165,237 in 1981 to 36,789 in 1987.[19]

The Union Pacific merger of the Missouri Pacific and the Western Pacific made UP able to offer shippers single line service from the Pacific Northwest and San Francisco area directly to the Southeast and the Gulf. The ICC attempted to offset Southern Pacific revenue losses by conditioning the merger on SP receiving trackage rights from Kansas City to St. Louis and the Rio

Grande receiving trackage rights to Kansas City.[20] But the Union Pacific estimated it would still divert $33.2 million in annual revenues from Southern Pacific.[21] The SP estimated the likely diversion of its revenues per year at $105 million with a net operating revenue loss of $30 million.[22] Because of the many factors affecting the demand for rail services, it is not possible to measure the actual diversion effects on each rival carrier. Many factors impeded the rise in freight revenues of the Southern Pacific in the 1980s. In 1978, the SP subsidiary, St. Louis Southwestern Railway, contracted to buy the bankrupt Rock Island Railroad's line between Santa Rosa, New Mexico and St. Louis, Missouri. This purchase for $57 million was finally approved by the ICC in June, 1980.[23] This so-called Tucumcari line enabled SP to reduce its route milage between Los Angeles and St. Louis by 400 miles. But the only part of the line that SP would use as a main line was the 604-mile route from Santa Rosa to Topeka, Kansas. Maintenance on this line had been so neglected SP had to spend $97 million on rehabilitation.[24] Traffic on the line had fallen off in the 1970s as shippers switched to rival Santa Fe. As of 1982, SP had to face the issue of how to convince shippers to divert traffic back to its new and restored route. Where possible, SP rerouted its traffic from its Cotton Belt route and from the Ogden gateway traffic to the Tucumcari route

Among the difficulties for the Southern Pacific were its investments in non-rail activities. SP controlled Sprint, one of the first long-distance telephone firms to enter competition with A.T.&T.[25] After deregulation in the telecommunications industry, SP sold Sprint because it did not have sufficient funds to expand the firm in a competitive market. Likewise, SP had invested in Ticor, a title insurance firm. But in the recession of the 1980s, the construction market for homes declined and Ticor also suffered. The most important factor affecting SP after 1980 was rate deregulation. Burlington Northern and combined Union Pacific-Missouri Pacific were larger carriers with more through routes. The new rate rivalry meant negotiation of contracts with individual shippers, but SP management was slow to meet the competition. One former marketing executive of SP was quoted as follows: "It was particularly frustrating if you were in marketing. Pricing, marketing and sales were all under different departments and all reported to different decision makers. It was almost impossible to make a coordinated marketing decision."[26]

PUBLIC INTEREST STANDARD APPLIED

The STB opinion reminds us that the first element of public interest is public benefits:

> Public benefits may be defined as efficiency gains such as cost reductions, cost savings, and service improvements. Cost reductions are public benefits because they permit a railroad to provide the same level of rail services with fewer resources or a greater level of rail services with the same resources. An integrated railroad can realize additional benefits by capitalizing on the economies of scale, scope, and density which stem from expanded operations.[27]

But cost reductions as public benefits are realized by consumers only if the carriers operate under workably competitive conditions, so that the STB must make some estimates of likely competitive effects of mergers. The STB concluded as follows:

> Despite significant parallel aspects examined below, the merger as conditioned clearly will be pro-competitive in the sense that it will stimulate price and service competition in markets served by the merged carriers. The merger will create a more efficient and competitive UP/SP system competing head-to-head throughout the West with BNSF, whose efficiency was greatly enhanced by its recent merger. UP/SP customers will benefit from tremendous service improvement brought about by reductions in route milage, extended single-line service, enhanced equipment supply, better service reliability, and new operating efficiencies.[28]

A key issue here is that the operating efficiencies of the UP-SP merger would not only enable service rivalry with BNSF but would also lead to innovations that made for more effective competition with motor carriers.[29] This would especially apply to intermodal traffic.

The estimated public benefits by the carriers that were approved by the STB are reported in Table 7.3. Since the estimated shipper savings were not internal to the railroads, the STB found the realizable public benefits from more efficient operations to be $534.3 million per year.[30] The merged firm would combine and consolidate operations at common terminals, establish new blocks of freight cars and new trains to lower costs and improve service, and consolidate functions such as transportation, maintenance of equipment, engineering, information, purchasing and marketing. Major savings in labor would result from combining administrative functions and departments, reducing staff and office space. The merging carriers estimated the labor impact of the merger would be 4,909 jobs abolished, 2,132 jobs transferred, and 1,522 jobs created.[31]

A key element of savings in operations is the creation of more efficient routes, which, in term mean more single-line service for shippers. As UP and SP combined to provide single-line service between points on both lines, shipping time would be markedly reduced. More than 350,000 cars, trailers and containers, carrying 26 million tons of freight, would gain single-line service each year.[32] BN-Santa Fe trackage rights over the new UP-SP would add single-line service for another 120,000 cars per year. A list of the key improved joint routings follows:[33]

Table 7.3. Union Pacific-Southern Pacific Merger Surface Transportation Board's Restatement of Cost Savings (Millions of Dollars).

Operating Benefits	
Labor Saving	$261.2
Car Use	12.2
Communications/Computers	14.2
Operations	116.5
General/Administrative	129.7
Subtotal	534.3
SHIPPER LOGISTICS SAVING	93.1
TOTAL BENEFITS	627.4

Source: Union Pacific Corp.-Control and Merger-Southern Pacific Rail Corp., 1 S.T.B. 376 (1996).

(1) California-Dallas-Memphis via SP from Los Angeles to El Paso and UP (MP) from El Paso to Memphis.
(2) Northern California-Midwest via SP from Oakland to Ogden and UP from Ogden to Fremont and over the North Western into Chicago.
(3) Southern California-Midwest: upgrade SP route from El Paso to Topeka with centralized traffic control and adequate sidings. UP-SP expected to spend over $360 million, an amount SP could not generate.
(4) Pacific Northwest-Texas by linking UP and SP route networks in Texas with SP route from Fort Worth to Denver and UP routes from Denver to the states in the Northwest.
(5) Colorado-Utah Coal Route via SP and UP to Denver, thereby avoiding steep grades, and over UP from Denver to Kansas City.
(6) Kansas City Bypass for coal and heavy grain unit trains using UP line in Central Kansas and upgrading UP's OKT Route from Wichita to Fort Worth.
(7) California-Laredo via SP from Los Angels to San Antonio and then UP line to Laredo.

Another key result of the merger would be financial rescue of the SP. As noted in Table 7.2, the SP had negative net revenue from operations in most prior years. The STB concluded that there was convincing evidence of SP's financial status as follows:

SP's competitive position is eroding, and will continue to do so, because of its inability to generate sufficient capital to provide quality service. Other than in one unrepresentative year, 1994, SP has historically been financially weak and unprofitable, relying heavily on large real estate sales to generate necessary cash flows. SP cannot continue to generate funds from this source, however, because it has a dwindling amount of marketable real estate for sale. As applicants note, SP's unsecured credit now has "junk bond status" and it is unable to secure additional funds from its lenders because it cannot meet the earnings test of its loan covenants.[34]

As a remedy, the merged UP-SP would spend $1.3 billion over four years to upgrade SP rail lines and facilities and build new terminals and yards.[35] UP-SP planned to invest $221.4 million to add over 100 miles of double trackage to the Sunset Route, $145.8 million to make the Tucumcari line a high-speed route, and $125.4 million to upgrade UP's Texas & Pacific (MP) line from El Paso to Memphis. UP would also invest more than $250 million in new intermodal terminals in Los Angeles, Kansas City and points in Texas. They would also expand intermodal facilities in major cities in the West. Thus, the former SP would become part of a large, healthy rail system with financial strength to sustain efficient operations and maintain investment in a functioning rail system.[36]

TRACKAGE RIGHTS TO MAINTAIN MARKET RIVALRY

The effects of the merger would be to reduce some shippers from having the choice of three rail carriers to only two rail carriers. A lesser number of shippers would be reduced from two possible rail carriers to one. The remedy to the possible loss of market rivalry between carriers was to assure shippers they would have at least two alternate carriers. This was accomplished by UP-SP granting trackage rights over 3,698 miles of its lines to BNSF.[37]

The longest trackage rights received by BNSF are over SP lines from Denver to Oakland, CA(1,385 miles), and over UP from Salt Lake City to Stockton, CA.[38] In eastern Nevada, these lines are paired so that one carries traffic west and the other carries traffic east. These are bridge rights for the movement of overhead traffic only except local access to industries served by UP and SP and no other railroad. This access illustrates the objective of assuring shippers the benefit of service by two carriers.

As to the route from Houston to New Orleans, BNSF was to exercise its option to acquire the SP line of 188.4 miles between Avondale, LA and Iowa Junction, LA, and receive trackage rights between Iowa Junction and Houston.[39] As to the route from Houston to Memphis and St. Louis, BNSF was to receive trackage rights over UP in Arkansas and over SP from Houston to Arkansas.[40] This trackage was unprecedented in that it covered an area of the South not previously served by the BNSF. In effect it carried out part of a settlement agreement between the carriers and the Chemical Manufacturers Association to assure that the plants of their members were served by both UP-SP and BNSF.[41] As to the route from Houston to Brownsville, BNSF trackage rights would enable it to offer rival service to Corpus Christe, Harlingen, and Brownsville, including interchange with Mexican carriers.[42] As to the route from Houston to San Antonio, BNSF received trackage rights over UP.[43]

In addition to trackage rights, BNSF was allowed to purchase the UP (former Western Pacific) line of 111.8 miles from Keddie, CA to Beiber, CA.[44] This created a second route from central California to Portland and thus gave shippers the possibility of new rival service to the SP and to motor carriers through California from Mexico to Canada.[45] In order to facilitate this new rivalry, BNSF agreed to grant UP-SP overhead trackage rights over a 68 mile line from Chemult, OR to Bend, OR.[46]

The effect of the extensive trackage rights for BNSF was to assure almost all shippers that they could be served by 2 carriers. Potential rate rivalry might not be the most important factor for assuring possible service from two carriers. Shippers are more concerned with having available service from two carriers because one carrier may have difficulties supplying freight cars, maintaining train schedules, offering terminal support, or other aspects of poor services. Thus, service rivalry of two financially strong carriers may be needed to promote efficiency.

The key issue raised by the Department of Justice and other protestants to the merger was whether reducing the number of western railroads from two financially strong carriers, BNSF and UP, plus one financially weak one, SP, to only two carriers would lessen competition.[47] Would the duopoly resulting form the merger be more likely to result in tacit collusion in rate making? The conclusion of the STB was No, as it pointed out that western rail service was a rapidly evolving market.[48] In its largest market, from Los Angles to Chicago, a financially weak SP faced increasing rivalry from the newly merged BNSF. On this route BNSF was investing substantial capital in double-tracking and improved signaling. A revitalized UP-SP would be in a much improved position to compete aggressively.

STB noted that efficiency savings expected from this merger were substantial. Since 1980, many railroads that have reduced costs through mergers and market incentives initiated by the Staggers Act. Consequently, they have met competition by passing those savings on to shippers in terms of lower rates and improved service. STB cited an ICC study that since 1980, the number of Class 1 railroads had decreased from 26 to 10 while average rail rates per ton had declined 37.7% on an inflation adjusted basis from its peak in 1981 through 1993.[49]

The high fixed costs of railroad operations and the resultant significant economies of density of traffic also reduce the likelihood of tacit collision.[50] An increment of main line traffic not only adds earnings but also contributes to lowering average costs. Consequently, there is an incentive to railroads to compete for higher volumes of traffic. The likelihood of rate rivalry was also encouraged by the Staggers Act of 1980 which terminated the requirement to file tariffs with the ICC for each class of commodity. The railroads could enter contracts with shippers to carry goods at any bargained rate. If the shipper chose not to reveal the rate to others, confidentiality clauses in such contracts mean that rates are not revealed to other carriers.[51]

In order to make sure that the trackage rights received by BNSF would result in effective service rivalry, the STB imposed a five-year oversight period to examine whether the specific conditions had effectively addressed the competitive issues.[52] It was essential that the UPSP train dispatchers not discriminate against BNSF trains on the almost 4,000 miles of trackage rights received. Dispatching times for trains were subject to a detailed written trackage rights protocol that would ensure equal treatment of all trains without regard to ownership. The protocol ensured that each railroad could monitor in real time the handling of its trains by the other. It allowed stationing supervising employees by the tenant railroad at the owner railroad dispatching center and dispute resolution procedures.[53] STB also retained review over the level of payments charged by the owner railroad to the tenant railroad.[54]

ABANDOMENTS

As a part of the merger application, the Union Pacific and Southern Pacific sought authorization to abandon 17 line segments totaling 584 miles.[55] The carriers asserted that the lines had been used primarily for overhead traffic that after merger would be rerouted over more efficient lines of the merged carrier. Local traffic on those lines was minimal and the lines could not be maintained by revenues from that traffic. A key example was the former Chicago and North Western line from the Chicago-Omaha line at Nelson, IL south to St. Louis that Union Pacific had acquired. This Chicago-St. Louis route was 318 miles while the alternative Union Pacific route that had been acquired with Missouri Pacific was only 257 miles from St. Louis to Chicago freight yards.[56] In addition, the Southern Pacific rival route was the old Gulf, Mobile and Ohio line of 272 miles.[57] Since the merged carrier planned to reroute all through traffic from Chicago to St. Louis to the shorter lines, local traffic from the Springfield, IL area to St. Louis on the North Western route would be insufficient to support that line. The merging carriers applied to abandon 68 miles of that line and STB approved.[58]

The longest proposed abandonment was UP's former Missouri Pacific line from Pueblo, Colorado to Herington, Kansas. In this proceeding the STB approved abandonment of the 122.4 miles of the line in Colorado.[59] This in effect terminated the interstate line. The Missouri Pacific line was a secondary main line with light traffic. This had also been true of the UP Kansas Pacific line between Kansas City and Denver. It seems clear that UP management found it inefficient to maintain two secondary lines. UP's Kansas Pacific Line was now carrying heavy coal traffic and required major upgrading.[60]

FINANCIAL RESULTS AFTER MERGER

In the merger proceedings, the two carriers submitted pro forma financial statements showing expected consolidated data of the merged railroad for each of the first five years after consummation of the merger. Those statements reflected the anticipated benefits of the merger, including cost savings and diversion of traffic from other railroads.[61] These projections estimated 1997 operating revenues of $10.7 billion and an operating ratio of 82.7.[62] The subsequent years estimations were operating revenues of $10.8 billion to $10.86 billion and operating ratios declining from 80 to 79.

The actual revenues reported by Union Pacific to the Surface Transportation Board were somewhat lower than the projections. These are compiled in Table 7.4.[63] The 1997 operating revenues were $9.8 billion and the operating ratio was 87.7. The 1998 operating revenues were $9.2 billion and the operating ratio was 95.9. The 1999 operating revenues were almost $10 billion and the operating ratio was 82.3. The 2000 operating revenues were $10.5 billion and the operating ratio was 82.8.

One must conclude that the pro forma operating ratios presented to the STB were not realistic for the early post-merger years. In 1995, the year before the merger, the operating ratio of the combined Union Pacific and Chicago & North Western was 78.9, but the operating ratio of the Southern Pacific was 100.7. If one combines the revenues of UP and SP for 1995 and also combines their expenses, a joint operating ratio would be 85.6. Since the merger implementation began in late 1996, the pro forma estimate that the combined operating ratio could be reduced to 82.7 in 1997 seems unreasonable. The fact that the UP expected to spend $1.3 billion over a period of years on the SP main lines in order to increase efficiency is not consistent with a quick drop in the operating ratio. As noted, the actual UP operating ratio in 1997 was 87.7.

Table 7.4. Union Pacific Railroad Company Income Statement (Millions of Dollars).

Year	2000	1999	1998	1997	1996
Operating Revenues	10,539	9,987	9,198	9,801	6,729
Operating Expenses	8,729	8,222	8.821	8.594	5,240
Operating Income	1,810	1,765	337	1,207	1,489
Other Income	296	269	357	332	329
Miscellaneous Deductions	83	90	106	103	34
Fixed Charges	594	624	616	480	329
Contingent Interest	9	4	4	9	10
Income Taxes	494	461	−19	326	482
Net Income	926	854	27	620	963

Source: Surface Transportation Board, *Statistics of Class I Freight Railroads in the United States* (1996–2000).

Beginning in the third and fourth quarters of 1997, the UP suffered great congestion of rail operations at Houston and the coastal areas of Texas and Louisiana. By the fourth quarter of 1997 the effects had spread throughout the entire rail system and this continued into 1998.[64] The financial impact was severe. In the fourth quarter of 1997, UP had an operating loss of $56 million, and in the first half of 1998, the operating loss was $64 million.[65] In spite of the merger plan to release about 5,000 employees in other tasks, there was a shortage of train and engine employees. In order to ease the system congestion, UP focused on hiring additional train and engine employees, accelerating locomotive purchases and leases, improving management of traffic, and using outside carriers for haulage and train switching in congested areas.

The system congestion on the merged UP began in Houston at the old SP Englewood switching yard.[66] The yard had been inadequate and overloaded before the merger, and SP did not have the capital funds to expand the yard. In order to compensate for Englewood's deficiencies, SP managers would route some cars to other cities for sorting. A few hundred cars were sorted in small satellite yards in Houston, some of which cars would be ordered back to Englewood and resorted. After merger, UP's managers decided these methods were inefficient and ordered that the bulk of SP's cars be sorted at Englewood. The presumed that they could cope with greatly more cars by sending more locomotives to haul them away. But SP had a shortage of locomotives and crews to execute this plan. UP's Stettegast Yard and smaller yards in Houston also became overloaded because of the booming petrochemical business and the growing NAFTA related trade with Mexico.[67] Congestion was aggravated because the old SP line east from Houston to New Orleans had to be shut down eight hours per day for repairs.

The financial recovery of Union Pacific in 1999 and 2000 must be attributed to the completion of capital investments in rail lines and locomotives from 1997 forward. The spending, including long-term leases of locomotives, exceeded $2 billion per year.[68] In 1999, nearly $500 million was spent on locomotives to replace 1,500 aging inefficient ones in the fleets of the Chicago & North Western and SP.[69]

The largest part of the capital investments were for engineering and maintenance-of-way projects. In 1999, UP completed a $327 million project to triple-track 108 miles of its main line from North Platte to Gibbon, Nebraska that carried the coal trains from the Powder River Basin in Wyoming to the main line cutting south to Topeka, Kansas City and power plants in the South.[70] This segment of the main line to Chicago was the busiest rail line in the United States, carrying 140 trains daily. In 2000, the plans were to finish double-tracking the 142-mile main line south from Gibbon to Marysville, Kan., the line to Kansas City.[71] This was part of the $187 million to be spent in 1999 to increase the capacity of rail lines from the Powder River Basin to Kansas City.

The next priority for UP was continuing the upgrading of the Tucumcari line.[72] This line plus the old SP Sunset line from Los Angeles to El Paso provided a shorter route from Southern California to Chicago than UP's main line through Salt Lake City. Furthermore, the grades were less and the weather better. Additional investments were to be made in centralized traffic control and more sidings. One short congested segment was to be double-tracked. Added investments to improve operations were continuing in the Gulf Coast and the Laredo gateway to Mexico.

CONCLUSION

The 1996 merger of the Union Pacific Railroad and Southern Pacific Transportation Co. created a combined carrier with 38,366 miles of line. Like some of the earlier mergers, this one was response. As shown in Chapter 6, the merger of the Burlington Northern and the Santa Fe created a carrier offering single-line freight service throughout the West. The Union Pacific acquisition of the Southern Pacific created a similar carrier able to offer single-line service across the West as a strong rival to the BN-Santa Fe.

A key financial factor in the background to this merger was the strong financial condition of the Union Pacific and the weak financial condition of the

Southern Pacific as a rival carrier. A key result of this merger was to provide the former Southern Pacific lines with sufficient funding to maintain those lines and their equipment at high standards. For example, rail service between the Midwest and Los Angeles had to compete with the high service standards of the former Santa Fe, now part of Burlington-Santa Fe.

The estimated cost reductions of $534 million per year were $90 million more than the Burlington Northern-Santa Fe estimated savings. Labor savings were the largest part for the new UP-SP, estimated at $26 million with over 4900 jobs abolished. Single line service on new joint routes of UP and SP were estimated to reduce shipping times greatly.

Trackage rights over 3,698 miles of line of the new UP-SF were granted to the BN-Santa Fe. The precedent for this was explained in chapter 6 where BN-Santa entered settlement agreement with UP and with SP to grant substantial trackage rights so that most shippers would be assured the services of two rival carriers. The most striking portion of these trackage rights were 1,385 miles from Denver to Oakland, CA. Because the UP had acquired the Western Pacific in 1982, the UP and the SP together owned the only two lines from Utah to northern California. The effect of these trackage rights was to give direct access from Colorado to the ports of the San Francisco area that neither the Burlington Northern nor the Santa Fe had ever had before. Similar unprecedented trackage rights were granted to BNSF over the UP lines in Arkansas to Houston. Neither the Burlington Northern nor the Santa Fe had previously served that area of the South.

NOTES

1. Union Pacific Corp.-Control and Merger-Southern Pacific Rail Corp., 1 STB 233 (1996) (Noted below as UP-SP).
2. Association of American Railroads, *Analysis of Class 1 Railroads* 60 (1995). The miles of road excluding trackage rights over other railroads was 20,154.
3. Union Pac. Corp.-Control-Chicago & N. W. Transp. Co., I.C.C. Docket No. 32133 (Feb. 21, 1995)(not printed). See David M. Cawthorne, *ICC Approves Union Pacific Control of C&NW*, 241 Traffic World 60 (Mar. 13, 1995).
4. See Chapter 2, *supra*, following text note 18.
5. Union Pacific RR. et al.-Trackage Rights Over CNW, 7 I.C.C. 2d 177 (1990).
6. *Id.*, at 184.
7. Union Pacific Corp., et al.-Control-CNW, 9 I.C.C. 2d 939 (1993).
8. Cawthorne, *ICC Approves Union Pacific Control, supra*, note 3, at 61.
9. See 243 Traffic World 25 (July 3, 1995).
10. Ass'n of Am. R. R., *Analysis, supra* note 2, at 61. The miles of road excluding trackage rights over other railroads was 11,860.
11. Rio Grande Industries et al.-Control-SPT Co. et al., 4 I.C.C. 2d 834 (1988), *affirmed*, Kansas City Southern Industries, Inc. v. I.C.C., 902 F.2d 423 (5th Cir. 1990).

12. Santa Fe Southern Pacific Corp.-Control-S. Pac. Transp. Co., 2 I.C.C. 2d 709, 726–807 (1986), *rehearing denied*, 3 I.C.C. 2d 926 (1987). See Allen R. Wastler and Bob Poos, *Santa Fe-Southern Pacific Merger Rejected by ICC as Anticompetitive*, 207 Traffic World 8 (July 28, 1986); Russell Pittman, *Railroads and Competition: The Santa Fe/Southern Pacific Merger Proposal*, 39 J. Industrial Economics 25 (1990).
13. 4 I.C.C. 2d at 844.
14. *Id.*, at 860-861.
15. *Id.*, at 876.
16. *Moody's Transportation Manual* 257 (1986).
17. *Id.* at 266 (1991).
18. Union Pacific-Control-Missouri Pacific; Western Pacific, 366 I.C.C. 462 (1982).
19. Rio Grande Industries-Control-SPT Co. et al., 4 I.C.C. 2d 834, 892 (1988).
20. See Chapter 6, notes 9 and 10 and accompanying text.
21. Union Pacific-Control- Missouri Pacific; Western Pacific, 366 I.C.C. at 712.
22. *Id.*, at 738.
23. St. Louis Southwestern Ry.-Purchase-Rock Island (Tucumcari), 363 I.C.C. 320, 328 (1980). The agreement included assignment to SP of Rock Island's trackage rights over the UP route from Topeka to Kansas City. *Id.*, at 364-366.
24. *Business Week* 120 (May 3, 1982).
25. Bob Poos, *Many Factors Contributed to Once-Mighty SP's Fall*, 211 Traffic World 10 (Aug. 10, 1987).
26. *Id.*, at 12.
27. UP-SP, *supra* note 1, at 363.
28. *Id.*, at 375. See Salvatore Massa, *Are All Railroad Mergers in the Public Interest? An Analysis of the Union Pacific Merger with Southern Pacific*, 24 Transportation Law J. 413, 425–427 (1997).
29. See Robert E. Gallamore, *Regulation and Innovation: Lessons from the American Railroad Industry*, in José A. Gómez et al., editors, Essays in Transportation Economics and Policy 511-516 (Washington D.C.: Brookings Institution Press, 1999).
30. UP-SP, *supra* note 1, at 376.
31. *Id.*, at 252.
32. *Id.*, at 381.
33. *Id.*, at 564.
34. *Id.*, at 383.
35. *Id.*, at 381.
36. *Id.*, at 381–382.
37. *Id.*, at 253, 562. See Massa, *Are All Railroad Mergers in the Public Interest?*, *supra* note 28, at 430–434.
38. UP-SP, *supra* note 1, at 562.
38. *Id.*, at 407-408.
40. *Id.*, at 408, 563.
41. *Id.*, at 254, 371, 394.
42. *Id.*, at 409–410.
43. *Id.*, at 410--411.
44. *Id.*, at 253.
45. *Id.*, at 564–565. As to increased rail rivalry for motor carriers, see John Gallagher, *Hitting the I-5*, 264 Traffic World 36 (Oct. 16, 2000).

46. UP-SP, *supra*, note 1, at 563.
47. *Id.*, at 350, 369.
48. *Id.*, at 370.
49. *Id.*, at 370, 387, citing U.S., I.C.C., Office of Economic and Environmental Analysis, *Rail Rates Continue Multi-Year Decline* (1995). In 1994, Class 1 railroads were redefined as those with operating revenues of at least $256 million per year.
50. UP-SP, *supra* note 1, at 570. See John M. Clark, *Studies in the Economics of Overhead Costs* 51–55 (Chicago: University of Chicago Press, 1923).
51. UP-SP, *supra* note 1, at 570.
52. *Id.*, at 373.
53. *Id.*, at 403.
54. *Id.*, at 413-417.
55. *Id.*, at 487-489.
56. U.S. Dept. of Transportation, *Final Standards Classification, and Designation of Lines of Class 1 Railroads in the United States*, Vol. 1, at A3-14 (1977).
57. *Id.* See Rio Grande-Purchase-Trackage Rights-Chicago, Missouri & Western between St. Louis and Chicago, 5 I.C.C. 2d 952 (1989); Ira Rosenfeld and James Abbott, *SP Buys CM&W St. Louis Line, Gets Second Foot in Chicago*, 219 Traffic World 17 (Aug. 14, 1989).
58. UP-SP, *supra* note 1, at 497–504. Norfolk and Western Railway had acquired trackage rights over a 15.4 mile segment of this line in 1981. Norfolk & Western Ry. Co.-Purchase-Illinois Term. R. Co., 363 I.C.C. 882, 894 (1981).
59. UP-SP, *supra* note 1, at 525. This abandonment was from Towner on the border with Kansas west to North Avondale. The additional 16 miles west to Pueblo was jointly operated with the Santa Fe and was part of the Santa Fe main line to Denver.
60. Lawrence H. Kaufman, *Capital Investment: UP's Catch-Up Strategy*, Railway Age 33, 35 (Nov., 1999).
61. UP-SP, *supra* note 1, at 457–459.
62. *Id.*, at 576.
63. The revenues and expenses of Union Pacific Railroad Co. and Subsidiaries, as reported to the Securities and Exchange Commission were somewhat higher. Stated in millions of dollars, these amounts were as follows:

Year	2000	1999	1998	1997	1996
Operating Revenues	$10,731	$10,140	$9,329	$9,981	$7,680
Operating Expenses	8,828	8,318	8,896	8,728	6,078
Operating Income	1,903	1,822	433	1,253	1,602

Source: Union Pacific Railroad Co., 10K Reports to the S.E.C. (1996-2000).
64. Union Pacific Railroad Co., 10K Report to the S.E.C. F21 (1998).
65. *Id.*, at F20.
66. Brian O'Reilly, *The Wreck of the Union Pacific*, 137 Fortune 94, 98 (Mar. 30, 1998).
67. *Id.*
68. Kaufman, *Capital Investment*, *supra* note 60, at 33.

69. *Id.*, at 34. As to the importance of the Electro-Motive Division of General Motors in the building of locomotives, see William C. Vantuono, *Power Play*, Railway Age 33 (July, 2000).
70. Kaufman, *Capital Investment*, *supra* note 60, at 34.
71. *Id.*, at 35.
72. *Id.*

APPENDIX: MAPS

CHICAGO, ROCK ISLAND AND PACIFIC RAILROAD

Chapter 2

CHICAGO, MILWAUKEE, ST. PAUL AND PACIFIC R.R.

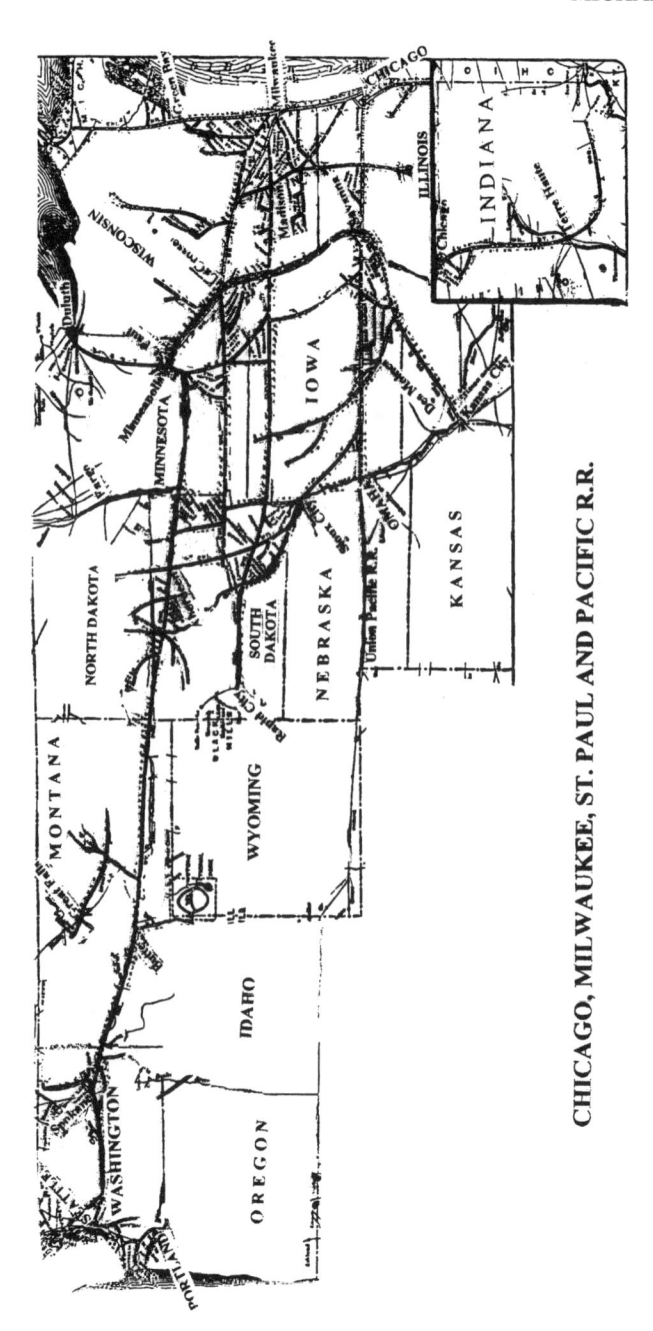

Chapter 3

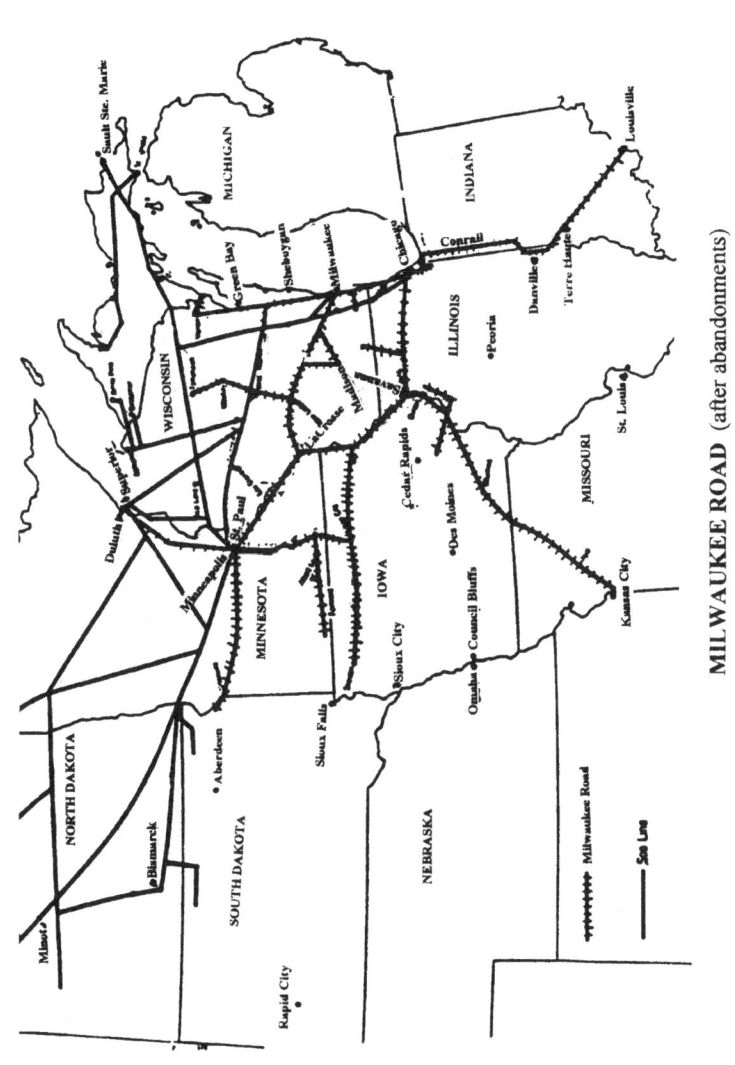

Appendix: Maps 137

MILWAUKEE ROAD (after abandonments)

SOO LINE ACQUISITION

Chapter 3

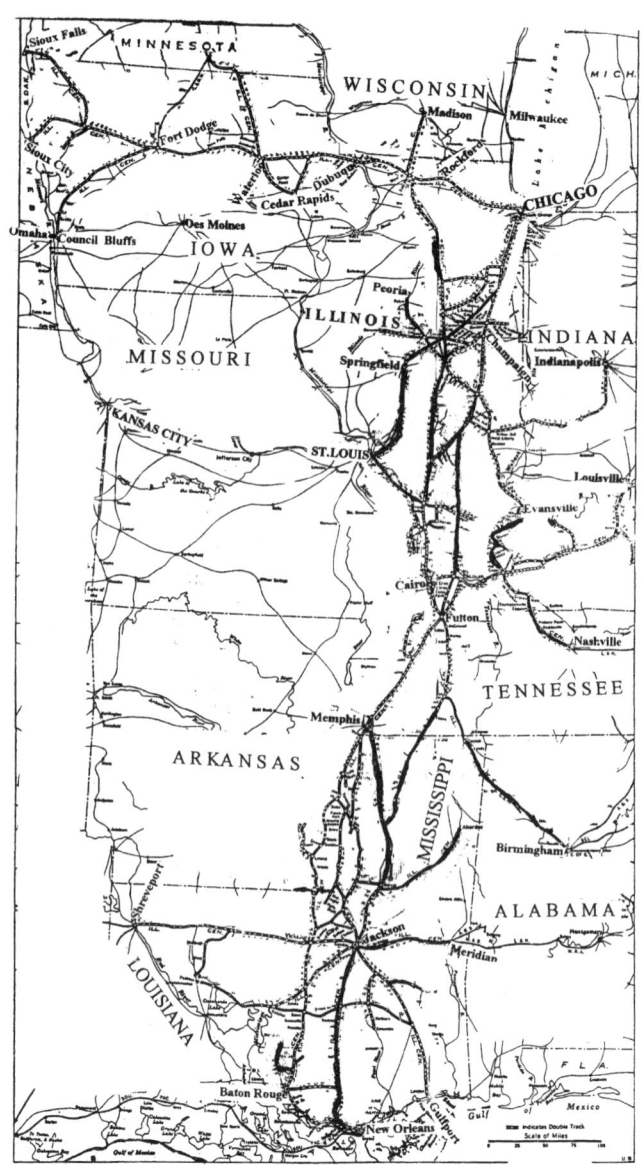

ILLINOIS CENTRAL RAILROAD
(Before merger of the Gulf, Mobile & Ohio)

Chapter 4

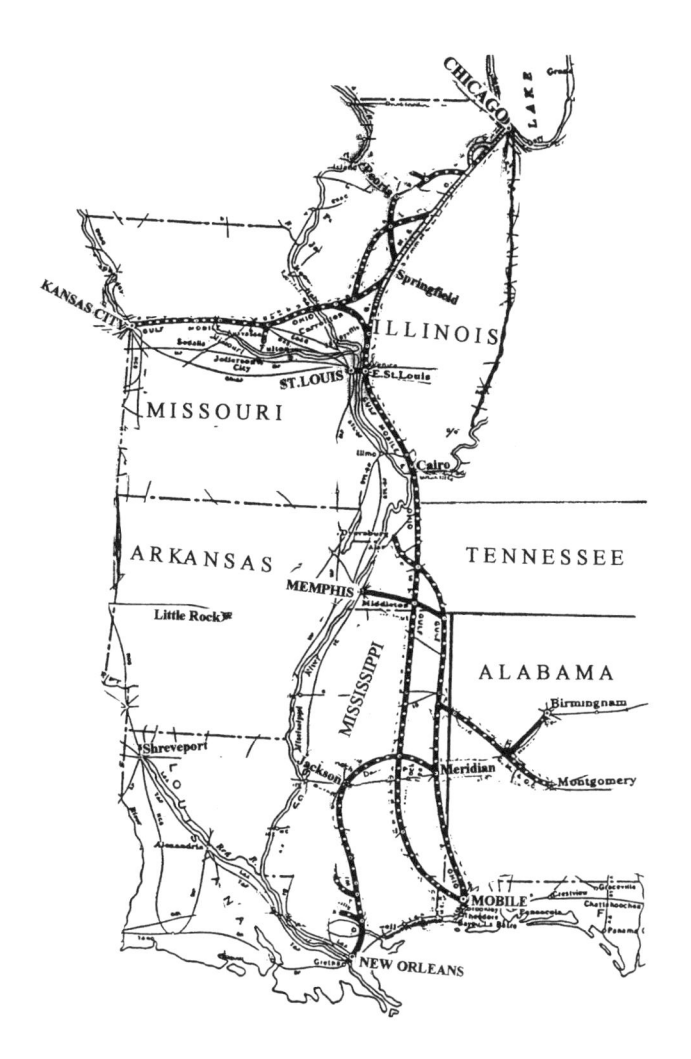

Appendix: Maps   139

GULF MOBILE AND OHIO R.R.

Chapter 4

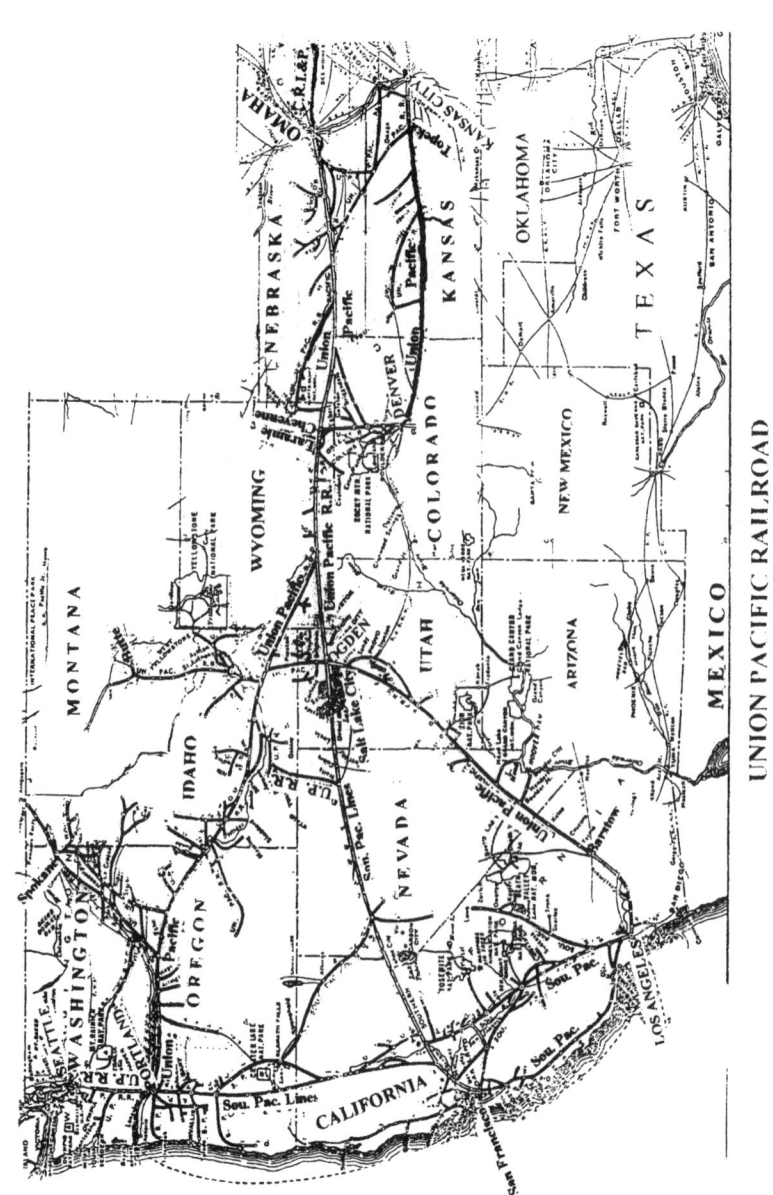

UNION PACIFIC RAILROAD

Chapter 5

Appendix: Maps

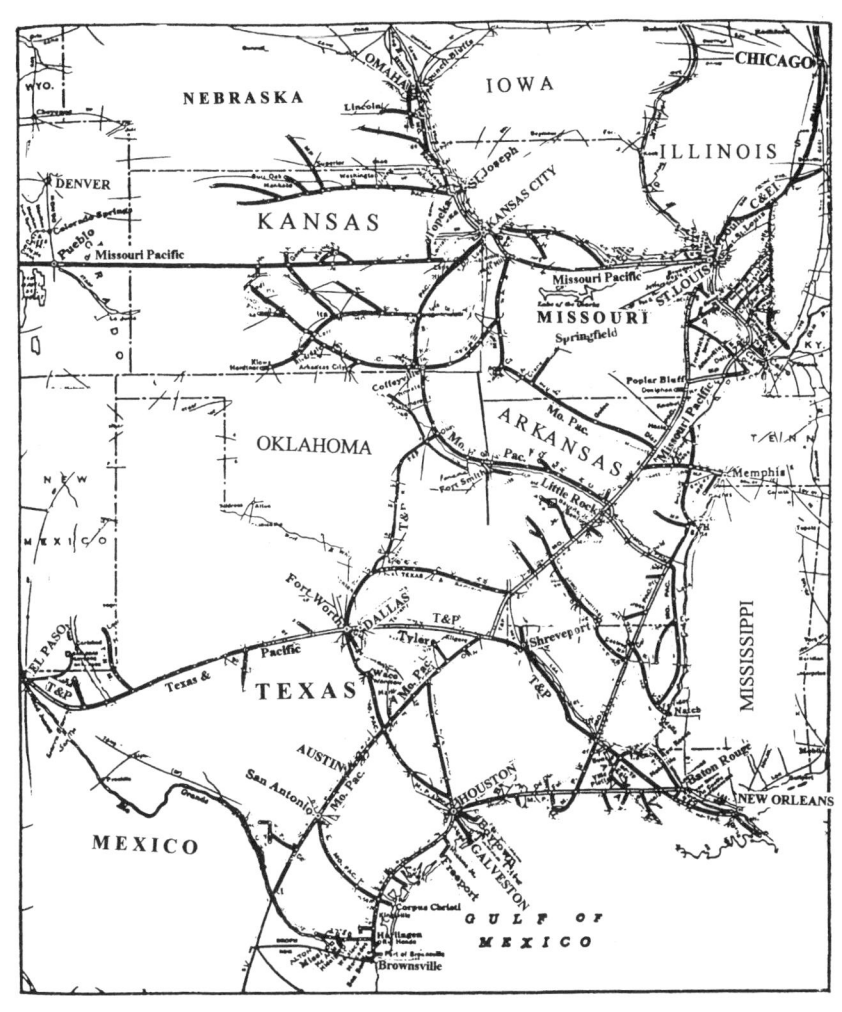

MISSOURI PACIFIC RAILROAD

Chapter 5

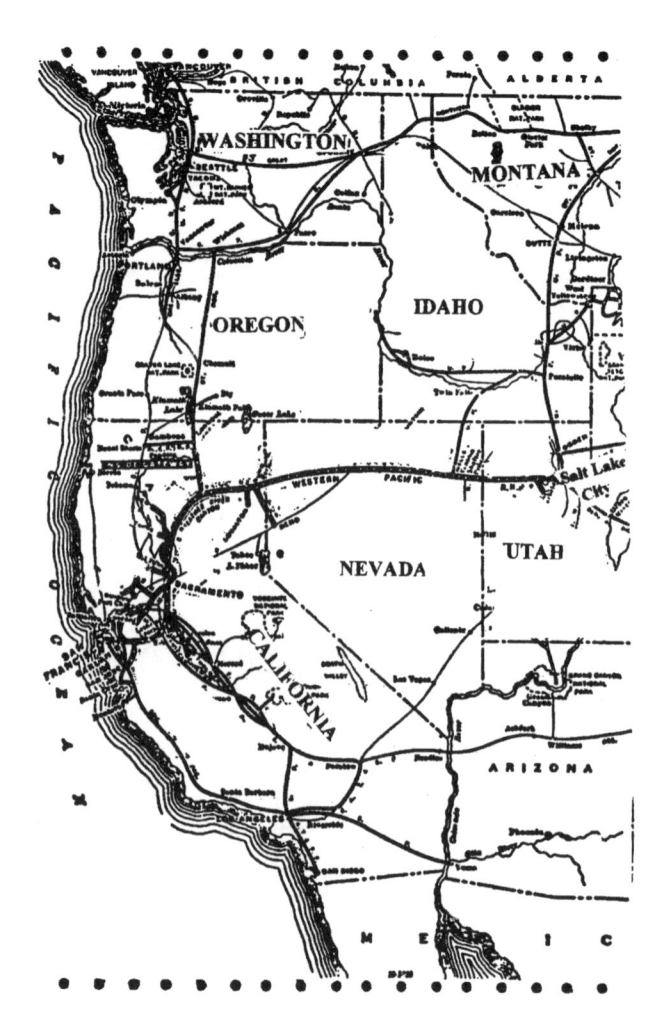

WESTERN PACIFIC RAILROAD

Chapter 5

Appendix: Maps 143

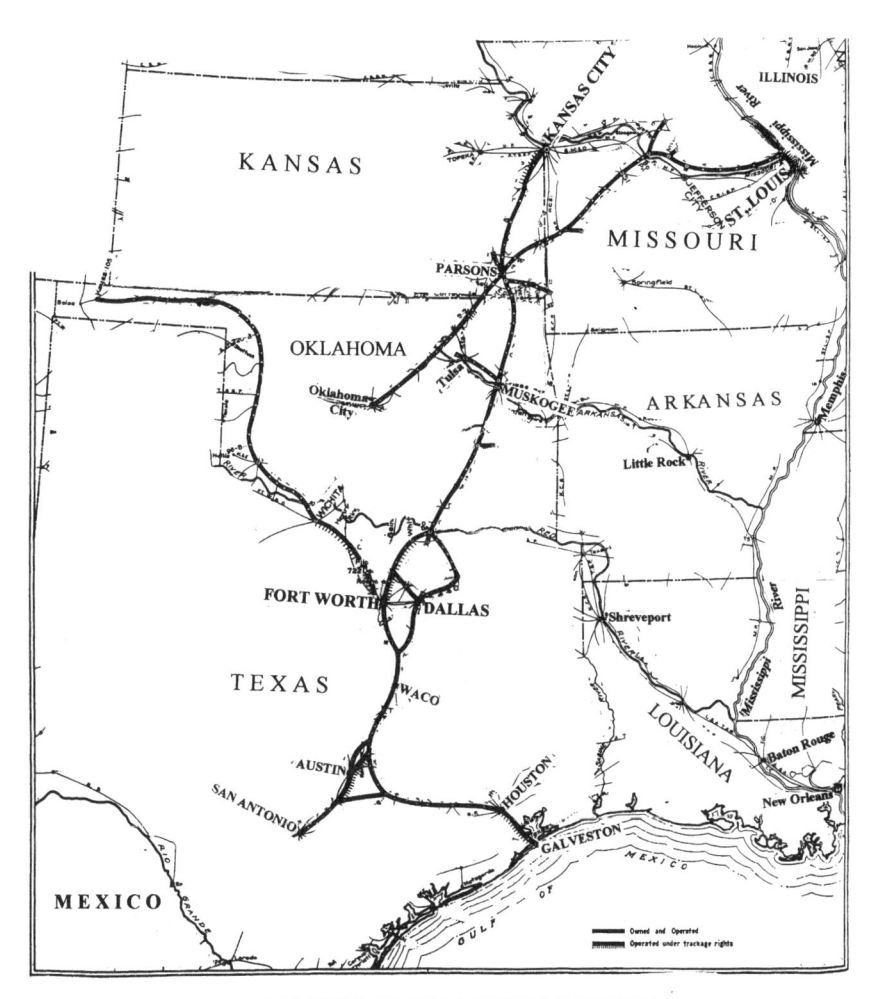

MISSOURI-KANSAS-TEXAS RAILROAD

Chapter 5

BURLINGTON NORTHERN

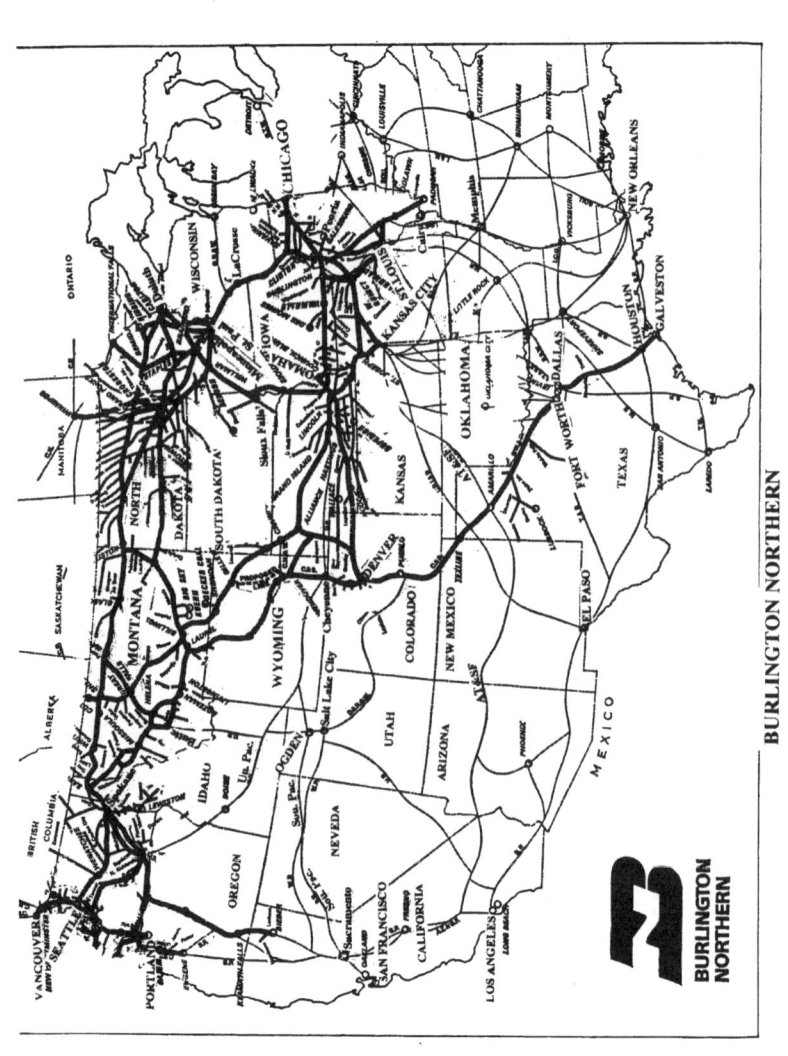

Chapter 6

Appendix: Maps

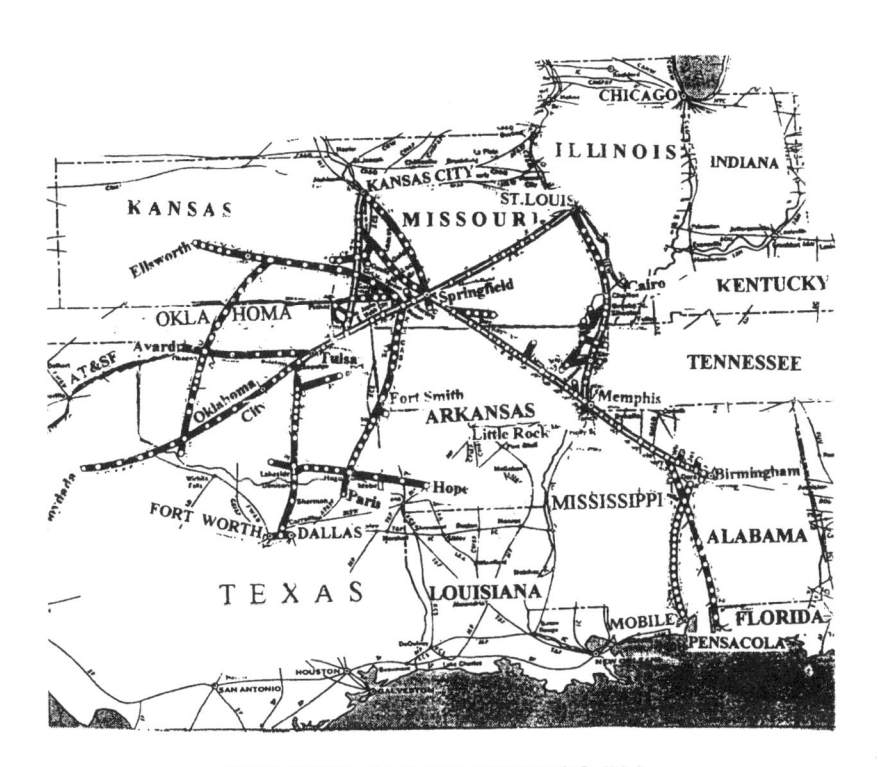

ST.LOUIS-SAN FRANCISCO RY.

Chapter 6

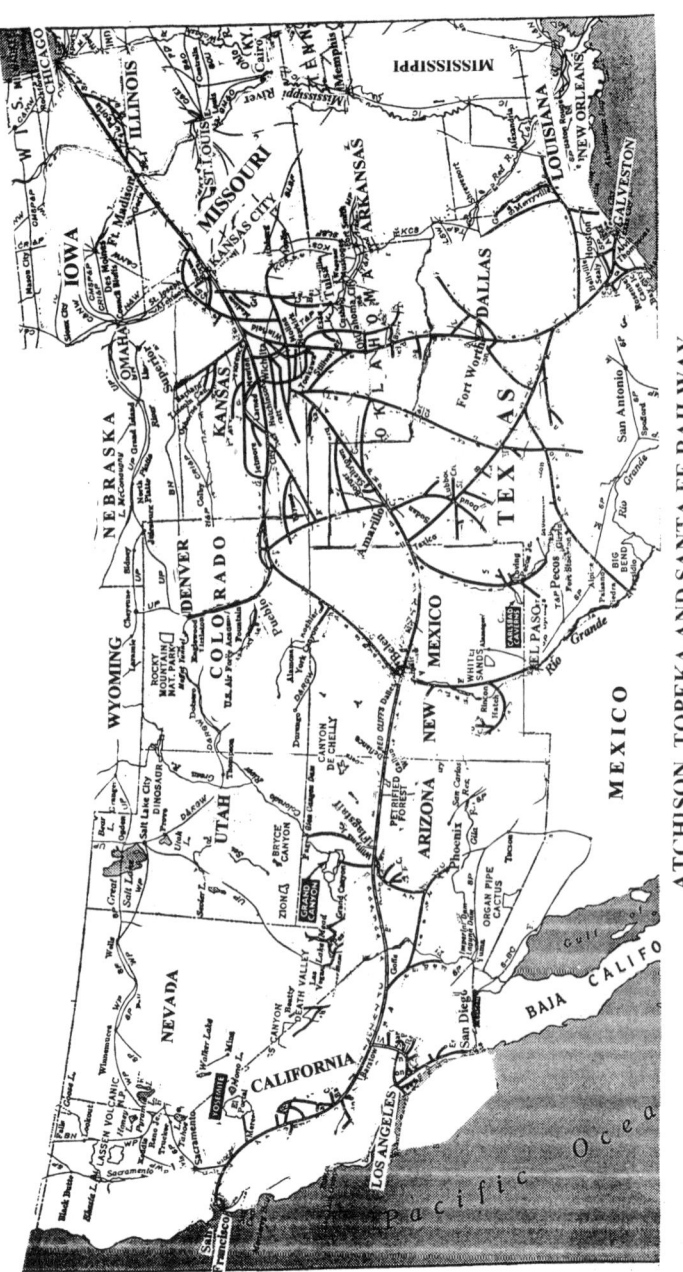

ATCHISON, TOPEKA AND SANTA FE RAILWAY

Appendix: Maps 147

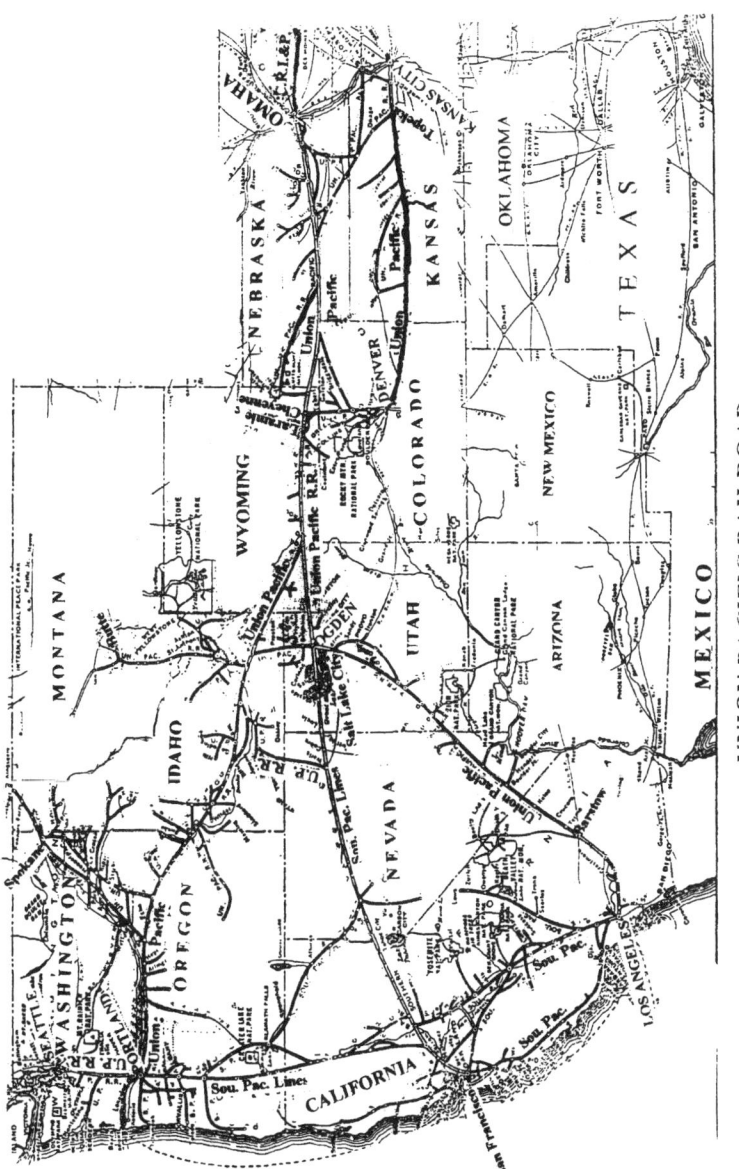

UNION PACIFIC RAILROAD

Chapter 7

CHICAGO AND NORTH WESTERN RAILWAY

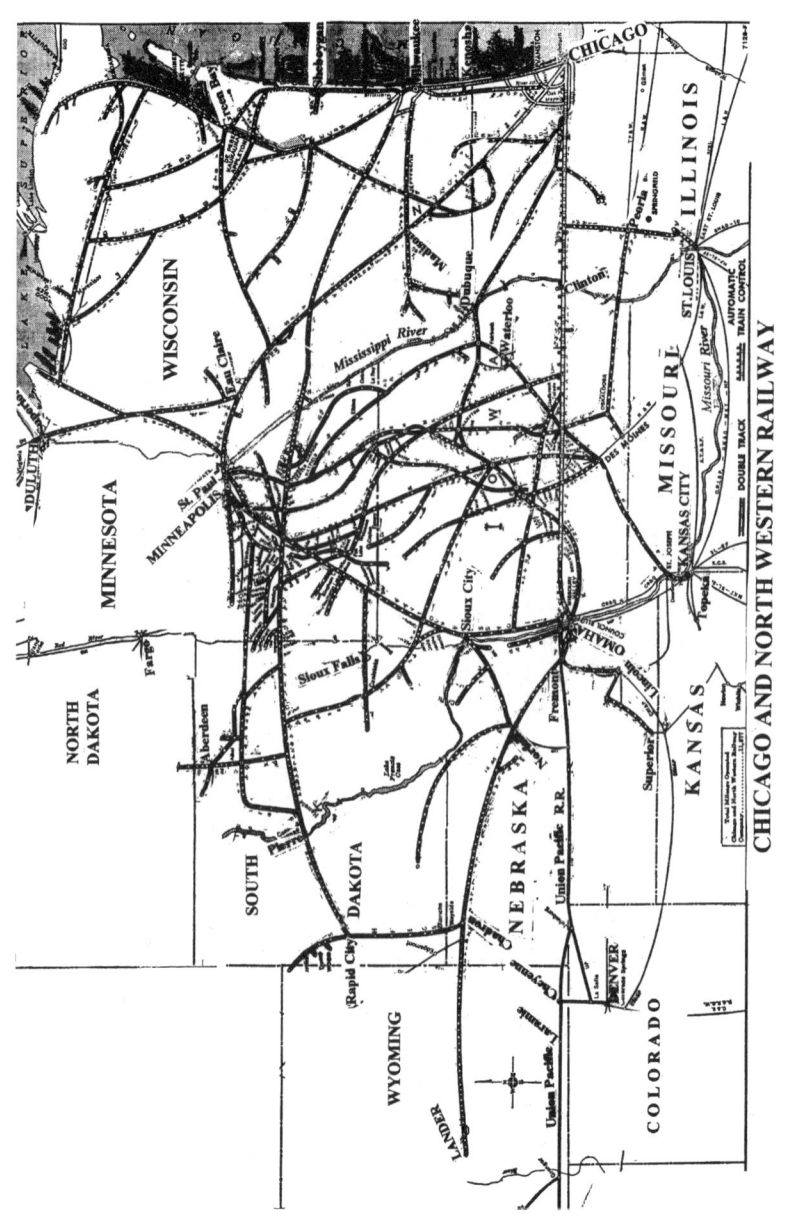

Chapter 7

Appendix: Maps 149

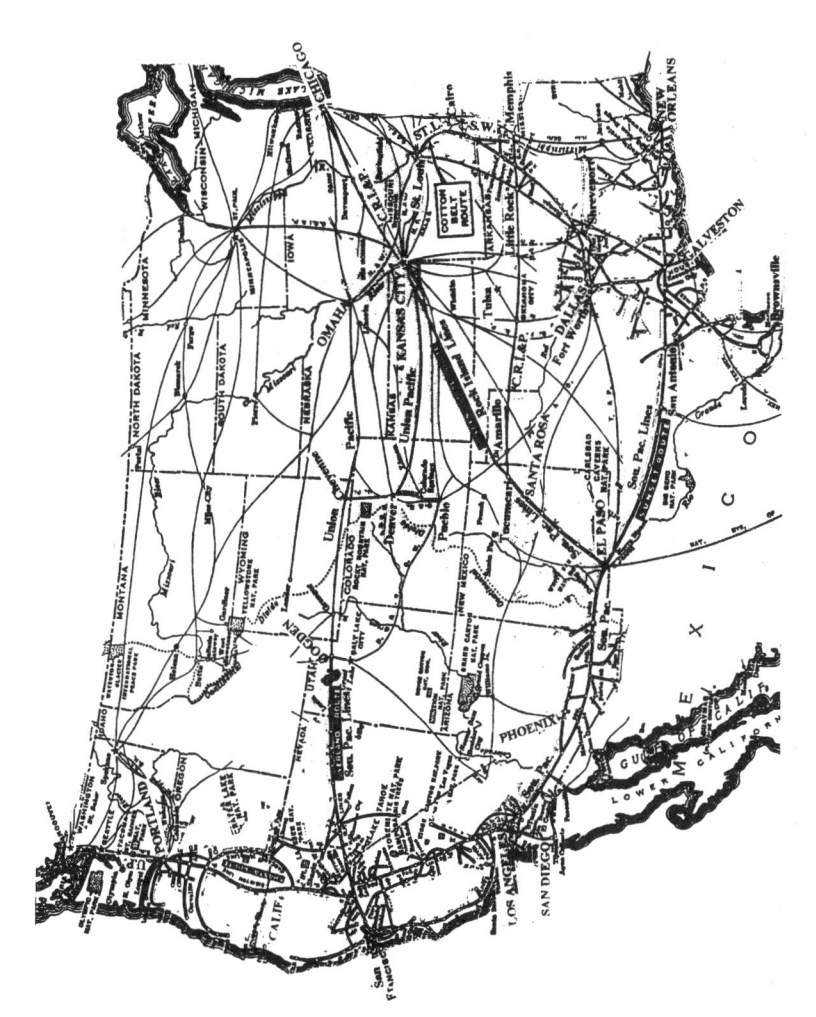

SOUTHERN PACIFIC RAILROAD
Chapter 7

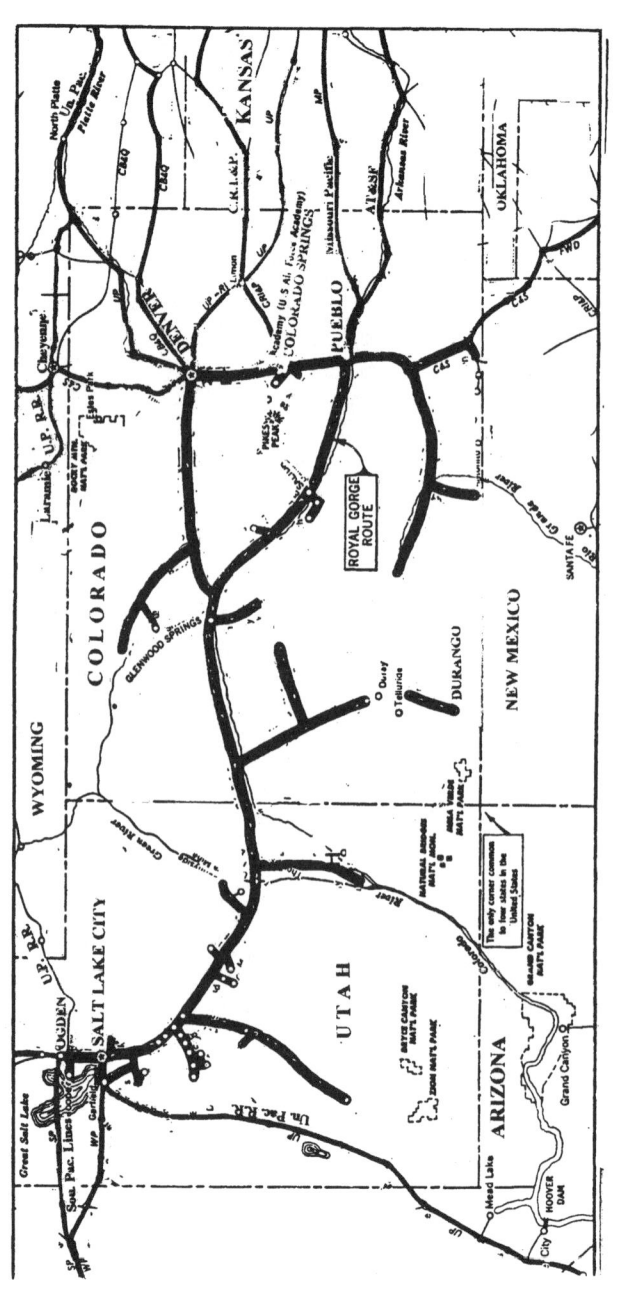

DENVER AND RIO GRANDE WESTERN RAILROAD

Chapter 7

INDEX

Abandonments, 3, 10, 14–16, 20, 21, 23, 33, 41, 43, 50, 56, 58, 60, 80, 86, 99, 116
Amtrak, 2, 21, 53, 72, 77
Antitrust Division, 73, 74, 105, 118, 125 [see Justcie Dep't]
Atchison, Topeka and Santa Fe Railway (*See* Santa Fe), 104

Bankruptcy reorganization
   Chicago, Missouri & Western, 79, 80
   Milwaukee Road, 5, 47, 55–58
   Rock Island Lines, 5, 27, 37–41
Booz, Allen & Hamilton, 56
Brooks-Scanlon v. Railroad Commission, 2
Burlington Northern, 5, 6, 7, 9, 16, 28, 30, 31, 39, 48–50, 52, 57, 59, 61, 63, 65, 68, 97, 100, 113–117, 119, 122, 130
   acquired St. Louis-San Francisco, 103–105
   acquired Santa Fe, 105, 106
   control in public interest, 106–109
   description, 105
   financial analysis, 109–110
   impact of merger, 110–113
   settlement agreements, 107, 108
   traffic density, 6
Burlington Northern Santa Fe, 109

Canadian National Railway, 58, 83–86, 88
Cedar Valley Railroad, 79, 82
Central Wisconsin Railroad, 79
Chemical Manufacturers Association, 125
Chicago & Alton Railroad, 72
Chicago & Eastern Illinois Railroad, 28, 91

Chicago & North Western Railroad, 5, 9, 10, 17, 24, 28, 30, 31, 37, 39, 41, 42, 44, 63, 65, 66
   acquired by Union Pacific, 117
   acquired Rock Island segment, 39
   bid for Milwaukee Road core, 58–61
   traffic density, 6
Chicago, Central & Pacific Railroad, 79, 81, 82, 84
Chicago Regional Transportation Authority, 33, 39, 53, 57
Chicago, Milwaukee, St. Paul & Pacific Railroad (*See* Milwaukee Road)
Chicago, Missouri & Western Railroad, 79, 80
Chicago, Rock Island & Pacific Railroad (*See* Rock Island Lines)
Colorado & Southern Railroad, 111
Consolidated Rail Corp. (Conrail), 2, 7, 11, 58, 68
Cost structures, 75, 115
Cross-subsidization, 1, 3, 9, 20

Dakota Minnesota & Eastern Railroad, 18, 24
Deferred Maintenance, 24, 30, 33, 40, 43, 50, 53, 54, 65, 78, 80, 95
Denver & Rio Grande Western Railroad, 40, 91
   acquired Southern Pacific, 118
Deregulation, 11, 24, 25, 61, 74, 85, 100, 122
   effects, 16–19
Dodge, Edwin, 63
DT&I Conditions, 15, 16, 24

Easterbrook, Judge Frank, 61
Economic efficiency, 1, 28–30, 92
Emergency Rail Services Act, 53
Eminent domain, 44, 67
   just compensation, 2
Excess capacity, 3, 7, 18, 19, 21, 28, 30–32, 47, 48, 61, 63, 65, 100

Farmrail Corp., 109, 110, 117
Federal Railroad Administration, 5, 11, 17, 33, 37, 40, 54, 56, 67, 78, 83
Financial analysis, 32, 53, 110
Fort Worth & Denver Railway, 111
Fox River Valley Railroad, 17

Gateway Western Railway, 80, 81, 88
Gibbons, William, 27, 28, 42, 44
Grainbelt Corp., 109, 110, 116
Grand Trunk Corporation, 58, 59, 64
Grand Trunk Western Railroad, 83
Gulf, Mobile & Ohio Railroad, 71–75

Haley, Jack, 79
Harris, Robert, 3, 21
Heartland, 39
Heartland Rail Corp., 39
Holmes, Justice Oliver W., 2

I&M Rail Link, 64, 70
Illinois Central Railroad, 6, 7, 72–85
   abandonments, 81
   control by Canadian National, 82–84
   financial results, 76
   merger of GM & O, 71–75
   sale of lines, 75–82
   traffic density, 6
Illinois Central Gulf Railroad, 31, 72, 75–77, 81, 82, 85–87
Illinois Department of Transportation, 45, 80, 81, 87
Indiana Rail Road Co., 79, 87
Intermodal transport, 97, 107
Interstate Commerce Commission, 3, 22, 27, 29, 34, 37, 41, 43, 44, 54, 66, 67, 72, 96, 104
Iowa Interstate Railroad, 39, 45
Iowa Rail Finance Agency, 39

Justice Department (see Antitrust Division)

Kansas City Southern,
Kansas City Southern Railway, 35, 72, 76, 77, 81, 84, 86, 99
Kansas City Terminal Railway, 38, 44
Keeler, Theodore, 3, 20, 21
Kyle Railroad, 40

Langdon, Jervis, 27, 28, 42
Levin, Richard C., 5, 6, 20, 22

Maintenance of way (*See* Deferred maintenance), 3, 18, 29, 36, 39, 40, 43, 44, 62, 64, 72, 75, 93, 94, 96–98, 102, 110–112, 115
McGarr Judge Frank, 27
Mergers, 7, 10, 13, 14, 16, 19–25, 35, 43, 86, 90, 100, 106, 115, 116, 123, 126, 130, 132
Mid States Port Authority, 40
Milwaukee Road, 5, 6, 9, 16, 20, 28, 30–32, 35, 40, 47–65
   abandonments, 56–58
   acquired Rock Island segment, 40
   bankruptcy, 55, 56
   denied inclusion in BN, 52, 53
   excess capacity, 48–50
   financial analysis, 53–55
   freight traffic densities, 6, 49
   historical background, 47, 48
   sale of lines, 57, 58
   search for merger, 50–53
Milwaukee Road Restructuring Act, 53, 56, 58, 61, 67
Mississippi R. R. Comm'n v. Mobile & O.R.R., 2
Missouri Pacific Railroad, 5–7, 28, 32, 38–40, 42, 44, 45, 75, 76, 86, 90–102, 118, 119, 121, 122, 127, 128, 132
   acquired Chicago & Eastern Illinois, 90
   control by Union Pacific, 89–92
   description, 90
   financial results after merger, 95, 96
   financial results before merger, 90
   traffic density, 6
Missouri-Kansas-Texas Railroad, 35, 40, 45, 90, 92, 106, 115, 116, 118

Index

acquired by Union Pacific, 96–100
  trackage rights over MP, 97
  traffic density, 6

National Rail Passenger Service Act of 1970, 2, 21
National Railroad Passenger Corp. (*See* Amtrak), 2, 53, 54
New York, New Haven & Hartford Railroad, 2
Norfolk Southern Corporation, 82
Northrup, Herbert, x

Operating Statistics of Class I Railroads
  intermodal traffic, 17
  miles of road, 17
  revenue per ton, 17
  revenue ton miles, 17

Paducah & Louisville Railway, 79, 87
Passenger Service, 1, 2, 21, 33, 53, 73, 74, 77
Penn-Central, 21, 25
Posner, Judge Richard, 16
Powder River Basin, 20, 107, 130
Public interest standard, 13, 14, 75, 106–109, 122

Railroad employment, 18, 19, 25, 56, 97, 100, 111
Railroad Revitalization and Regulatory Reform Act of 1976, 4, 9, 52, 90
Railroad workers, 16, 19, 27, 57, 58, 61, 63, 78, 79, 85, 96, 97, 114, 115
Regulatory policy, 7, 10, 11, 14, 15, 61, 63
Riley, John, 17
Rock Island lines, 27–42, 50, 51, 65
  abandonments, 37–41
  bankruptcy, 27
  cancelled UP merger, 34–37
  description, 30
  directed service, 38
  dismemberment, 37–41
  economic performance, 28–30
  excess capacity, 30–32
  financial analysis, 32–34
  sale of lines, 41
  traffic density, 6

Rock Island Railroad Transition and Employee Assistance Act, 38, 39

Santa Fe, 5, 7, 9, 16, 28, 32, 35, 41, 50, 63, 91, 92, 99, 118
  acquired by Burlington Northern, 105–114
  control in the public interest, 106–109
  description, 105, 106
  financial analysis, 109, 110
  impact of merger, 110–113
  traffic density, 6
Settlement agreements, 108, 109, 114
Short-line railroads, 2, 14, 17, 24, 40, 41, 45, 72, 75, 78, 85, 87, 109
Soo Line Railroad, 6, 7, 47, 70
  acquired core of Milwaukee Road, 58–61
  financial impact of merger, 61–63
  sale of rail lines, 63, 64
  traffic density, 6
Southern Pacific Lines, 5, 6, 16, 28, 32, 34, 35, 37–39, 41, 44, 63, 80, 82, 92, 95, 99, 101, 102, 108–111, 114, 116
  acquired by Rio Grande Industries, 118
  acquired Rock Island segment, 38
  description, 118
  financial status in 1995, 118–121
  merged into Union Pacific, 117, 118
  protection in UP-MP merger, 91
  traffic density, 6
Sprint, 122
St. Louis-Southwestern Railway, 38, 41, 44, 116, 122, 132
St. Louis-San Francisco Railway, 6, 7, 35, 41
  acquired by Burlington Northern, 103–105
  description, 104
  traffic density, 6
Staggers Rail Act of 1980, 11–19, 22, 24, 78, 82, 90, 98, 100, 102, 126, 127
Surface Transportation Board, 17, 19, 24, 25, 64, 81, 83, 85, 107, 116, 118, 123, 128

Technological change, 1
Trackage rights, 1, 4, 7, 9, 10, 14–16, 23, 30, 38–40, 44, 48, 52, 58, 60, 63, 64, 66, 68, 80–82, 87, 90, 92, 97, 99, 105, 108, 109, 111, 114, 116, 118, 119, 121, 124–127, 131–133
Traffic density, 2, 3, 5, 7, 14, 21, 29, 72
Transportation Act of 1920, 13
  1940, 13

Union Pacific Railroad, 5, 6, 7, 10, 16, 27–31, 34–45, 51, 57, 58, 66, 76, 77, 107–110, 114
  abandonments, 126, 127
  acquisition of Chicago & North Western, 117
  acquisition of Missouri-Kansas-Texas, 96–100
  compared to Rock Island, 29
  control of Missouri Pacific, 89–92
  critique of Western Pacific purchase, 92–95

financial analysis of MP merger, 92
financial background in 1995, 118–121
financial results of SP merger, 95–96, 127–129
protection for Southern Pacific, 117, 118
STB public interest standard, 121–124
trackage rights to maintain rivalry, 124–126
traffic density, 6

Washington Central Railroad, 113
Western Pacific Railroad, 6, 7, 44, 90–96, 108, 116, 118, 121, 126
  critique of UP purchase, 92–95
  financial status before merger, 90
  traffic density, 6
Western Resources, Inc. v. Surface Transp. Bd., 109
Wisconsin Central Railroad, 61, 63

Set up a Continuation Order Today!

Did you know you can set up a continuation order on all JAI series and have each new volume sent directly to you upon publication. For details on how to set up a continuation order contact your nearest regional sales office listed below.

To view related **Transportation** series
visit

www.socscinet.com/transportconnect

30% Discount for Authors on all Books!

A 30% discount is available to Elsevier book and journal contributors **ON ALL BOOKS** plus standalone **CD-ROMS** except multi-volume reference works. To claim your discount, full payment is required with your order, which must be sent directly to the publisher at the nearest regional sales office listed below.

ELSEVIER REGIONAL SALES OFFICES

For customers in the Americas:

Elsevier Science
Customer Support Department
Regional Sales Office
P.O. Box 945 New York
N.Y. 10159-0945, USA
Tel: (+1) 212 633 3730
Toll Free number for North-America
1-888-4ES-INFO (4636)
Fax: (+1) 212 633 3680
Email: usinfo-f@elsevier.com

For customers in all other locations:

Elsevier Science
Customer Support Department
Regional Sales Office
P.O. Box 211
1000 AE Amsterdam
The Netherlands
Tel: (+31) 20 485 3757
Fax: (+31) 20 485 3432
Email: nlinfo-f@elsevier.nl

For customers in the Far East & Australasia:

Elsevier Science
Customer Support Department
3 Killiney Road, #08-01/09
Winsland House I,
Singapore 239519
Tel: +(65) 63490200
Fax: + (65) 67331817/67331276
Email: asiainfo@elsevier.com.sg